# FACT-FINDING
# IN
# THE MAINTENANCE OF
# INTERNATIONAL PEACE

by
WILLIAM I. SHORE

Preface by
A.J.P. TAMMES

1970/Oceana Publications, Inc. Dobbs Ferry, New York

Manufactured in the United States of America

# PREFACE

Recent diplomatic initiatives in the United Nations have caused an increasing academic interest in the investigation of facts as a contribution to the settlement of international questions. This new interest may be compared with the attention to fact-finding in scientific literature after the Hague Peace Conferences in 1899 and 1907, where for the first time rules were drafted for fact-finding as an independent means of regulating conflicts. Not always has the relevance of the investigation of facts been recognized as an independent and preliminary procedure of the settlement of international conflicts, which is the main theme of this book. Such procedures as conciliation, mediation and negotiations imply the need for inquiry into the relevant facts. The initiative of the Netherlands Government in the United Nations concerning the establishment of a permanent and independent organ of fact-finding once again puts emphasis on the independent contribution fact-finding may make to the solution of conflicts.

Since the First Hague Peace Conference of 1899 a great variety of experience has been obtained with regard to the investigation of facts. From the excellent historical survey in this book it should be clear how much the area of the application of fact-finding procedures has been shifted over the years from the mainly maritime incidents between nations in a wartime situation before the First World War to the important territorial and ideological conflicts with which the League of Nations and the United Nations have had to deal. Recent examples of fact-finding do reveal, however, that in comparison with the first years in the United Nations history, the area of application of investigation has shifted to peripheral questions of the international society although there are better guarantees now for impartiality as the Secretary General of the United Nations is increasingly involved in fact-finding activities. Fact-finding has lost in relevance but gained in impartiality. Fact-finding covers a variety of activities with regard to the collection of relevant information, which is referred to as inquiry, observation, inspection, supervision and safeguards. The application of these procedures is relevant for a variety of purposes such as the regulation of international conflicts, the decision-making in international organizations in their role aiming at international peace and security, and the observance of international agreements. Since, in the 19th century, states for the first time accepted the supervision of international bodies on their territory, the area of application has been extended progressively. International negotiations on arms control measures have increased the attention given to fact-finding activities of international bodies. Progress in this area, however, is difficult because of the unwillingness and fear of states to accept the supervision of foreign persons and international organs where their national security may be involved. This book, too, shows the large gap between the many schemes for the application of fact-finding and its practical realisation. The unwillingness of states to sacrifice a part of their national sovereignty was the most important limiting factor. Hence, the application of procedures for the independent inquiry into facts is closely related to the basic principle of international society: the sovereign equality of states. This principle is the origin of the limitation that investigation is dependent upon the free consent of states, while the area of investigation is restricted by the rule of non-interference in matters which are essentially within the domestic jurisdiction of states.

This book fills an important gap in the legal literature of the peaceful settlement of international conflicts. It offers a fine survey of the
application of fact-finding and a review of the relevant juridical problems. This book, therefore, is an important contribution to the further
research into these and related problems of conflict solution.

A.J.P. Tammes,
Amsterdam.

TABLE OF CONTENTS

TABLE OF CONTENTS (Cont'd)

# CHAPTER I

## INTRODUCTION

The Hague Convention of 1899 introduced a novel and unique procedure for pacific settlement - the independent international commission of inquiry. The distinguishing features of this new procedure were the use of fact-finding on an ad hoc basis, in an independent form, with complete freedom on the part of the States parties to a dispute with respect to the initiation of the procedure. In addition, any such State party to the creation of a commission of inquiry was at liberty to accept or reject the results of the investigation as it saw fit.

If the procedure was unique for its time, the reasons supporting the introduction of the concept to the Hague Conference were even more remarkable. Professor de Martens, the principal legal advisor of the Russian Foreign Ministry which introduced the proposal to the Conference, advanced the idea in the belief that it would be extremely helpful as a preliminary effort to subsequent arbitration. Although this motive was not suggested in the arguments advanced in support of the proposal to the Conference, Professor de Martens' experience with difficulties in fact-finding which he encountered in arbitration proceedings over which he had just previously presided leads to this as a possible motive.

In subsequent years, the strongest proponent of the concept of independent international commissions of inquiry was the Honorable William Jennings Bryan, the United States Secretary of State under President Wilson. Mr. Bryan's motives for supporting the concept of an independent international commission of inquiry can at best be only the subject of conjecture. The possibility has been advanced that Mr. Bryan's motive in promoting the idea of the independent international commission of inquiry arose from his experiences in labor negotiations in which he had encountered major obstacles in reaching settlements through lack of determinations of fact acceptable to all parties.

It is thus remarkable that the two strongest advocates of the concept of the independent international commission of inquiry appreciated the need for the impartial determination of fact as a result of their experiences in two entirely diverse situations - one on the international level and one on the domestic level. The need for some impartial means of finding the facts as a preliminary step in either a quasi-judicial procedure as arbitration or in the equally laborious process of direct negotiations was thus recognized by these two individuals whose experiences in each of these areas had brought them in direct contact with the problems involved in the determination of fact. Their diverse experiences also served to emphasize to them the importance of finding the facts as a prerequisite to the efficient functioning of the procedure of settlement with which each was most familiar.

Nevertheless, it is to be noted that Professor de Martens' proposal was for an independent fact-finding body and not for a fact-finding effort attached to an arbitration procedure. Likewise, Secretary of State Bryan's proposals also envisaged an independent fact-finding body which

1

was unrelated to any requirement for negotiation, although it is probable that Mr. Bryan hoped that an independent determination fact would open the way to direct negotiations between the parties. Both Professor de Martens and Mr. Bryan were cognizant of the limitations arising out of international political realities which surrounded the introduction of any proposal for compulsory procedures for pacific settlement. Both men, therefore, were careful to stress the voluntary and isolated nature of the independent international commission of inquiry which they promoted.

The introduction of the concept of the independent ad hoc commission of inquiry in international relations can be described as a great experiment. Advancing the idea that States parties to a dispute should, without committing themselves to a predetermined course of procedure, seek to determine the facts in the dispute through an independent and impartial agency was a breathtaking experiment in an uncharted area of international relations. Operating within the framework of a system that was based on the principle of sovereign equality of States, it opened tremendous possibilities for progress towards constructive efforts to promote pacific settlement of international disputes.

The instances in which commissions of inquiry have been used in international disputes have been few. Nevertheless, if the implementation of the concept of the independent international commission of inquiry contained in the Hague Conventions of 1899 and 1907 has been disappointing, the nurture and preservation of the idea by all States has presented an encouraging and enheartening example of the light of constructive thought in international relations. Those obstacles which have prevented greater use of commissions of inquiry in international disputes stem from the political realities of international relations based as they are on the principle of sovereign equality of States. The failure to implement the fact-finding provisions of many treaties for pacific settlement or to enter in arrangements providing for commissions of inquiry under the Hague Conventions is due to operation of the principle of sovereign equality of States rather than to any inherent defect in the concept of the independent international commission of inquiry.

A study of the history of the development of the Hague concept of the independent international commission of inquiry becomes highly interesting and important for the insight which it develops into the basic problems of promoting pacific settlement of international disputes. Such a study should also promote a greater appreciation of the usefulness of fact-finding in the peaceful settlement of international disputes and of the various forms which attempts to determine the facts can assume in international relations. Above all, any study of fact-finding in international disputes must lead to a continuing evaluation of the use of independent inquiry in the promotion of orderly and constructive procedures for maintaining and developing peaceful relations among the member States of the world community. The best and only place to begin such a study is with the Hague Convention of 1899 which incorporated the concept of the independent international commission of inquiry.

The history of inquiry in international disputes as a concept introduced at the Hague Conference of 1899 is distinguished by three main trends. These are (1) the great interest which has been displayed in inquiry as an independent procedure for the pacific settlement of international disputes; (2) the failure to use inquiry in this sense in the pacific settlement of international disputes, with the exception of a very few limited instances, to the present day; and (3) the use of inquiry by the League of Nations, the United Nations and the Organization of American States as a procedure in exercising their responsibility for the maintenance of international peace.

With respect to the first trend, the concept of independent investigation or inquiry as a method or procedure for the pacific settlement of international disputes has in the past more than six decades found various expression both in treaties and in the constitutional basis of international organization.

Various studies have also been undertaken under the auspices of the League of Nations and the United Nations in order to determine how to promote the greater use of independent inquiry in the pacific settlement of international disputes. The most recent efforts in this direction were initiated by the General Assembly of the United Nations which adopted, on December 16, 1963, resolution 1967 (XVIII) entitled "Questions of methods of fact-finding", requesting the Member States to submit their views concerning, and the Secretary-General to study, the methods of fact-finding in international relations.[1]

As a result of the General Assembly's resolution, a conference was held in Mexico City by the Special Committee on Principles of International Law Concerning Friendly Relations and Co-operation Among States. The Special Committee devoted its thirty-sixth and thirty-seventh meetings, held on September 25 and 29, 1964, to consideration of the methods of fact-finding.[2]

The small amount of time which the Special Committee was able to devote to the subject, and the realization by the members of the Special Committee that information concerning fact-finding was still incomplete, led to the adoption by the Committee of a draft resolution which had been submitted by the Netherlands representative. The draft resolution proposed that further study be made of the subject.[3]

Subsequently, the General Assembly adopted a resolution on December 20, 1965, recalling its earlier resolution 1967 (XVIII) of December 16, 1963 on methods of fact-finding and noting with appreciation the report of the Secretary-General[4] on the question. The Assembly resolution also referred to the comments submitted by Governments and the views expressed at its twentieth session[5], as well as Chapter VII of the report of the Special Committee[6], dealing with fact-finding. The Assembly, taking into consideration all of these factors, expressed the belief that further study of the subject was required.[7]

---

[1]The resulting report of the Secretary-General is U. N. Doc. A/5694 (May 1, 1964).

[2]U. N. Docs. A/AC.119/SR. 36 and A/AC.119/SR. 37. The Special Committee was established under resolution 1966 (XVIII) of December 16, 1963 to study the four principles of international law concerning friendly relations and cooperation among States listed in resolution 1815 (SVII) which had been adopted by the General Assembly, December 18, 1962. Resolution 1967 (XVIII) requested the committee to include in its deliverations "...the feasibility and desirability of establishing a special international body for fact-finding or of entrusting to an existing organization fact-finding responsibilities complementary to existing arrangements..."

[3]U. N. Doc. A/AC.119/L. 29

[4]U. N. Doc. A/5694 (May 1, 1964).

[5]U. N. Doc. A/6165 (December 18, 1965). Report of the Sixth Committee on agenda items 90 and 94.

[6]U. N. Doc. A/5746 (November 16, 1964).

[7]U. N. General Assembly resolution 2103 (XX), December 20, 1965. Reaffirmed in resolution 2182 (XXI), December 12, 1966.

The General Assembly resolution, accordingly, requested the Secretary-General to supplement his study so as to cover areas of international inquiry envisaged in some treaties.[8] At the same time, Member States were invited to submit in writing to the Secretary-General, before July 1966, any views or further views they might have on the subject. The General Assembly, on September 23, 1967, again decided to include in the agenda of its twenty-second session the item entitled "Question of methods of fact-finding. The item was referred to the Sixth Committee which, after a general debate on the item and consideration of the proposals of a Working Group of Sixteen which had been set up to reconcile different views, submitted a draft resolution to the General Assembly. On December 18, 1967, the General Assembly adopted the proposals of the Sixth Committee as resolution 2329 (XXII). The resolution invited the Member States to take into consideration the possibility of entrusting the ascertainment of fact to competent international organizations and bodies established by agreement between the Parties concerned, and drew special attention to the possibility of resort by States to procedures for the ascertainment of facts, in accordance with Article 33 of the Charter. It also requested the Secretary-General to prepare a register of experts in legal and other fields, whose services the States parties to a dispute might use by agreement for fact-finding in relation to the dispute, and requested the Member States to nominate up to five of their nationals to be included in such a register. The General Assembly's request has been transmitted to the Member States and as of August 31, 1968, thirty-three Member States had responded to the request.

The present interest in pursuing the study of methods of fact-finding in the pacific settlement of international disputes and General Assembly resolution 2329 (XXII) on the subject is further evidence of the possibilities of inquiry in the maintenance of international peace. The historical survey of inquiry in the pacific settlement of international disputes, beginning with the Hague Convention of 1899, covered in Chapter II infra, also provides ample evidence that, despite its infrequent use, the possibilities inherent in the use of fact-finding refused to let the concept wither.

Noted international jurists have also stressed the need to find the facts in anticipation of settling a dispute as basic to concepts of law and order. Judge Jessup has pointed out that the importance of finding the facts in the pacific settlement of disputes has been widely recognized.[9] In a more specific sense, Professor Lauterpacht has asserted that the manner in which the facts are marshalled may be decisive for the elaboration of legal principles.[10]

Perhaps the best consensus of the attitude of states with regard to the possibilities of inquiry were the opinions expressed in the meetings at Mexico City, referred to earlier, of the Special Committee on Principles of International Law Concerning Friendly Relations and Co-operation Among States. The opinions expressed in the Sixth Committee, during the course of the discussions on the subject, at the twentieth session of the General Assembly also provide evidence of such interest in the possibilities of fact-finding.

At Mexico City, the United States delegate took the position that

---

[8]U. N. Doc. A/6228 (April 22, 1966) is the resulting report of the Secretary-General.

[9]Philip C. Jessup, The Use of International Law, (Ann Arbor: University of Michigan Law School, 1959), p. 38.

[10]H. Lauterpacht, The Development of International Law by the International Court of Justice, (New York: Longmans, Green, and Co., 1958), p. 36.

4

While no procedure was of any use without the requisite will to employ it in good faith, the mere availability of well-designed machinery set up for the specific purpose of fact-finding might induce States or United Nations organs to use it.[11]

The Canadian representative stated that

his delegation was convinced that the establishment of impartial fact-finding machinery was in the long run inevitable. It was part of the process of the elaboration of rules of international law, and responded to a need of the international community at the present stage of development.[12]

The Italian delegate noted that his delegation

believed that the attitude of Governments towards the institutionalization of fact-finding procedures would in the long run prove a far more decisive test of good-will in international relations than any degree of enthusiasm for proliferation of general principles or rules of conduct.[13]

The representative of India noted that

The close inter-connection between fact-finding and peace-keeping operations had helped to ensure the maintenance of international peace and security; . . .[14]

In arguing for flexibility in investigation, the delegate of the Union of Soviet Socialist Republics said

That did not mean that the Soviet Union in any way under-estimated the importance of determining the facts of a dispute or situation; on the contrary, it felt that objective inquiry into the facts was of utmost importance in reaching correct decisions aimed at bringing about peaceful settlements.[15]

During the meetings of the Sixth Committee, the United Kingdom representative noted that his delegation

considered, however, that any advance in the field of fact-finding could be a useful service to the cause of strengthening peace and the settlement of disputes between States and would support any proposal that could command international support or strengthen the facilities available to the international community in the field.[16]

Regardless of the positions taken by the various delegations concerning the establishment of a permanent fact-finding body, either at Mexico City or in the Sixth Committee, all were apparently agreed in principle, that fact-finding was an accepted procedure and method in the pacific settlement of disputes.[17] In light of this favorable view of fact-finding, the question arises as to how often and with what effect inquiry has been resorted to in international disputes.

---

[11] U. N. Doc. A/AC.119/SR.36, p. 12.

[12] Ibid., p. 20.

[13] Ibid., p. 22.

[14] Ibid., p. 10.

[15] Ibid., p. 14.

[16] U. N. Doc. A/C.6/SR.881, p. 10.

[17] U. N. Docs. A/C.119/SR.36, A/C.119/SR.37, A/C.6/SR.87 to A/C.6/SR.893 and A/C.6/SR.898, meetings held November 5 to December 8 and December 17, 1965.

As the survey of the history of inquiry in the pacific settlement of international disputes in Chapter II herein shows, the framework of treaty provisions incorporating methods of inquiry is far more impressive than their implementation.

The accumulation of fact-finding experience in international disputes has been mostly confined to the activities of the League of Nations, the Organization of American States and the United Nations which are surveyed in Chapter III herein.

This last point directs attention to the relationship between fact-finding and the concepts upon which the present international political structure is based as they apply to fact-finding in international disputes.

Before proceeding further it would be well to clarify the terms "inquiry", "enquiry", "investigation" and "fact-finding". "Inquiry or "enquiry", it appears, is a term used by the Hague Conventions and instruments subsequently created based upon the concepts of the Hague Conventions. "Investigation" is the term by which investigations of fact are described in the Covenant of the League of Nations[18] and the Charter of the United Nations[19] with respect to disputes endangering peace referred to the League Council, in the first case, and to the Security Council, in the second case.

With respect to "inquiry" as used by the Hague Conventions, the Covenant of the League refers to "inquiry" in Articles 12 and 17 while the United Nations Charter uses the term "enquiry" in Article 33.

"Fact-finding" is a term that appears to have been used in recent years by the United Nations General Assembly in resolutions initiating studies of methods of investigation.[20] The term has been used, accordingly, by the Secretariat in the studies it has undertaken in accordance with the instructions of these and subsequent resolutions of the General Assembly on the subject.[21]

In this study, investigations of fact will be designated by the use of any of the above terms without distinction and without any differences in meaning implied.

Returning to the discussion of the political principles upon which international relations are structured, it should be noted that the dominant principle is the equality under international law of sovereign and independent states. This principle is incorporated in Article 2, paragraph 1 of the United Nations Charter which states "The Organization is based on the principle of the sovereign equality of all its Members."

In the wording of Article 2, paragraph 1 the concepts of sovereignty and equality are combined.[22] Since the limitations upon fact-finding can be inferred from the attributes of the concept of sovereignty, the follow-

---

[18] Article 15, para 1.

[19] Article 34.

[20] U. N. General Assembly resolution 1967 (XVIII), December 16, 1963 and resolution 2104 (XX), December 20, 1965.

[21] U. N. Docs. A/5694 (May 1, 1964) and A/6228 (April 22, 1966).

[22] Leland M. Goodrich and Edward Hambro, Charter of the United Nations, (Boston: World Peace Foundation, 1949), p. 98; See discussion of Article 2 (1). On the concept of equality of States, see E. D. Dickinson, The Equality of States in International Law, (Cambridge: Harvard University Press, 1920).

ing discussion will be confined to the subject of sovereignty.[23]

The principle of state sovereignty as it affects the concept of inquiry in international disputes can be expressed simply as independence from any other authority. It is external independence with regard to liberty of action outside its borders in its relations with other States which a State enjoys.[24] It is internal independence with regard to the liberty of a State inside its borders.[25]

What is of concern here is the effect of such liberty of action upon the use of inquiry in the pacific settlement of international disputes. At the time of the first Hague Convention in 1899, the concept of the external and internal independence of the States which were parties to the Convention was expressed in Article IX of Title III which provided that the role of a fact-finding commission was to be applicable only in disputes "involving neither honor nor vital interest".

The expression of the external and internal attributes of sovereignty of States, also appeared in Article 9 of the Hague Conventions of 1907. Treaties providing for arbitration, concluded prior to World War I, similarly, contained a clause excluding from the pacific procedure disputes "affecting the vital interests, the independence or honor of the two contracting parties".[26]

The Bryan Treaties eliminated the qualifying phrase "involving neither honor nor vital interests" in their jurisdictional clauses. The great majority of treaties concluded since World War I also abandoned the reservation as to vital interest, independence and honor as antiquated and out of harmony with the post-war systems of pacific settlement.[27]

The elimination of the qualifying phrase "involving neither honor nor vital interest" did not impose any greater restrictions upon the liberty of action of the parties to a treaty as far as inquiry was concerned. This was so because inquiry is one of the methods used in peaceful settlement which is based upon the principle of voluntary acceptance of the terms of settlement.[28]

This principle of voluntary acceptance was not completely incorporated in the Covenant of The League of Nations.[29] The Council, after examining the facts, if unable to settle a dispute, which had been brought before it, was to publish a report containing a statement of the facts and its recommendations. Failure to comply with the recommendations of the report left a party open to possible action by Members of the League.[30]

As in the Covenant of the League of Nations, with respect to Members of the League[31], the Charter of the United Nations, in Article 33, imposes

---

[23] An excellent treatment of sovereignty as a limiting factor on voting rights in international conferences and organizations is found in Wellington Koo, Jr., Voting Procedures in International Political Organs, (New York: Columbia University Press, 1947).

[24] L. Oppenheim, International Law, Eighth Edition, (London: Longmans, Green and Co., 1955), Vol. 1, p. 286.

[25] Idem.

[26] M. Habicht, Postwar Treaties for the Pacific Settlement of International Disputes, Cambridge: Harvard University Press, 1931, p. 992.

[27] Ibid., p. 993.

[28] Goodrich and Hambro, op. cit., p. 240. Also see Habicht, op. cit., p. 1001.

[29] Article 15.

[30] Article 15 (6) and (7).

[31] Article 12.

upon Members of the United Nations the obligation to seek a solution of their peace endangering disputes by peaceful methods. The principle of voluntary acceptance of the results of an inquiry reappears in Articles 36, 37 and 38 of the Charter.[32] In Article 36, the Security Council "may recommend appropriate procedures or methods of adjustment" and under Article 37, the Security Council may "recommend such terms of settlement as it may consider appropriate". The word "recommendations" is also used in Article 38.

The obligation under the Charter, therefore, to submit disputes which endanger international peace and security to solution by peaceful methods applies to inquiry. Acceptance of the terms of settlement proposed by the Security Council based upon such inquiry, however, is, under the Charter, on a voluntary basis.

It is interesting to note the difference between the effect of the Charter of the United Nations upon voting procedures and upon inquiry.[33] With respect to voting procedures, sovereign States can, by agreement in constituting international organizations, substitute voting by majority for the unanimity rule applicable to international conferences. The voting provisions for the General Assembly in Article 18 and for the Security Council in Article 27 of the Charter provide support for this statement. Similarly, by agreement, the sovereign States which created the United Nations could have provided for compulsory acceptance of the terms of a settlement based upon inquiry.

As was shown earlier herein this waiver of sovereignty was not incorporated in the Charter.

Another qualification which has served to limit the application of procedures of pacific settlement is the reservation which excludes matters solely within the domestic jurisdiction of the contracting parties. This qualification is also an expression of the attributes of sovereignty which independent states possess and which act as limiting factors on the use of inquiry in international disputes.

Many treaties for the pacific settlement of international disputes contained such provisions excluding matters solely within the domestic jurisdiction of states.[34] The Covenant of the League of Nations, also, in Article 15(8), expressed this limitation as follows:

If a dispute between the parties is claimed by one of them, and is found by the Council, to arise out of a matter which by international law is solely within the domestic jurisdiction of that party, the Council shall so report, and shall make no recommendation as to its settlement.

This reservation was also listed by the General Act for the Pacific Settlement of International Disputes of 1928 among the permissible reservations.[35] In the Pact of Bogatá of 1948, it is stated as "matters which, by their nature, are within the domestic jurisdiction of the State." [36]

Recognition of the realities of state sovereignty - and its expression - was reflected similarly in the United Nations Charter in Article 2, paragraph 7, which states

---

[32]Goodrich and Hambro, op. cit., p. 260. For discussion of Articles 33 to 38, see pp. 237-261.

[33]On voting procedures, see Wellington Koo Jr., op. cit.

[34]Habicht, op. cit., pp. 996-8. See also United Nations, Systematic Survey of Treaties for the Pacific Settlement of International Disputes 1928-1948, Lake Success: New York, 1948, p. 24.

[35]L. of N., Treaty Series, Vol. 93, No. 2123, p. 345.

[36]U. N. Treaty Series, Vol. 30, p. 55 and p. 84.

Nothing contained in the present Charter shall authorize the United Nations to intervene in matters which are
essentially within the domestic jurisdiction of any state
or shall require the  Members to submit such matters
to settlement under the present Charter; but this principle
shall not prejudice the application of enforcement measures
under Chapter VII.[37]

The principle of state sovereignty as a limiting factor on the use of
inquiry and other procedures in the pacific settlement of international
disputes is thus well documented in the Hague Conventions and in treaties
for pacific settlement of international disputes, as well as in the League
of Nations Covenant and in the United Nations Charter.

It is for this reason, that fact-finding, particularly with respect to
peaceful change, in contrast to its acceptance in principle apparently has
not made the contribution to pacific settlement of international disputes
that it should have made.  In further support for this position, one authority has cautioned that where claims are of a political nature it is doubtful
whether disinterested factual investigation is effective in disposing of
claims for peaceful change.[38]

Professor Kaplan and Nicholas de B. Katzenbach have framed this
idea more directly in stating that

. . . disputes that effect the security or continued existence
of a state cannot be put in the hands of a third party, however
impartial, if any alternative is feasible.[39]

Probably the best expression of the limitations which the sovereignty
of the Member States places upon the United Nations, especially in political matters - and also the reason for inclusion of Article 2, paragraph
7 in the charter - is the following statement contained in the report of
Committee I/1 to Commission I of the San Francisco Conference on International Organization:

The Organization we are developing is assuming, under
the present Charter, functions wider in scope than those
previously assumed by the League of Nations or other international bodies and even wider than those which were first
contemplated at Dumbarton Oaks; especially in the economic,
social and cultural fields.  The tendency to provide the United
Nations with a broad jurisdiction is, therefore, relevant and
founded.  The necessity, on the other hand, to make sure that
the United Nations under prevalent world conditions should
not go beyond acceptable limits or exceed due limitation called

---

[37]See Goodrich and Hambro, op. cit., pp. 110-121, for a discussion of Article 2 (7).

[38]Frederick S. Dunn, Peaceful Change: A Study of International
Procedures (New York:  Council on Foreign Relations, 1937), p. 113.
Judge Hudson, also, while acknowledging the appearance of fact-finding
provisions in international conventions since the Hague Conventions of
1899, points out that in the subsequent forty years only three commissions
of inquiry of a limited nature were created.  (Manley O. Hudson, The
Permanent Court of International Justice 1920-1942 (New York:
Macmillan, 1943, pp. 40-41.

[39]Morton A. Kaplan and Nicholas de B. Katzenbach, The Political
Foundations of International Law, (New York: John Wiley and Sons Inc.,
1961).

for principle 8 (Article 2 (7) as an instrument to determine the scope of the attributes of the Organization and to regulate its functioning in matters at issue.[40]

The principle of State sovereignty must therefore be considered in our study of the possibilities of fact-finding in the pacific settlement of international disputes.[41] This principle has been and still remains a limiting factor on the use of fact-finding in international disputes.

There remains the third trend which is the use of inquiry by international organs in exercising their responsibility for the maintenance of international peace. It is in this area that the bulk of experience in investigation in international disputes is found.

The question that arises is to what extent are sovereign rights limited, if at all, by international political organs in the exercise of their right of investigation as a procedure in fulfilling their collective responsibility for maintaining international peace? For example, how has the Organization of American States dealt with the issue of the sovereignty of its member States and its collective responsibility for international peace with respect to the use of inquiry?[42] It is hoped that this study will be helpful in clarifying this point and in delineating the parameters of this trend.

We have been discussing up to this point possible limitations on the use of inquiry in international disputes arising from the constitutional conflict between State sovereignty and collective responsibility for maintaining international peace. The reference to such collective responsibility may be bilateral or multi lateral. Another approach in our search for limitations upon the use of inquiry in international disputes can be directed toward the operational aspect of inquiry.[43]

One purpose of this study is to examine the available information in order to discover what procedures and practices of investigating bodies have proved most satisfactory. By improving the technique of fact-finding it is hoped that it will find readier acceptance in the procedures used for the pacific settlement of international disputes.[44]

---

[40]U. N. C. I. O. , Supplement to Report of Rapporteur, Committee I/1 to Commission I, Doc. 1070, 1/1/34(1) (d), p.1 (Documents, VI, p. 486. For a discussion of the limitations of Article 2(7) see Hans Kelsen "Limitations on The Functions of the United Nations" in Yale Law Journal, Vol. 55 (1946), pp. 997-1006.

[41]Georg Schwarzenberger, International Law, Third Edition, Vol. 1, London: Stevens, 1957, pp. 114-115.

[42]See Marjorie M. Whiteman, Digest of International Law, Washington: United States Government Printing Office, 1965, Vol. 5, pp. 134-135 for recent treatment of equality and sovereignty concepts in the inter-American Peace System.

[43]In Goodrich and Hambro, op. cit., p. 240, the statement is made that enquiry, strictly speaking, is not a means of settlement at all but rather an effort to find a basis for a settlement.

[44]Improvement of the technique of fact-finding will also be valuable in conjunction with the policy of crystallizing into treaty form with fact-finding or inspection provisions certain specialized areas of international relations. See U. N. Doc. A/6228, April 22, 1966, study of the Secretary-General, entitled "Methods of fact-finding with respect to the execution of international agreements." Also, see James Simsarian "Inspection Experiences under the Antarctic Treaty and the International Atomic Agency," American Journal of International Law, Vol. 60 (1966), pp. 502-510.

At the same time, it would be naive to assume that improvement of techniques, alone, will induce readier acceptance of methods of inquiry. The limitations upon co-operative action in the area of international peace also act upon attemps at investigation.

As was pointed out earlier, the experiences of the League of Nations and of the United Nations, as well as of the Organization of American States, provide many instances in which investigation has been employed in dealing with international disputes in a diversity of situations. As a result, a valuable body of information has accumulated in these agencies concerning the methods of investigation applied in such cases. This information will provide the basic material of this study with respect to techniques of investigations which have taken place in international disputes.

The use of military observers will not be examined except where military observation formed a part of developments which included investigation. In such cases, an account of the military observation becomes necessary to preserve continuity in the treatment of the development of the situation involving investigation.

Finally, some of the investigations pursued by United Nations organs, which are noted herein, have dealt with violations of human rights or investigations of circumstances surrounding the death of an outstanding public figure or of a political leader. These investigations have been included, in this study because it was felt they were pertinent in their bearing on procedures for the initiation and operation of commissions of investigation.

The recognition of finding the facts as a prerequisite to intelligent action is apparently accepted as a basic philosophic principle. In the complex arena of international political relations, the application of that principle is beset with obstacles. There have been collections of the fact-finding experiences of the League of Nations, the United Nations and the Organization of American States.[45] The attempt that will be made here is to approach the available material regarding fact-finding experiences of international political organs from the dual perspective of constitutionalism and functionalism. The purpose will be to isolate the limitations upon the use of inquiry in the maintenance of international peace. Once isolated, perhaps steps might be taken towards eliminating these limitations within the political framework of international relations as it now exists.[46]

---

[45]See sources cited herein in Chapters II and III.

[46]For a discussion of the practical limitations upon the activities of United Nations political organs in peaceful settlement and adjustment of international disputes, as well as on the possibilities inherent in the United Nations system, see Leland M. Goodrich, The United Nations, New York: Thomas Y. Crowell Co., 1959, pp. 190-214.

# CHAPTER II

## HISTORICAL SURVEY OF FACT-FINDING

### A. The Hague Conventions

From the time of the adoption of the Hague Conventions of 1899, many treaties and conventions for the pacific settlement of disputes have been adopted. All of these have contained provisions providing for the use of fact-finding techniques either in the form of commissions of inquiry or of conciliation.[1]

It should be pointed out that, although commissions of investigation had been used before 1899[2] the Hague Convention of 1899 was the first attempt toward institutionalization of fact-finding in the pacific settlement of international disputes. The essence of this initial step is contained in Title III, Article IX, of the Hague Convention of 1899 entitled "International Commissions of Inquiry" which outlined the role and nature of a fact-finding commission in the following terms:

> In differences of an international nature involving neither honor nor vital interest and arising from a difference of opinion on points of fact, the Signatory Powers recommend that the parties who have not been able to come to an agreement by means of diplomacy, should as far as circumstances

---

[1]Several compilations of such treaties published. See League of Nations, Systematic Survey of the Arbitration Conventions and Treaties of Mutual Security Deposited with the League of Nations, (prepared by the Legal Section of the Secretariat, Geneva, 1927); M. Habicht. Postwar Treaties for the Pacific Settlement of International Disputes (Cambridge: Harvard University Press, 1931); United Nations, Systematic Survey of Treaties for the Pacific Settlement of International Disputes 1928-1948 (Lake Success, New York: 1948), Ivan N. Efremov, Les traites internationaux de conciliation (Paris: Les Editions Internationales, 1932) is more limited; Francis C. deWolf, General Synopsis of Treaties of Arbitration, Conciliation, Judicial Settlement, Security and Disarmament actually in force between countries invited to the Disarmament conference (Washington, D. C.: 1933) lists the contractual obligations of states existing with respect to the type of treaties as entitled; as to the Bryan Treaties, see J. B. Scott, Treaties for the Advancement of Peace Between the U. S. and Other Powers Negotiated by the Honorable William J. Bryan (New York: Oxford University Press, 1920) and C. L. Lange, The American Peace Treaties (Kristiana: Aschehoug, 1915)

[2]In 1894, a commission composed of representatives of Britain, France and Turkey investigated the origin and responsibility for the massacre of Armenians at Sassoun, Turkey, Revue générale de droit international public, vol. 1, (1896), pp. 89-91, 101-103.

allow, institute an International Commission of Inquiry to facilitate a solution of these differences by elucidating the facts by means of an impartial and conscientious investigation.[3]

It is difficult because of the incomplete records of the First Hague Conference to trace accurately and specifically the origins of the concept of inquiry as proposed and adopted in the form of Articles 9 - 14 of the Hague Convention of 1899. The records do reveal that the draft proposal for commissions of inquiry was presented to the Conference by Russia as prepared under the direction of Professor Frederick de Martens, the principal legal advisor to the Russian Foreign Ministry.[4]

From the Conference remarks of Professor de Martens, little can be gleaned as to his source of the idea of an international commission of inquiry except from a general statement which he made to the Conference. In his general statement on the subject, Professor de Martens pointed out that the commission of inquiry was not novel but that it had already been proved to be of service in situations where states, acting in good faith became involved in a controversy, perhaps over boundary matters.[5]

It is reasonable to assume that Professor de Martens experience as an arbitrator had impressed him with the difficulties involved in obtaining a clarification of fact in complex controversies before arbitral tribunals of which he was a member. In addition to this aspect of inquiry, Professor de Martens considered a commission of inquiry as a safety valve given to governments to enable excited and ill-informed public opinion to be held in check.[6]

Professor de Martens and the other delegations to the Conference could very likely have been influenced in their attitudes toward inquiry by the events of the times. The boundary dispute in British Guiana between Great Britain and Venezuela, involving possible infringement of the Monroe Doctrine as a result of certain British actions such as the dispatch of naval forces to the Venezuelan coast, resulted in the appointment by the United States of a national commission of inquiry.[7] Although the inquiry was never prosecuted, the arbitral tribunal which was subsequently created in 1897 met, with Professor de Marten as chairman, in Paris at about the same time as the Peace Conference at the Hague.[8] The complexity of the facts presented to the arbitral tribunal and the possibility that a commission of inquiry, which nearly functioned, might have been better able to cope with the staggering amount of evidence presented possibly could have influenced Professor de Martens and the other delegates to the Peace Conference at the Hague.[9]

---

[3]William M. Malloy, (comp.) Treaties, Conventions, International Acts, Protocols and Agreements between the United States and Other Powers, 1776-1909 (Washington, 1910, 1923), Vol. 2, p. 2022.

[4]James Brown Scott, The Proceedings of the Hague Peace Conferences: The Conference of 1899 (1920), p. 800.

[5]Ibid., Committee of Examination, 9th meeting, June 23, p. 730.

[6]Ibid., Third Commission, 6th Meeting, July 19, p. 641.

[7]Papers Relating to the Foreign Relations of the United States, 1895, vol. 1, p. 542.

[8]John Bassett Moore, History and Digest of International Arbitrations to which the United States Has Been a Party. (1898), vol. 5, pp. 5017-5018.

[9]The Collected Papers of John Bassett Moore (1944) vol. 2, pp. 203 ff.

The delegates to the Hague Peace Conference may have also been influenced by one other event which occurred at about the time of the Conference. The sinking of the Maine in February 1898 illustrated the inadequacy of national commissions of inquiry. The inquiries made by the disputants resulted in contradictory reports and the lack of impartial information was considered by some to have intensified the controversy.[10]

The report of the rapporteur of the third commission, M. Chevalier Deschamps, to the plenary session summarized the reasons why the Conference decided to establish a system of inquiry as follows:

(1) in any international dispute there is a need both for an elucidation of the facts and for time to allow passions to subside;

(2) the procedure of inquiry offered a special appeal because of its completely voluntary character and its non-binding reports; and

(3) the commissions were not innovations in international practice, but had already proved their usefulness.[11]

In referring to the concept of inquiry as not novel but rather an old idea, M. Deschamps, in his report, pointed out that mixed commissions had long been in existence and operation.[12] Whether or not mixed commissions can be considered as the predecessors of the international commission of inquiry is open to question. Some writers have considered them as too ancestral.[13] Others have, following the opinions expressed by the majority of delegates at the Hague Conference, attributed a closer relationship between mixed commissions and the newer international commission of inquiry.[14] There are many differences between mixed commissions and international commissions of inquiry as envisaged by the Hague Peace Conference of 1899. It is not important to discuss these differences here. What is important is that the proponents of the concept of international inquiry felt it necessary to stress that it was not an innovation.

But aside from the fear of innovation, several other criticisms of the concept of international commissions of inquiry were raised at the Hague Conference which indicated why the procedure was not developed earlier and why it was not implemented more frequently, subsequently.

The Balkan delegates were opposed to a system of inquiry for several reasons.[15] First, they feared that the commissions might be used by the larger powers as a pretext for intervening into the internal affairs of smaller states. Second, it was feared that international inquiries which revealed administrative shortcomings might cause humiliation to a state.[16]

---

[10] A. Beaucourt, Les commissions internationales après la paix. (Thesis, Paris, Arras: Repesse, Cassel, 1909), pp. 36-39; M. Bokanowski; Les commissions internationales d'enquête. (Thesis, Paris: Pedone, 1925), pp. 36-37; A. Le Ray, Les commissiones internationales d'enquête au XXme siecle. (Saumur: Godet, 1910), pp. 33-34.

[11] James Brown Scott, The Proceedings of the Hague Peace Conference: The Conference of 1899, 7th Plenary Session, July 25, pp. 114-118.

[12] Ibid., Third Commission, 6th meeting, July 19, p. 640.

[13] A. Le Ray, op.cit., p. 20; A. Beaucourt, op.cit., p.11.

[14] M. Bokanowski, op.cit., p.11.

[15] See James Brown Scott, Proceedings of the Hague Peace Conferences: The Conference of 1899, Third Commission, 6th meeting, July 19, pp. 626-637.

[16] Ibid., 16th meeting, July 18, p.781.

A third objection advanced was that a state might be forced by means of moral pressure to participate in an international inquiry when it deemed such action inadvisable.[17]  A fourth objection was directed at the inclusion of a third party on the commissions.[18] Another objection raised was that, although the commission's report was not binding on the parties, it might place them in a position where they could not avoid arbitration without encountering further problems.[19]

Notwithstanding all of the objections raised, the concept of international commissions of inquiry was incorporated into the Hague Convention of 1899.  That concept incorporated the following elements distinguishing it from other procedures for settlement.  First, the commission is an international agency containing some impartial members or a third party; second, its purpose is, through investigation, to establish and elucidate the facts and thereby contribute toward clarifying the issues in a dispute; and third, the report of a commission of inquiry has no binding effect. Those instances in which inquiry was subsequently used in the promotion of peaceful settlement rarely conformed to this format because of failure to adhere to the letter of the second purpose.  Commissions of inquiry that were constituted and operated under the Hague Convention aegis attempted to define responsibility and assess damages - activities which reached beyond a simple elucidation of fact.

The second major step taken toward encouraging fact-finding as an instrument for the pacific settlement of international disputes was part III of the Convention for the Pacific Settlement of International Disputes, concluded at the Hague on October 18, 1907, entitled "International Commissions of Inquiry."[20]

The second Hague Convention continued the concept of fact-finding embodied in the earlier Hague Convention but whereas the earlier convention had contained only six articles, the second convention contained twenty eight articles.  Of these twenty eight articles, nineteen contained rules of procedure which, as was pointed out in Article 17, were designed to facilitate the constitution and working commissions of inquiry.

With the exception of seven commissions of inquiry that were actually created and used, there appears no other evidence of specific implementation of the fact-finding provisions of the Hague Conventions.

The first such commission of inquiry was created as a result of the Dogger Bank episode which occurred on October 21, 1904 during the Russo-Japanese War.[21]  The Russian Baltic Fleet, which was on its way

---

[17]Ibid., 6th meeting, July 18, pp. 626-637.

[18]This was not surprising since the Conference marked the first acceptance into international relations of the principle that the offer of good offices to disputants was to be considered a friendly act.

[19]James Scott Brown, The Hague Peace Conferences of 1899 and 1907, vol. 2 (1909), p. 267.

[20]United States, Treaty Series, No. 536 (Washington D. C., U. S. Government Printing Office).  Entered into force for the United States, January 26, 1910.  See Appendix A, infra, for text of Title III of Hague Convention I of 1907.  Arguments in favor of the institution of fact-finding set forth at the Hague Conference can be found in Carnegie Endowment for International Peace, The Reports to the Hague Conferences of 1899 and 1907.

[21]James Brown Scott (ed.). The Hague Court Reports. New York: Oxford University Press for Carnegie Endowment for International Peace, 1916, 1932, 2 vols. pp. 403-412.  For discussions of the Dogger Bank Commission, see A. Beaucourt, op. cit., M. Bokanowski, op. cit., A. Le Ray, op. cit.

to the Far East, fired into the Hull fishing fleet off Dogger Bank in the North Sea whereby two fishermen were killed and considerable damage was done to several trawlers. Great Britain demanded from Russia not only an apology and adequate damages but also severe punishment of the officer responsible for the outrage. As Russia maintained that the firing was caused by the approach of some Japanese torpedo boats and that she could therefore not punish the officer in command, the parties agreed upon the establishment of an international commission of inquiry as suggested by France. This Commission was charged not only to ascertain the facts of the incident, but also to pronounce an opinion concerning the responsibility for the incident, and the degree of blame attaching to the responsible persons.

The Commission, consisting of five naval officers of high rank from England, Russia, The United States of America, France and Austria-Hungary, sat at Paris from December 22, 1904 to February 26, 1905, on which date it rendered its report. The report of the Commission stated that no torpedo boats had been present and that the opening of fire on the part of the Baltic Fleet was not justifiable. The report also stated that Admiral Rojdestvensky, the commander of the Baltic Fleet, was responsible for the incident but that these facts were not of a nature to cast any discredit upon the military qualities or the humanity of Admiral Rojdestvensky or the personnel of his squadron. In consequence of the last part of the report, Great Britain could not insist upon punishment of the responsible Russian officer. However, Russia did pay the sum of 65,000 British pounds to indemnify the victims of the incident and the families of the two dead fishermen.

The success of the fact-finding effort in the Dogger Bank case in alleviating a dangerous situation resulted in a more determined effort to develop the use of fact-finding techniques in the peaceful settlement of international disputes. The outcome of such efforts appeared in the second Hague Convention of 1907.

Subsequent to 1907, six commissions of inquiry were constituted and functioned in accordance with the provisions of the second Hague Convention. The first such commission was set up on 1912 to determine the facts in disputes between France and Italy arising out of the incidents involving the French ships Tavignano, Camouna and Gaulois. The Tavignano had been captured by an Italian vessel and the Camouna and Gaulois had been fired upon by an Italian torpedo boat. A commission was created under an agreement of May 20, 1912 between the parties to consist of naval officers named by the French, Italian and British Governments, the last being President. The Commission submitted its report on July 23, 1912, which contained no definite conclusion. The matter was then submitted to arbitration but no decision was rendered. The matter was finally settled by a special agreement under which Italy agreed to pay an indemnity of 5,000 francs to the French Government for distribution among the various individuals who suffered losses. [22]

The second commission was formed, in 1921, in a dispute between the Netherlands and Germany to determine responsibility for the torpedoing of a Dutch steamship, the Tubantia, on March 16, 1916. The Commission, established by an agreement of March 30, 1921, consisted of naval officers of Dutch, Danish, Swedish and German nationality presided over by a former member of the Swiss Federal Council. After holding sessions at the Hague, from January 18 to February 10, 1922, the Commission established the fact that the Dutch ship had been sunk by a torpedo launched by a German submarine but could not determine whether the

---

[22]James Brown Scott, (ed.) The Hague Court Reports (New York: Oxford University Press for Carnegie Endowment for International Peace 1916), pp. 413-420.

torpedoing had been willful or unintentional.[23]

Three additional commissions of inquiry that were set up in accordance with the provisions of the Hague Convention of 1907 were concerned with incidents at sea involving German ships engaged in hostilities during World War I. In the first such dispute, between Spain and Germany, a commission of inquiry was set up to determine whether the Norwegian ship Tiger had been in Spanish territorial waters when sunk by a German submarine. It appears that a report in favor of Spain was issued on November 8, 1918.[24]

The remaining two such inquiries concerned a determination of fact upon which the international law with respect to the seizure of ships and the internment of prize crews entering neutral waters could be applied. In the first of these inquiries, an international commission, composed of naval officers of Denmark, Sweden, Argentina, Netherlands and Germany, was constituted to determine, in a dispute between the Netherlands and Germany, whether two German submarines which at different times had entered Dutch waters and had been detained with their crews by Dutch authorities had been lawfully detained. The Commission concluded, on July 20, 1917, that one submarine had entered Dutch waters through the neglect of its captain and should be detained while the other submarine had entered such waters by accident and should be released.[25]

In the second inquiry, involving Germany and Denmark, a German prize crew on a captured Spanish ship, the Igotz Mendi, was stranded in Danish waters on February 24, 1918 and later seized by the Danish authorities. An international commission of investigation, established by Germany and Denmark, rendered a decision, on August 19, 1918, that the case of the prize crew of the Igotz Mendi was not so similar to that of British officers who had previously been released by Danish authorities that the differing decisions could be regarded as violating neutrality. The factual basis for the Commission's decision referred to a previous incident involving two neutral vessels which had been stopped at sea by a British cruiser and ordered to proceed to British ports. British officers had been placed on the two vessels which remained under their own flags and their own officers and had not been treated as prizes. Bad weather preventing their calling at British ports of inspection to which they had been directed to go, the British officers agreed that the vessels should proceed to their original destinations. The British officers, assuming the status of ordinary passengers, were liberated upon the arrival of the two vessels in Denmark, since the arrival of the British officers had no direct connection with hostile acts. Such was not the case with the German prize crew whose internment was therefore continued.[26]

---

[23]Ibid., 2nd Series, 1932, pp. 135-145.

[24]U. N. Doc. A/AC.18/64, June 15, 1948. According to M. O. Hudson, The Permanent Court of International Justice 1920-1942 (New York: 1943) p. 40n, no report was published by the commission in this matter. Nor does J. B. Scott, The Hague Court Reports, op. cit., contain a report of the Tiger Inquiry. Also see Ralston, J. H., International Arbitration from Athens to Locarno (Stanford: University Press, 1929), pp. 294-295.

[25]Green H. Hackworth, Digest of International Law. (Washington: Government Printing Office, 1940-1944), vol. 7, p. 462.

[26]Ibid., p. 583.

The sixth case, of recent date, in which a Commission of Inquiry was constituted and operated was the "Red Crusader" incident.[27] The case revolved about the arrest by Danish authorities of a British trawler, on May 29, 1961, alleged to have been fishing in Danish waters in violation of an Agreement of April 27, 1959 between the Danish and United Kingdom Governments. According to the Agreement, which related to the temporary regulation of fishing around the Faroe Islands, a limit had been agreed upon referred to as "the blue line". Under the Agreement, vessels registered in the United Kingdom were excluded from fishing in the area between the coast of the Faroe Islands and the blue line. According to the exchange of notes of November 15, 1961, the Commission of Inquiry which was established had to decide whether the "Red Crusader" was fishing or with her fishing gear not stowed was present inside the blue line on the night of May 29, 1961 and to elucidate the circumstances of the arrest of the "Red Crusader". The case was further complicated by the attempt of the "Red Crusader" to escape from the Danish frigate escorting her and the alleged interference by British naval vessels in the pursuit of the "Red Crusader" by the Danish frigate. The question was also raised as to whether the act of the Danish frigate in firing several loaded rounds at the "Red Crusader" thereby inflicting some damage was necessary.

The Commission was constituted on November 21, 1961 in The Hague and consisted of Professor Charles de Visscher (Belgium), President, Professor Andre Gros (France) and Captain C. Moolenburgh (Netherlands), Members. After holding hearings from March 5 through March 16, 1962, the Commission issued its report on March 23. In its report, the Commission found that (1) no proof of fishing within the blue line had been established although the "Red Crusader" was in water inside the blue line for fourteen minutes on May 29, 1961; (2) during such time, the "Red Crusader" was within the blue line her fishing gear was not stowed; and (3) all signals to stop given by the Danish frigate were given outside the blue line. The Commission further found that the "Red Crusader" was in fact arrested, that it did attempt to escape and that in the process the Skipper of the "Red Crusader" took steps to seclude the two naval personnel placed on board by the Danish frigate. In addition, the Commission noted that the firing of solid shot by the Danish frigate exceeded the legitimate use of armed force. With respect to the British naval vessel involved, the Commission found that the Commanding Officer of that ship made every effort to avoid any recourse to violence between the "Red Crusader" and the Danish frigate and that his conduct and the conduct of his officers were impeccable. The Danish Government agreed that the damages assessed by the Commission of Inquiry were not unreasonable.

The work of the seven commissions described above was very specialized. In all cases, the subject matter, consisting of facts concerning incidents at sea, was reviewed by commissions composed of naval officers (with the exceptions of the President of the Tubantia inquiry and the President and one member of the Red Crusader inquiry). The inquiries consisted of an evaluation of written and oral statements submitted by the parties as well as a study of maps to determine the location of the incidents in question. With the exception of the Dogger Bank case, no other case was of sufficient importance to have endangered peace if not re-

---

[27] Report of The Commission of Enquiry in the "Red Crusader" Incident, Bureau International De La Cour Permanente d'Arbitrage, The Hague: Van Langenhuijsen Brothers, March, 1962. Also see Gerard Timsit "Le fonctionnement de la procédure d'enquête dans l'affaire du 'Red Crusader'" Annuaire Francaise de Droit International, vol. IX, (1963) p. 460.

solved.[28]

B. The Bryan Treaties
The Bryan Treaties, concluded by the United States in 1913 and 1914, marked a step forward in the development of basic commitments and procedures for the use of fact-finding in the settlement of international disputes. Important among the innovations were the change from ad hoc to permanent commissions appointed in advance and the extension of jurisdiction to cover disputes of every nature which either diplomacy had failed to adjust or where the parties did not have recourse to arbitration. The innovations included, also, a provision that recourse to the commission was binding and that the commission was entitled to initiate action. In addition, an obligatory cooling-off period was introduced through the requirement of a report from the commission within one year during which time no war was to be declared nor hostilities permitted. The recommendations of the commission, however, were to be without binding force on the parties.

The source of Mr. Bryan's inspiration for his idea was a plan he had supported to be used in domestic labor disputes.[29] Mr. Bryan projected onto the level of international relations his objections to compulsory arbitration of labor disputes. These objections stemmed from what he felt was public opposition in the United States to the compulsory nature of arbitral decisions.[30] He hoped that by providing for compulsory investigation, the parties would be induced by the weight of public opinion to reach agreement. Mr. Bryan was of the opinion that arbitration was often avoided because of the parties' fear that questions affecting their vital interests or honor might arise in the course of the proceedings.[31] The exclusion of matters concerning vital interests and honor in many treaties was also a limiting factor on the use of the arbitration procedure, Mr. Bryan felt.

It is interesting to note that in advocating his plan for the use of inquiry in the pacific settlement of international disputes, in 1905, Mr. Bryan was not familiar with the Hague Convention of 1899's provisions regarding commissions of inquiry.[32] Nevertheless, although based on different experiences, the reasoning of Mr. Bryan and Professor de Martens in support of the use of inquiry in international disputes was remarkably similar. Another point of interest is that Mr. Bryan felt strongly enough about his plan to make his acceptance of the Office of Secretary of State conditional on a promise by President Wilson to make the plan an integral part of his foreign policy.[33]

Authorities agree that many of the subsequent developments in international inquiry are to be found in features incorporated in the Bryan Treaties.[34] Yet the record of accomplishment under the Bryan format for setting up bilateral fact-finding commissions under a series of treaties each of which was entitled "Treaty For The Advancement of Peace"

---

[28]M. O. Hudson, op. cit., p. 40n.

[29]James Brown Scott, Treaties for The Advancement of Peace, p. XXVIII.

[30]Idem.

[31]Ibid., pp. XXX-XXXII

[32]Proceedings of the American Society of International Law, vol. 23, (1929), p. 172.

[33]Ibid., pp. 171-172.

[34]Manley O. Hudson, The Permanent Court of International Justice, (1943), pp. 40-41. Also see Max Habicht, op. cit., p. 1001 and John Brown Scott in Proceedings of The American Society of International Law (1929), p. 174.

was disappointing. Of the thirty treaties concluded by Secretary of State Bryan, only twenty-eight entered into effect. Only ten of the permanent commissions were ever constituted and of these none are in existence, today. Nor were any of the commissions provided for by the Bryan Treaties ever called upon to investigate a dispute.[35] The Bryan Treaties incorporated, by referral, provisions of the Hague Convention of 1907 with regard to the appointment of commissioners under Article 45 and to procedure under Articles 9 to 36. The "cooling-off period" provisions of the Bryan Treaties also exercised an influence on the drafters of the League Covenant. For example, under Article 12, Members of the League agreed "in no case to resort to war until three months after the award by the arbitrators or the judicial decision, or the report by the council".

The unique aspect of the Bryan Treaties was that they provided for compulsory submission of disputes although still retaining the Hague concept that the reports of the commissions of inquiry did not have an obligatory effect on the parties.[36] The essence of the Bryan Treaties was that in view of the desire of nations to retain control over the solution of controversies to which they were parties, arrangements could be made for compulsory investigation of disputes, with the understanding that both states would be at liberty to disregard the findings of the tribunal.[37]

Considering the stage of international legal and organizational development at the time, the idea was radical and, while the results were disappointing, did furnish material that was used in the League of Nations' subsequent approach to the problems of investigating the facts in international disputes.

The Bryan Treaties while not identical were basically similar. The following is a summary in topical form of their basic provisions:[38]

Jurisdictional clause. There were four variations of the jurisdictional clause, of which one was the following:

> All disputes of every nature whatsoever to the settlement
> of which previous arbitration treaties or agreements do
> not apply in their terms or are not applied in fact.

A variation was "All disputes of every nature whatsoever which diplomacy shall fail to adjust". The elimination of the Hague provision "involving neither honor nor vital interest" was an important step forward.

Postponement of hostilities. One of the innovations made by the Bryan Treaties consisted of an agreement not to declare war or begin hostilities during the investigation of the commission and before its report was submitted.

Composition of the commission. Each commission consisted of five members. The manner of appointment was most frequently specified as follows:

> One member shall be chosen from each Contracting Country
> by the Government thereof; one member shall be chosen by
> each Government from some third country; the fifth member
> shall be chosen by common agreement between the two
> Governments, it being understood that he shall not be a citi-
> zen of either country.

---

[35]N. L. Hill, "International Commissions of Inquiry and Conciliation", International Conciliation No. 278, (1932), pp. 85-134.

[36]C. C. Hyde, "The Place of Commissions of Inquiry and Conciliation Treaties in The Peaceful Settlement of International Disputes", British Yearbook of International Law (1929), pp. 96-110.

[37]N. L. Hill, op. cit.

[38]Taken from J. B. Scott, Treaties for the Advancement of Peace, op. cit.

The attempt to include representatives of each party as well as apparently impartial members from other countries was basically a sound formula which was followed in the practice of appointing assessors to League of Nations' commissions.

Only seven treaties provided for removal of commissioners and, six of these also provided for withdrawal of approval of the fifth commissioner. The other treaties made no provision on these points.

All the Bryan Treaties, with minor exceptions, provided that vacancies should be filled according to the manner of the original appointment.

Most of the treaties made no reference to the tenure of office of the commissioners, it apparently being understood that the term of office was indefinite. The treaties with China, France, Russia, Spain and Sweden provided for appointment for one year, the commissioner, however, to remain in office until superseded or reappointed or until the work in which he was engaged at the time his office expired was completed. The treaty with Italy provided for a four year term.

The indefiniteness of the term of office of the commissioners underlines one of the problems that confronts the use of bilateral permanent commissions of investigation. This is one aspect inviting the criticism made by Judge Jessup that bilateral arrangements like the Bryan Treaties involving so many commissions would be unwieldy if the plan were used by every state because there would not be enough commissioners to fill all the positions.[39]

Procedure and Functioning. The procedure of the commission is not always provided for in the treaties, although several refer the commission to the Hague Convention of 1907 for guidance.

With respect to assumption of jurisdiction, the treaties usually contained an apparently simple provision that the dispute should be referred to the international commission by the contracting parties. However, the commission could assume jurisdiction independently. Six treaties stated that the commission might act on its own initiative by notifying both governments and requesting their cooperation in the investigation. Five treaties required that the commission assume such initiative only by unanimous agreement. Three treaties specified that if the majority of the members of the commission consented and one of the contracting parties agreed, then the commission would have jurisdiction of the case. The principle of compulsory submission of disputes to investigation was a radical innovation made by the Bryan Treaties.

Only five of the treaties provided for a place of meeting of the commission and these stipulated that it should be determined by the commission itself.

Although most of the treaties were silent on the vote required for a decision, five treaties provided that the terms of the report and the conclusion of the commission should be adopted by a majority.

All treaties were uniform in providing that the contracting parties should furnish the commission with the means and facilities required for its investigation and report. The treaty with Italy contained the additional clause

> provided that in their judgment this does not conflict with
> the laws or with the supreme interests of the State, and
> provided that the interest and rights of third States shall
> not thereby suffer damage.

The stipulation concerning expenses was generally that the expenses of the commission should be paid by the two governments in equal proportion. Some of the treaties contained, in addition, a provision that agreement on the compensation of the commissioners must be arrived at beforehand. This provision was an equitable one and the practice of

---

[39]Philip C. Jessup, International Security, New York: Council of Foreign Relations, (1935), pp. 89-90.

having governments share in the expenses has been followed in recent years in investigations conducted at the request of member states by the Secretary-General of the United Nations.

The treaties usually provided that the report of the commission should be completed within one year after the date on which it declared its investigation to have begun. Some treaties added that the contracting parties might either extend or shorten this period by mutual agreement.

The usual provision with regard to duration was that the treaty would remain in force for five years. Some treaties provided for automatic renewal unless denounced within a period six months or one year, as the case might be, prior to the end of the five year period.

Implementation. Only three treaties incorporated articles on provisional measures. With respect to implementation, the usual stipulation was that the parties reserved the right to act independently on the subject matter of the dispute after the report of the commission had been submitted. Some of the treaties contained, in addition, an expression that the parties would, on the basis of the report, endeavor to adjust the dispute directly.

The importance of the Bryan Treaties, although they were not implemented, lay in their nurture of the concept of fact-finding in international relations. In addition, the innovations they added such as compulsory submission and the idea of a "cooling-off" period appeared in the League of Nations Covenant. The institutionalization of fact-finding begun in the Hague Convention of 1899 was thus further developed by the efforts of Mr. Bryan. Fact-finding as a technique also found its way, subsequently, into procedures of conciliation which were incorporated into treaties and conventions created under the auspices of the League of Nations, as well as in the procedures of the League Council itself. The material of the Hague Conventions and of the Bryan Treaties was, in this manner, woven into the texture of subsequent developments in the use of fact-finding in international disputes.

C. League of Nations

The contribution of the League of Nations to fact-finding was two-fold: 1. the new international organization used fact-finding as a basis for action by the League Council and Assembly, and 2. the development of the technique of inquiry as a means of pacific settlement of disputes between states continued. Under the first heading, the use of inquiry became a preliminary measure in the procedures followed by the Council and Assembly of the League in bringing about a cessation of hostilities or in acting as an organ of conciliation. Under the second heading, fact-finding was absorbed into the procedure of conciliation.

In this latter connection, the importance of the resolution adopted by the Third Assemply of the League of Nations, on September 22, 1922, lies in the trend which it both initiated and signalled--a trend away from the Bryan independent commissions of inquiry and toward absorption of fact-finding techniques into conciliation procedures. This trend was carried foward by the Locarno Treaties of 1926 and the General Act for the Pacific Settlement of International Disputes of 1928. Thus the adoption by the Third Assembly of its resolution of September 22, 1922 and the adoption by the Ninth Assembly of the General Act in 1928 laid their impress on the large number of bilateral treaties created between 1919 and 1940 in which provision was made for commissions of conciliation rather than of inquiry.

1. Resolution of Third Assembly 1922

Paralleling the use of fact-finding commissions by the League of Nations, itself, was the incorporation of fact-finding procedures in a large number of bilateral and multilateral treaties concluded after the first World War. Recognizing this development, the League Council initiated studies of the bilateral and multilateral treaties concluded after

World War I which contained provisions establishing procedures for the investigation and conciliation of disputes. These studies were performed by the Committee on Arbitration and Security of the Disarmament Commission in conjunction with the Secretariat of the League.[40] As a result, a series of studies were prepared and published by the Secretariat of the League on the procedure for pacific settlement as incorporated in the many existing bilateral and multilateral treaties for pacific settlement.[41] Commitments of such a character as were contained in such treaties were not regarded as conflicting with the obligations of members of the League under the Covenant.

The Committee's findings, which were slightly modified by the Council, became the basis of a resolution adopted by the Third Assembly, on September 22, 1922, recommending that the members of the League conclude separate agreements for the establishment of commissions of conciliation "subject to the rights and obligations mentioned in Article 15 of the Covenant".[42] The Assembly expressed the hope that

The competence of conciliation commissions will extend to the greatest possible number of disputes and that the practical application of particular conventions between States, as recommended in the present resolution, will, in the near future, make possible the establishment of a general convention open to the adhesion of all States.[43]

Members of the League were further authorized to request the assistance of the Secretary-General in the conclusion of such agreements.[44]

Article 5 of the "Rules" of the Assembly resolution provided for inquiry in the following language:

Both parties shall be heard by the Commission. The parties shall furnish the Commission with all the information which may be useful for the enquiry and the drawing up of the report, and shall in every respect assist it in the accomplishment of its task.

The Commission shall itself regulate all details of procedure not provided for in the Convention, and establish rules of procedure for the obtaining of evidence.

However, Article 7 of the "Rules" stated that "in the proper cases the report shall include a proposal for the settlement of the dispute". The step away from the Bryan commissions of inquiry had been taken.

2. Locarno Treaties

At the same time that the Treaty of Mutual Guarantee was concluded at Locarno, October 16, 1925, four separate arbitration treaties were concluded between Germany and Belgium, France, Poland and Czechoslovakia. [45] What is of interest here is that in each of these arbitration agreements, the contracting parties stipulated that disputes of every kind between them with regard to which they were in conflict as to their respective rights and which it might not be possible to settle amicably by the normal methods of diplomacy might, prior to resort to arbitral procedure, be submitted by agreement to a permanent conciliation commission.

---

[40] L. of N., Records of 3rd Assembly, Plenary Meetings, vol. I (Geneva, 1922), p. 199.

[41] L. of N., Systematic Survey, op. cit.

[42] L. of N., Records of 3rd Assembly, Plenary Meetings, vol. I (Geneva, 1922), p. 199.

[43] Idem.

[44] Idem.

[45] League of Nations, Treaty Series, vol. 54, pp. 304, 316, 328, 342.

This permanent conciliation commission was to be composed of five members, one chosen by each party and three others of different nationalities to be chosen, by common agreement from among the nationals of third powers. The task of the permanent commission was to elucidate questions in dispute, to collect with that object all necessary information by means of enquiry or otherwise, and to endeavor to bring the parties to an agreement. The parties undertook to facilitate the work of the commission and to supply it with all relevant documents and information as well as to allow it to proceed in their territory and in accordance with their laws to summon and hear witnesses and visit the localities in question. If no amicable settlement had been reached before the commission, provision was made for subsequent resort to arbitral and judicial procedures.

    3.   General Act for the Pacific Settlement of
           International Disputes [46]

The General Act for the Pacific Settlement of International Disputes, adopted by the Ninth Assembly of the League of Nations, September 26, 1928, and which entered into force, August 16, 1929, dealt in its first chapter with conciliation.

As under the Locarno Pacts, the task of the conciliation commission was to elucidate the questions in dispute, to collect with that object all necessary information by means of enquiry or otherwise, and to endeavor to bring the parties to an agreement. In its procedural provisions, the General Act followed substantially the provisions of the bilateral Treaties of Locarno discussed above. Similarly, in regard to enquiries, the commission, unless it decided unanimously to the contrary, was to act in accordance with the provisions of Part III of the Hague Convention of October 18, 1907 for the Pacific Settlement of International Disputes. The absorption of fact-finding into conciliation procedures had thus become fully accepted.

Although many bilateral treaties incorporating fact-finding in procedures for conciliation had been entered into since the resolution of September 22, 1922 of the Third Assembly,[47] only ten commissions of conciliation were actually constituted and functioned.[48] When these ten instances are added to the seven cases referred to earlier, in which commissions of investigation had been established and had operated under the Hague Conventions, the score for the implementation of fact-finding provisions in treaties is rather low.

It appears that greater progress in the use of fact-finding in international relations has been made by international organizations in the maintenance of international peace. The first example, of course, was the League of Nations with the establishment of which, fact-finding became a part of the new legal and political framework of a permanent international organization. The distinguishing factors in this picture were the obligation to submit the dispute under Articles 12 and 15 of the Covenant and the transfer of responsibility for constituting and operating the commission of inquiry from the parties directly concerned to a third party, i.e., the League Council or Assembly. This method of handling inquiries could result in the parties not being members of the fact-finding body at all. However, the parties retained the right to appoint "assessors" to assist the commission, the assessors not being members of the commission and only representing the parties before the commission.[49]

[46]L. of N., *Treaty Series*, Vol. 93, No. 2123, p. 345.

[47]see footnote 1

[48]U. N. Doc. A/5694, (May 1, 1964).

[49]Examples are the Lytton Committee (L. of N. Doc. C663.M320. 1932 VII, p. 6) and the Chaco Commission (L. of N. Doc. C154, M64, 1934 VII, p. 7).

Of particular interest is Article 5, paragraph two of the Covenant, which provides that the appointment of committe to investigate a particular matter is a matter of procedure and may be decided by a majority. Although this would appear to obviate the Hague Convention requirement of consent of the parties to the investigation, in practice no commission of inquiry was established by the League of Nations without the prior consent of both parties to the dispute, thus assuring their cooperation in the investigation.

The provisions of the League Covenant concerned with inquiry are contained in Articles 12, 15 and 17 in addition to Article 5 to which reference has already been made. Concepts developed in the Bryan Treaties with respect to a "cooling-off period" now provided one more basis for determining when a party's acts violated international law.[50] In this connection, Article 16 provided for sanctions to be imposed should any member of the League resort to war in disregard of its covenants under Articles 12, 13 or 15.

With regard to the obligatory nature of the report of a commission of inquiry, Article 15 provided that a report adopted unanimously by the Council (or a report adopted by the Assembly concurred in by the representatives of members of the Council and by a majority of the other members) containing a statement of the facts of the dispute and recommendations which are deemed just and proper in regard thereto, created the obligation for the members of the League not to go to war with any party to the dispute which complied with the recommendations of the report. The votes of the parties were excluded in arriving at unanimity. In the event that no such unanimity was reached by the Council or Assembly on a report, Paragraph 7 of Article 15 provided that the members of the League were free to "take such action as they shall consider necessary for the maintenance of right and justice".

The Secretary-General, under Article 15, paragraph 1, was bound, after having received a notice from a party of the existence of a dispute, to make all necessary arrangements for a full investigation and consideration thereof. In practice, that included the creation of a committee for an inquiry on-the-spot, preceding and preparatory to consideration of the merits by the Council.[51] In many cases, the Council appointed a rapporteur who was one of its members or a small committee of such members to gather information, try to settle the dispute and report to the Council. [52]

---

[50]Under Art. 12 para. 1, the members of the League of Nations agree "in no case to resort to war until three months after . . . the report by the Council".

[51]See Shanghai Committee, L. of N. Official Journal, 1932 XIII, p. 343; also, L. of N. Official Journal, Special Supp. No. 101, p. 194.

[52]For accounts of the L. of N. activities, see T. P. Conwell-Evans, The League Council in Action (London: 1929), F. P. Walters, History of the League of Nations - 2nd vol. (London: 1952), C. Howard-Ellis, The Origin, Structure and Working of the League of Nations (Boston: 1928). As to cases considered formally by the League of Nations for the purpose of political settlement, the Information Section of the League lists 43 issues dealt with by the League under the heading "Political Questions Dealt with by the League of Nations" in the 10th ed. of Essential Facts about the League of Nations (1939). Adding the appeal of the Finnish Government in Dec. 1939 would make 44. In not all cases was fact-finding resorted to.

4. Geneva Protocol of 1924

In order to plug up loopholes in the Covenant of the League of Nations, with respect to League action in international disputes, the Protocol for Pacific Settlement of International Disputes (Geneva Protocol) was adopted by the Fifth Assembly on October 2, 1924.[53] The purpose of the Geneva Protocol was to make war illegal and by providing detailed procedures for Council action, to render more complete and effective the provisions of the Covenant contained in Articles 4, 5, 6, 7, 11, 12, 13, 14 and 15. The members also agreed at the time to work to amend the Covenant of the League to include the concepts contained in the Geneva Protocol.

The Geneva Protocol provided in Article 7 that if the Council was of the opinion that a complaint required investigation, it would if it deemed it expedient, arrange for enquiries and investigations in one or more of the countries concerned. Such enquiries would be carried out with the utmost possible dispatch and the signatory states undertook to afford every facility for carrying them out. If the result of such enquiries and investigations was to establish an infraction of the provisions of Article 7, it would be the duty of the Council to summon the state or states guilty of the infraction to put an end thereto. In addition, Article 10 of the Geneva Protocol stated that every state which resorted to war in violation of the undertakings contained in the Covenant or in the Protocol was an aggressor.

By providing a legal definition of aggression coupled with fact-finding procedures to determine if the conditions of aggression were present, the Geneva Protocol was a unique attempt to strengthen the League of Nations, in its role of maintaining international peace and security. The Geneva Protocol failed to obtain the required number of ratifications and never came into force.

D. The United Nations

The creators of the United Nations Charter drew heavily upon the experience of the League of Nations as well as the provisions for fact-finding contained in prior treaties and conventions. The power to conduct investigations of fact is therefore woven into the fabric of the Charter both explicitly and implicitly.

With respect to fact-finding in the Hague tradition, Article 33 of the Charter accepts the concept of inquiry as a method of peaceful settlement upon which the fact-finding provisions contained in many treaties and conventions were based. Article 33 provides that:

1. The parties to any dispute, the continuance of which is likely to endanger the maintenance of international peace and security, shall, first of all, seek a solution by negotiation, enquiry, mediation, conciliation, arbitration, judicial settlement, resort to regional agencies or arrangements or other peaceful means of their own choice.

2. The Security Council shall, when it deems necessary, call upon the parties to settle their dispute by such means.

It is in the newer concept of fact-finding, as a basis for action by an international organ, that the Charter has found more application. The Security Council, General Assembly and the Secretary-General have from time to time engaged in fact-finding of this nature thereby building a useful body of experience. The powers and practices of United Nations organs in conducting investigations in international disputes will be analyzed in detail in Chapters V and VI herein.

E. The Inter-American Peace System

Among the American States of the Western Hemisphere, several multilateral treaties providing, among other procedures of pacific set-

---

[53]League of Nations Doc. C606, M211.1924 IX. Also see M. Habicht, op. cit., p. 929.

tlement, for fact-finding and conciliation make up what can be termed the Inter-American Peace System.[54]  While the operations and effects of inquiries in disputes between states of the western hemisphere are shaped by the regional character of the Inter-American Peace System, a study of fact-finding in international disputes would not be complete without including the fact-finding experiences of the Inter-American Peace System.

The first instrument in the western hemisphere, of a conventional nature, which incorporated the concept of inquiry was the Treaty on Compulsory Arbitration, signed on January 29, 1902, at the Second International American Conference.[55]  The treaty was signed by nine countries, ratified by six and entered into force on January 31, 1903.[56]  In addition to establishing procedures of good offices and mediation, the treaty provided for the establishment of an ad hoc International Commission of Inquiry for those controversies arising from a difference of opinion on points of fact.

The inter-American efforts in the area of pacific settlement of disputes incorporating fact-finding techniques received a second impetus with the Central American Treaty of 1923.[57]  The preamble of the treaty produced by the Central American Conference in Washington, February 7, 1923, consisting of Costa Rica, Guatemala, Honduras, Nicaragua, Salvador and the United States, stated that it was the desire of the parties to "unify and recast in one single convention" the treaties that had preceded it.[58]  However, unlike the Bryan Treaties, to which it referred, which had provided for permanent commissions, the Central American Treaty provided for ad hoc commissions.

Shortly thereafter, the American republics entered into the so-called "Gondra Treaty", signed at Santiago, Chile on May 3, 1923.[59]  Like the Bryan Treaties, the Gondra Treaty provided for the submission to a commission of inquiry of all controversies between the contracting parties which it had been impossible to settle through diplomatic channels or to submit to arbitration in accordance with existing treaties.  Based in respect to its general objectives on the Bryan Treaties, the Gondra Treaty sought to give a collective character to the obligation to submit controversies of whatever nature to the procedure of investigation and report.[60]

Although the Gondra Treaty provided for ad hoc commissions of inquiry, it also provided for the designation of two permanent commissions, one in Washington and one in Montevideo, to be composed of the three American diplomatic agents longest accredited in those capitals. The functions of these commissions were declared to be limited to re-

---

[54]See for texts of conventions and resolutions of Inter-American Conferences, Carnegie Endowment for International Peace, The International Conferences of American States 1899-1928, (1931), and First Supplement 1933-1940, (1940), London: Oxford University Press; Pan American Union, Department of Legal Affairs, International Conferences of American States, Second Supplement, 1942-1954, Washington: 1958 (hereinafter referred to as International Conferences).

[55]International Conferences, 1899-1928, pp. 100-104.

[56]Pan American Union, Inter-American Treaties and Conventions, Washington: 1954, p. 11.

[57]U. S. Treaty Series, No. 717.

[58]Idem.

[59]L. of N. Treaty Series, Vol. 33, p. 25.

[60]Charles G. Fenwick, The Organization of American States, The Inter-American Regional System, Washington: Kaufman Printing, Inc., 1963, p. 53.

ceiving from the interested parties the request for convocation of the ad hoc commission of inquiry and to notifying the other party thereof immediately.

Under the General Convention of Inter-American Conciliation, signed at Washington, on January 5, 1929, the commission of inquiry provided for under the Gondra Treaty was expanded to a commission of conciliation.[61] The General Convention thus represented an attempt to strengthen the commission created by the Gondra Treaty by adding to its investigatory powers the further power to propose bases for the settlement of controversy.[62]

One provision of particular interest in the General Convention of Inter-American Conciliation was that which provided that the permanent commissions established under Article III of the Gondra Treaty should exercise conciliatory functions either on their own motion or at the request of a party to the dispute until the various commissions of conciliation could be organized.

The Protocol to the General Convention of Inter-American Conciliation, signed at Montevideo, on December 26, 1933 provided that the signatories, by means of bilateral agreement, should name those members of the various commissions provided for in Article IV of the General Convention.[63] Those commissions were declared to have a permanent character and were to be called "Commissions of Investigation and Conciliation". The commissions organized under Article II of the Gondra Treaty were to be called "Permanent Diplomatic Commissions of Investigation and Conciliation".

The complete submergence of fact-finding into conciliation procedures is apparent in the Inter-American Anti-War Treaty of Non-Agression and Conciliation, sometimes referred to as the "Saavedra Lamas Treaty", which was signed by certain American republics at Rio de Janeiro, on October 10, 1933.[64] The emphasis was now on securing conciliatory settlement of the disputes rather than on elucidating the facts. According to Professor Habicht, explaining this emphasis on conciliation, the purpose is to endeavor to bring the parties to agreement so that there is a

new definition of the task of the commission, according to which the presentation of conclusions and proposals in a report is no longer essential and can even be omitted if the commission prefers.[65]

Perhaps the desire to reduce costs by eliminating the investigation procedure resulted in the greater stress on conciliation found in the treaties among the American states.[66] More likely, the nature of the inter-American system, it was felt, did not require the impartial and full investigation of all the facts, developed in the light of all the contentions of every kind advanced by the states at variance, as the phraseology of the prior treaties providing for commissions of inquiry had stated. The European approach should be contrasted with this which, as Professor Hyde has observed, required such impartial and full investigation in order

---

[61]L. of N. Treaty Series, Vol. 100, p. 401.

[62]Charles G. Fenwick, op. cit., p. 55.

[63]U. S. Treaty Series No. 887.

[64]L. of N. Treaty Series Vol. 163, p. 393.

[65]M. Habicht, op. cit., p. 1027.

[66]Charles E. Hughes, as the United States delegate, urged the expense of a long inquiry as a reason for eliminating the prerequisite of investigation required by the Gondra Treaty. (Proceedings of the International Conference of American States on Conciliation and Arbitration, held at Washington, December 10, 1928 to January 5, 1929. Washington: United States Government Printing Office, 1929, p. 362.

to establish the recommendations of the conciliators as worthy of respect. [67]

Two further treaties in the inter-American system should be mentioned in passing. The Inter-American Treaty on Good Offices and Mediation, signed by the United States and other American states at Buenos Aires, on December 23, 1936, provided that if the procedures for good offices and mediation provided for under the treaty failed to achieve agreement, then the controversy was to be submitted to the procedure of conciliation, provided for in existing inter-American agreements. [68]

The second treaty was the Inter-American Treaty on the Prevention of Controversies which was signed at Buenos Aires, also, on December 23, 1936. This treaty provided for creation of bilateral mixed commissions to study with the primary object of eliminating as far as possible the causes of future difficulties or controversies and to propose additional or detailed lawful measures which it might be convenient to take in order to promote the due and regular application of treaties in force between the respective parties. [69]

The present framework of the Inter-American Peace System is provided by the Inter-American Treaty for Reciprocal Assistance (Treaty of Rio) of September 2, 1947, [70] the Charter of the Organization of American States, signed April 30, 1948, [71] and the American Treaty on Pacific Settlement (Pact of Bogota), also signed April 30, 1948. [72]

Chapter IV of the Charter of the Organization of American States provides that all international disputes that may arise between American states shall be submitted to the peaceful procedures set forth in the Charter.

Chapter III of the Pact of Bogota, to which many of the American states have not adhered, deals with the "Procedure of investigation and conciliation". One of the important features of Chapter III of the Pact of Bogota is the ability of one party to initiate the procedure of investigation and conciliation by addressing a request to the Council of the Organization of American States to convoke a commission of investigation and conciliation. The parties may also establish a commission of investigation and conciliation by mutual agreement.

The Pact of Bogota places the choice of conciliation or investigation in the hands of the parties. Article XXII, which refers to the usual concept of conciliation incorporating fact-finding states that

It shall be the duty of the Commission of Investigation and Conciliation to clarify the points in dispute between the parties and to endeavor to bring about an agreement between them upon mutually acceptable terms. The Commission shall institute such investigations of the facts involved in the controversy as it may deem necessary for the purpose of providing acceptable bases of settlement.

Article XXVI of the Pact of Bogota reverts to the concept of fact-finding expressed in the Bryan Treaties and the earlier Hague Conventions in providing that

---

[67] C. C. Hyde, op. cit., p. 108.

[68] L. of N. Treaty Series, Vol. 188, p. 75.

[69] Ibid., p. 53.

[70] U. N. Treaty Series, Vol. 21, p. 77.

[71] U. N. Treaty Series, Vol. 119, p. 50.

[72] U. N. Treaty Series, Vol. 30, p. 55 and p. 84. The treaty came into force on May 6, 1949. Costa Rica, Dominican Republic, El Salvador, Haiti, Honduras, Mexico, Nicaragua, Panama and Uruguay had ratified it by January, 1964.

If, in the opinion of the parties, the controversy relates
exclusively to questions of fact, the Commission shall
limit itself to investigating such questions, and shall
conclude its activities with an appropriate report.

However, the treatment of the report and of the proceedings of the
commission, in both cases, is designed to promote conciliatory efforts.
Article XXVII, for example states that if agreement is reached by conciliation, the final report of the commission shall be limited to the text of
the agreement. If no agreement is reached, then the final report shall
contain a summary of the work of the commission.

The various treaties with respect to the application of fact-finding
techniques and procedures, entered into by the states of the western hemisphere, as in the case of the European treaties of the same nature, found
scarce implementation on a bilateral basis. It was in the framework of
the regional system for maintaining the peace and security of the western
hemisphere that fact-finding found the greatest application.

Within the Inter-American Peace System, today, fact-finding can be
engaged in by the Council of the Organization of American States, the
Inter-American Peace Committee and the Meeting of Consultation of
Foreign Ministers. The first body, when acting in a dispute constitutes
itself a Provisional Organ of Consultation until the ministers of foreign
affairs can meet as Organ of Consultation. Under the Rio Treaty, which
is in force with respect to all members of the Organization of American
States, the Organ of Consultation may conduct investigations as necessary
in accordance with its powers, under the Treaty, to deal with a dispute.
A decision to conduct an investigation, under the Rio Treaty, requires a
two-thirds vote of the Organ of Consultation, on which all members of the
Organization are represented.[73] The Council of the Organization of American States, acting as a Provisional Organ of Consultation under the Rio
Treaty has a similar power to investigate in the exercise of its functions
under that Treaty.

The Inter-American Peace Committee was created in pursuance of
Resolution XIV adopted at the Second Meeting of Consultation of Foreign
Ministers in 1940. Resolution XIV recommended to the Governing Board
of the Pan American Union that it

organize, in the American capital deemed most suitable
for the purpose, a committee composed of the representatives of five countries, which shall have the duty of keeping
constant vigilance to insure that States between which any
dispute exists or may arise, of any nature whatsoever, may
solve it as quickly as possible, and of suggesting, without
detriment to the methods adopted by the parties or to the
procedures which they may agree upon, the measures and
steps which may be conducive to a settlement[74]

The scope of the Committee has varied. Prior to 1956, the Committee
had wide latitude in initiating action insofar as it could act without the consent of the parties concerned and on the request of any American State.
After 1956, the Committee's jurisdiction was limited to cases where all
the parties concerned had consented to its action or where a state directly
concerned requested the Committee to act.[75] This jurisdiction was once

---

[73]Organization of American States, Inter-American Treaty of Reciprocal Assistance, Applications, Volume 1, 1948-1956. Pan American
Union, Washington: 1964, p. II.

[74]International Conferences, First Supplement, 1933-1940. p. 360.

[75]Annals of the Organization of American States, vol. 8, (1956),
pp. 194-196.

again expanded to permit the Committee to initiate action[76]

In this last development which was contained in Resolution IV adopted by the Fifth Meeting of Consultation of Ministers of Foreign Affairs, the Committee was specifically entrusted with the study of the following three questions: [77]

a. Methods and procedures to prevent any activities from abroad designed to overthrow established governments or provoke instances of intervention or aggression as contemplated in instruments such as the Convention on Duties and Rights of States in the event of Civil Strife, without impairment to: (i) the rights and liberties of political exiles recognized in the Convention on Territorial Asylum; (ii) the American Declaration of the Rights and Duties of Man; and (iii) the national constitutions of the American states;

b. The relationship between violations of human rights or the non-exercise of representative democracy, on the one hand, and the political tensions that affect the peace of the hemisphere, on the other; and

c. The relationship between economics underdevelopment and political instability.

As was pointed out earlier, the incidents requiring inquiry in the maintenance of international peace which have occurred in the western hemisphere have taken place within the framework of the regional system for maintaining the peace and security of the western hemisphere. The Pact of Bogota, which was signed on April 30, 1948, has been ratified by only ten of the signatories. Action taken by the Organization of American States in matters affecting the peace and security of the western hemisphere, therefore, must be based upon the Charter of the Organization of American States and the Treaty of Rio which all twenty one signatories have ratified.

Within this framework, the Inter-American Peace Committee occupies a unique position as an autonomous conciliatory agency. In the exercise of its conciliatory functions, the Inter-American Peace Committee has had to resort to investigations of varying scope. The Council of the Organization of American States may also direct the Inter-American Peace Committee to conduct an investigation as it did, in 1961, in connection with the complaint that the subversive activities of the Castro regime in Cuba constituted a threat to the peace of the hemisphere. The Committee is required to report to the Council of the Organization of American States, the Meeting of Consultation of Ministers of Foreign Affairs and the Inter-American Conference on its activities and the result of its efforts. It is also obligated to keep the Security Council informed of its activities under Article 54 of the United Nations Charter.

The use of fact-finding procedures by the Council of the Organization of American States acting as a Provisional Organ of Consultation and of the Meeting of Consultation of Ministers of Foreign Affairs serving as Organ of Consultation under the Inter-American Treaty of Reciprocal Assistance (Treaty of Rio) has produced a valuable accumulation of experience on the use of inquiry in the maintenance of international peace. The experiences in fact-finding of the Inter-American Peace Committee, especially when related to the efforts of the Council and the Organ of Consultation, also provide material for further analysis.

It is experiences of this nature in investigation by international organizations such as the Inter-American Peace System, the League of

---

[76] American Journal of International Law (1961) Vol. 56, pp. 539-540. Resolution IV of the Fifth Meeting of Consultation of Ministers of Foreign Affairs, Santiago, August 8, 1959, text.

[77] Idem.

Nations and the United Nations which provide the most important source of information on fact-finding techniques. Information from these experiences should throw light on the limitations and problems involved in investigating the facts in international disputes. These experiences will be reviewed in the following chapter.

F. Treaties of Inquiry and Conciliation since 1919.

After the close of World War I and prior to World War II, a large number of treaties providing for inquiry and conciliation were concluded. In all, 225 of such treaties were concluded which with several multilateral conventions and the Bryan Treaties created obligations for recourse to some 766 permanent or ad hoc commissions.[78] It is impossible to determine all the commissions that have operated but available records indicate only ten such commissions have reached the attention of publicists since the first World War including five since 1945.[79]

The restrictions on publicity which are contained in many of the treaties or which have been adopted by the Commissions have prevented the accumulation of data concerning the activities of all the commissions which may have functioned and also the nature of the operation of those commissions concerning which some information has been published. For that reason, the listing following of those commissions which have been publicized is not to be considered complete. For the same reason, the extent of the investigative function of the commissions whose activities are described is also left unclear.

Bolivian-Paraguayan Commission, 1929.[80]

Just prior to the opening of the 1929 Conference of American States on Conciliation and Arbitration in Washington, a series of border incidents occurred in the Chaco region, an area in which Bolivia and Paraguay had had a long simmering territorial dispute. A committee assigned by the Conference arranged for the parties to submit the dispute to a special commission of inquiry and conciliation. The commission was instructed to establish the facts with regard to the attack by Paraguayan troops, December 5, 1929, on the outpost, Vanguardia, and to submit proposals to settle the incident. The commission was further instructed that if no agreement were possible, it was to establish the facts and the responsibilities in the situation.

The commission was composed of one representative each from the United States, Mexico, Uruguay, Colombia and Cuba, and two each from Paraguay and Bolivia. It met ten times in Washington, D. C. between March and September 1929. Through the neutral representatives on the commission, an agreement was reached. In addition, the commission arranged for the supervision and repatriation of prisoners. Two subcommittees were sent to the area and their findings were incorporated in the records of the commission. No report was issued by the commission in view of its success in producing agreement between the parties to the dispute. Ten years passed before the substance of the dispute was disposed of by agreement between the parties.

---

[78]Jean Efremoff, "Organization de la conciliation comme moyen de prevenir les guerres, "Recueil des Cours l'Académie de droit international de la Haye, vol. 59 (1937), pp. 139-140.

[79]See Manley O. Hudson, International Tribunals, Past and Future (1944) p. 228; H. Rolin, European Yearbook, vol. 3 (1957), p. 7; United Nation Document A/5694, May 1, 1964.

[80]Proceedings of the Commission of Inquiry and Conciliation, Bolivia and Paraguay, March 13, 1929-September 13, 1929.

German-Lithuanian Commission, 1931.[81]

Under the terms of a 1928 treaty, a five member commission was created to resolve a dispute arising over the interpretation of a clause of the German-Lithuanian Commercial Treaty of 1928 pertaining to the reciprocal rights of immigration and settlement. The commission's recommendations submitted in September of 1931, were accepted by both parties.

French-Portuguese Commission.[82]

A commission was created under a 1928 treaty to resolve a trade dispute involving the interpretation of a treaty. The dispute was settled before the issuance of the report.

Belgium-Luxembourg Commission, 1934.[83]

In accordance with a treaty of 1927 a conciliation commission, with M. Max Huber of Switzerland, was created to consider a case of smuggling. It's recommendations were accepted by both parties. No report was published.

Danish-Lithuanian Commission, 1937-1938.[84]

A conciliation commission was created under the terms of a 1925 treaty. Its task was to resolve the differences regarding the mode of payment for work in connection with a railroad. Convening at the Hague on November 12, 1937 and adopting procedural rules on the following day, the commission adjourned to May 19, 1938, to await the conclusion of the written phase of its examination. The commission terminated its activities on September 30, 1938 with a report noting the failure of the parties to reach agreement.

French-Siamese Commission, 1946-1947.[85]

France and Siam had concluded an agreement, signed November 17, 1946, to submit to a commission of conciliation in accordance with a 1937 treaty, a controversy concerning numerous incidents which had occurred on the border between Siam and Indo-China since France had reoccupied Indo-China in 1946.

The 1946 accord contained the legal stipulation that the Convention of Tokyo, forced on France in 1941, delineating the borders between Siam and Indo-China was considered repudiated and that the status quo existing before the war was to be accepted by the parties as the basis for negotiation. Siam took the position that the prewar status should be changed and the commission was directed to examine the ethnic, economic, and geographic arguments with reference to the bases for revision if any existed. The members of the commission included diplomats experienced in Asian affairs from the United States, Great Britain, Peru, France and Siam with the United States representative as chairman. The commission held its deliberations in Washington, D. C.

The report of the commission supported the continuance of the status quo and advised against revision of the treaties in question. It included a resume of the dispute, conclusions as to the arguments presented by the parties and recommendations. Siam refused to accept the recommendations and reserved the right to place the matter before a political body. The Siamese government subsequently declared the matter closed.

---

[81]United Nations Document A/AC. 18/64, June 1948, p. 17.

[82]Idem.

[83]Ibid., p. 18.

[84]Idem.

[85]Suzanne Bastid, "La commission de conciliation franco-siamoise," La technique et les principes du droit public; études en l'honneur de Georges Scelle. vol. 1, (1950), pp. 3-4.

Belgian-Danish Commission, 1952.[86]

The permanent commission for Denmark and Belgium, created by treaty in 1927, was called to function for the first time on January 29, 1952. Presented for its consideration was a dispute in which Denmark sought reparations arising out of the internment and disposition of the crews and cargoes of two Danish merchant ships, the Gorm and Svava, by Belgian authorities in 1940.

The commission was composed of nationals of Sweden, Belgium, Germany, France and Denmark. It met in Stockholm under the chairmanship of the Swedish member. After examining the documents submitted by the parties and an oral examination of their agents, the commission submitted its recommendations which both parties accepted. According to the commission's proposals, Belgium was to pay indemnity to Denmark.

Franco-Swiss Commission, 1954-1955.[87]

On August 20, 1954, two legal disputes were referred by the Swiss and French governments to the permanent commission of conciliation established by treaty in 1925. One case involved a Swiss charge that the French customs officials had violated Swiss sovereignty in the course of investigating customs fraud. The second dispute related to a difference in the rebate of the costs of wartime internment in Switzerland of a Polish division which had fought on the French border.

The commission was composed of nationals of Switzerland, France, Spain, Great Britain and Belgium. Under the chairmanship of the Belgian member, the commission held its deliberations at the Peace Palace in the Hague. As eight years and fifteen years had elapsed respectively, from the inception of the disputes, the commission found it unnecessary to conduct investigations on-the-spot or to take the testimony of witnesses. It relied, instead, on documents which had been submitted by the parties and on oral interrogation of the agents of the parties. On November 18, 1955, the two governments, in identical letters, notified the commission of their acceptance of its recommendations.

Italian-Greek Commission, 1956.[88]

In 1956, Greece and Italy created a conciliation commission composed of nationals of Belgium (chairman), Greece and Italy. The task of the commission was to consider the matter of reparations for the sinking on August 3, 1940 of the Greek ship, Roula, off the coast of Crete by an Italian submarine while Greece was still enjoying the privileges of neutral status. The commission met at the Hague under the auspices of the Permanent Court of Arbitration and on March 20, 1956, submitted its proposals. Both parties informed the chairman of the commission in October 1956, that they had accepted the proposals of the commission and on the basis of such proposals had reached agreement.

---

[86]Henri Rolin "Une conciliation belgo-danoise," Revue générale de droit international public, vol. 24, series 3 (1953), pp. 353-371.

[87]F. M. van Asbeck, "La tâche et l'action d'une commission de conciliation," and "La procèdure suivie par la commission permanente de conciliation franco-suisse." Nederlands Tijdschrift voor international recht, vol. 3 (January and July 1956), pp. 1-9 and 209-219.

[88] J. P. A. Francois "Le Palais de la Paix en 1955." Nordisk Tijdschrift voor international recht, vol. 3 (January 1956), p. 72.

French-Moroccan Commission, 1957-1958.[89]

An ad hoc commission of inquiry was set up, under a special agreement of January 5, 1957, by France and Morocco to investigate the seizure by France of the plane carrying Ben Bella, the Algerian nationalist leader, while en route from Rabat to attend a conference in Tunis. Composed of nationals of Belgium (chairman), Morocco, Lebanon, France and Italy, the commission convened, on June 26, 1957, in Geneva.

The legal issues involved in the dispute concerned the nationality of the plane and the application of international convention. The Moroccan agent objected to a premature press release attributed to M. Charles de Visscher, the chairman of the commission. He also criticized the commission's decision not to include Ben Bella and his aides on the list of witnesses to be heard. The commission meeting on February 28, 1958, decided to adjourn permanently. The Moroccan commissioner noted that his government had ordered him home. The work of the commission was thus terminated.

In passing, mention should be made of the attempt made by Switzerland in 1957 to initiate a conciliation effort under a treaty of 1931 between the United States and Switzerland. At the time of the conclusion of the treaty, Secretary of State Stimson had agreed with the Swiss interpretation that "it is well understood that for all conflicts not of a juridical character, or that would be excluded from arbitration by virtue of Article 6 of the treaty, recourse to the commission of conciliation would be obligatory in all cases...." When, in 1957, Switzerland attempted to submit a dispute to the commission, the United States refused assent to the procedure. Among the reasons advanced by the United States in support of its position was that the purpose of conciliation was to enable the parties to compose differences arising from a lack of clarity as to the nature and basis of a claim. Where the positions of the parties were clearly understood, the United States argued, as in this case, there was no need for a conciliation commission.[90]

The implementation of the provisions in treaties for the pacific settlement of international disputes, adopted since 1919, with respect to provisions for conciliation and inquiry has been as disappointing as the implementation of the earlier Hague Conventions and Bryan Treaties with respect to commissions of inquiry.

From the few examples listed above, it is possible to make certain observations. First, the absorption of inquiry into conciliation procedures since 1919 has resulted in a deemphasis on the issuance of a report by a commission. This distinction between a conciliation function and an investigative function was noted in the Pact of Bogotá. The Bogotá Pact directs that a commission engaged solely in investigating questions of fact conclude its activities with a report. But the Pact of Bogotá does not make provision for the reporting of investigatory functions if the commission engages in conciliation.

Another major point to be noted in connection with the examples of commissions of conciliation and inquiry mentioned above is that their use is subject to the same limitations of the principle of national sovereignty which were responsible for the failure to implement the earlier Hague Conventions and the Bryan Treaties with respect to commissions of inquiry. Again, the similarity in this respect also extends to a strict limi-

---

[89]Charles Rousseau, "Échec de la procédure d'enquête et de conciliation dans l'affaire du réroulement de l'avion transportant de Rabat à Tunis les chefs nationalistes algériens le octobre 1956," Revue générale de droit internationale public, vol. 29, series 3 (October-November 1958), pp. 691-696.

[90]United States Papers Relating to the Foreign Relations of the United States (1931), vol. 2, p. 1026.

tation of the subject matter in those instances where commissions of inquiry or of conciliation and inquiry, were utilized successfully.

Nevertheless, the experience in operation of the several instances in which commissions of conciliation and inquiry have functioned has served to refine operating procedures of such commissions. The lack of full information as a result of the inadequacy of the reporting of the activities of such commissions of conciliation and inquiry is to be regretted.

# CHAPTER III

## FACT-FINDING EXPERIENCE IN INTERNATIONAL DISPUTES OF INTERNATIONAL ORGANIZATION

A. The League of Nations

The experience of the League of Nations in fact-finding, in its earlier years, covered a number of situations in which the League Council was called upon to use its prestige to arrange the delimitation of frontiers. These frontier disputes arose out of unresolved territorial questions as a result of the Protocols of London and Florence of 1913 and the World War I peace treaties. Among these disputes, the League was successful in the following instances in bringing about a settlement:

(1) Question of Albanian Frontiers, 1921.[1] Taken up by the Council of the League of Nations after the appeal of Albania under Article II of the Covenant because of the refusal of its neighbors to accept the boundaries as laid down by the Conference of Ambassadors, in the Protocols of London and of Florence of 1913.

(2) The Upper Silesian Question, 1921.[2] Referred to the Council of the League of Nations by the Supreme Allied Council under Article 11, paragraph 2, of the Covenant of the League of Nations.

(3) Frontier Dispute between Austria and Hungary, 1922.[3] Under the Treaty of Trianon, June 4, 1920, a Delimitation Commission was set up to trace the new frontiers of Hungary. The covering letter to the Treaty of Trianon provided for the referral to the League of Nations Council of questions involving injustice. The matter was referred on the basis of the Protocol of Venice of October 13, 1921.

(4) Frontier Dispute between Hungary and Czechoslovakia, 1923.[4] Based on the covering letter to the Treaty of Trianon, the matter was referred to the Council of the League of Nations with both parties agreeing in advance to accept the decision of the Council of the League.

(5) Frontier Dispute between Hungary and Yugoslavia, 1922.[5] Based on the covering letter to the Treaty of Trianon and the request of Hungary, the Conference of Ambassadors referred the dispute to the Council of the League of Nations.

(6) Frontier Dispute between Poland and Czechoslovakia, 1923.[6] Based on the covering letter to the Treaty of Trianon, the Conference of Ambassadors requested the Council of the League of Nations to consider the matter.

---

[1] L. of N., Official Journal, 1921, 5-6, p. 474.

[2] L. of N., Official Journal, 1921, 9, p. 982.

[3] L. of N., Official Journal, 1923, (PII), pp. 1330-1333.

[4] L. of N., Official Journal, 1923, p. 209.

[5] L. of N., Official Journal, 1922, (PII), p. 808.

[6] L. of N., Official Journal, 1923, p. 1472.

The League of Nations' experience in using fact-finding in the solution of international disputes, even in its early years, however, was not confined to matters of boundary delimitation. The following situations contain examples of more diversified fact-finding experiences of The League of Nations.

The Aaland Islands. The Aaland Islands dispute, in 1920, between Finland and Sweden, was concerned with the question as to whether the people of Swedish descent living in the Aaland Islands wished to remain under Finnish sovereignty.[7]  A commission of jurists was set up by the League Council to pass upon the legal questions involved. [8] Subsequently, a second investigating body, the Commission of Rapporteurs, was appointed to obtain information on the factual aspects of the question, which had not been covered by the judicial opinion supplied by the Committee of Jurists.[9]

The report of the Commission of Rapporteurs reviewed all the geographic, ethnic, political, economic and military factors present in the dispute.[10]  As a result of the report, the League Council, on June 14, 1921, decided upon the following terms of settlement covering three points, viz., 1. The sovereignty of the Aaland Islands was recognized as belonging to Finland; 2. Certain guarantees were to be given to the islanders and 3. Certain arrangements were to be concluded for non-fortification and neutralization of the archipelago.[11]

The Mosul Territory. Another dispute confronting the League in its early years was the Mosul dispute, in 1924-1925, between the United Kingdom and Iraq, on one hand, and Turkey, on the other. The dispute was submitted to the Council of the League of Nations on August 30, 1924, on the basis of Article 3, paragraph 2, of the Treaty of Peace, signed at Lausanne, July 24, 1923. The Treaty of Lausanne provided that the frontier between Turkey and Iraq was to be laid down in a friendly arrangement to be concluded between Turkey and Great Britain within nine months and that in the event of no agreement being reached between the two Governments within the time mentioned, the dispute was to be referred to the Council of the League of Nations.[12]

The League Council, on September 30, 1924, appointed a commission to make a thorough investigation of the facts including an investigation on-the-spot.[13] The Commission was to present to the Council all information and all suggestions which might be of a nature to assist it in reaching a decision. It was to receive all communications which the parties might wish to transmit to it and to give due consideration to the existing documents and to the views expressed by the interested parties with regard to procedure and substance. The Commission was empowered in its investigation on-the-spot to make use of the services of advisers appointed respectively by the governments of Turkey and Great Britain.

The Commission consisted of three members appointed by the Acting President of the Council in accordance with the Council's decision. These were Count Teleki, former Prime Minister of Hungary, Mr. af Wirsen, Minister Plenipotentiary of Sweden, and Count Paulis, of Belgium. Mr.

[7] L. of N., Official Journal, 1920, No. 5, p. 248.

[8] Ibid., pp. 249-250. The Permanent Court of International Justice would have been the appropriate body to render an advisory opinion on the legal questions involved but it did not come into existence until September 1, 1921, after the incidents referred to had occurred.

[9] L. of N., Official Journal, 1920, No. 8. p. 29.

[10] L. of N., Official Journal, 1921, No. 7. p. 699.

[11] Idem.

[12] L. of N., Official Journal, 1924, p. 1465.

[13] L. of N., Official Journal, 1924, p. 1360.

af Wirsen was elected President by the Commission. The Secretary-General was instructed to furnish the necessary staff and to advance funds as needed. The advances were to be refunded to the League in equal proportions by the two Governments concerned. The Commission was to set its own procedure.

In a report of ninety pages, signed by all three members, on July 16, 1925 the Commission described its work and analysed the question from geographical, ethnic, historical, economic, strategic and political standpoints. The report, which contained the Commission's conclusions and recommendations, was submitted to the League Council.[14]

As a result of a decision of the Permanent Court of International Justice declaring that the decision of the Council would be binding upon the parties,[15] the Council, using the report of its Commission of Investigation as a basis for its decision, decided that the Mosul Territory should be united with Iraq subject to guarantees to the Kurdish population.[16] These guarantees were considered as ensured by the continuance of the mandatory regime of Great Britain for twenty five years.[17]

The Demir Kapu Incident. On October 19, 1925, a clash occurred between frontier troops of Bulgaria and Greece as a result of a combination of a lack of proper organization of frontier forces and poorly disciplined troops. According to a Bulgarian telegram, dated October 22, 1925, to the Secretary-General, a Greek soldier on Bulgarian territory had fired on a Bulgarian sentry who killed him. Thereupon a Greek detachment advanced into Bulgarian territory to remove the body and firing began.[18] The Greek Government, in a telegram addressed to the Secretary-General, October 24, 1925, claimed this version was inaccurate.[19]

Upon receiving from both parties confirmation that they would carry out its recommendations concerning cessation of hostilities and the withdrawal of troops, the Council, on October 29, 1925, decided to appoint a commission to carry out a full inquiry into the incidents on the frontiers between Bulgaria and Greece to the northeast of Salonica, and to ascertain as exactly as possible the origin of these incidents and all the facts in relation thereto which had given rise to the intervention of the Council. According to the resolution

> The Commission shall in particular establish the facts
> enabling the responsibility to be fixed, and to supply the
> necessary material for the determination of indemnities
> or reparation which may be considered appropriate.[20]

Further, in order to permit the Council to be in a position to make suitable recommendations to the Governments concerned, the Commission was to submit to the Council any suggestions as to measures which in its opinion would eliminate or minimize the general causes of incidents similar to that referred to the Council or prevent their recurrence.

The Commission was composed of Sir Horace Rumbold, British Ambassador at Madrid, General Serrigny from France, General Ferrario from Italy, Mr. De Adlercrentz, Swedish Minister at The Hague, and Mr. Fortuyn, Member of the Netherlands Parliament. Sir Horace was elected President.

The Secretary-General appointed the secretary and assistant secretaries from among the staff of the League Secretariat as requested by the

---

[14]L. of N., Doc. C.400, M. 147. 1925, VII.

[15]Permanent Court of International Justice Reports, Series B, No. 12.

[16]L. of N., Official Journal, 1926, p. 192.

[17]Ibid., pp. 502-503

[18]L. of N., Official Journal, 1925, No. 11, (PII), p. 1696.

[19]Ibid., p. 1697.

[20]Ibid., pp. 1712-1713.

Council.

The Commission was directed to assemble at Geneva on November 6, 1925. It was asked to conduct its investigations both on-the-spot and at the seats of the two Governments concerned. The report of the Commission, which was submitted to the Council on November 28, 1925 consisted of fourteen pages containing three main sections entitled "Enquiry", "Responsibilities and Indemnities", and "Recommendations". It was signed by all five members of the Commission.

The Commission of Inquiry decided that it was impossible to determine who fired first and whether the Greek soldier killed was or was not in Bulgarian territory. It was apparent to the Commission that the local commanders had attempted to stop the affray but the state of mind of the Greek refugees from Bulgaria, affecting the mentality of the soldiers living in their midst, had inflamed the Greek troops. Nevertheless, the Commission held that while the Greek Government's military action in occupying a part of Bulgarian territory was not premeditated, it was also unnecessary. [21] Accordingly, the Commission's recommendations, based on its findings, included the payment of reparations by the Greek Government to Bulgaria, reorganization of the frontier guard systems on both sides and expediting the liquidation of property in accordance with the voluntary exchange of populations as well as an end to all vexatious measures. [22] These recommendations with slight modifications agreed to by the parties were subsequently adopted by the Council. [23] The Council's decision was accepted by the two Governments concerned.

Manchuria. As a result of the disturbance of the status quo by Japanese forces in Manchuria through military occupation of certain centers, the question of Manchuria was brought to the attention of the League Council on September 22, 1931. [24] The representative of the Chinese Government had, on September 21, 1931, addressed a note to the Secretary-General of the League requesting him to bring to the attention of the Council the dispute which had arisen between China and Japan because of Japanese actions at Mukden during the night of September 18 and 19. He asked the Council to take immediate steps, on the basis of Article 11, to prevent the further development of a situation endangering the peace of nations.

The Council, on December 10, 1931, on the proposal of the representative of Japan, adopted a resulution which, among other provisions, provided for the appointment of a commission

. . . of five members to study on-the-spot and to report to the Council on any circumstances which affecting international relations, threatens to disturb peace between China and Japan, or the good understanding between them, upon which peace depends . . . [25]

In the event that the two parties initiated any negotiations, these did not fall within the scope of the Commission, nor was it within the competence of the Commission to interfere with the military arrangements of either party.

The five members of the Commission, selected by the President of the Council with the approval of the two parties, were Count Aldrovandi

---

[21] L. of N., Official Journal, 1926, No. 2, pp. 197-205.

[22] Idem.

[23] Ibid., p. 177.

[24] L. of N., Official Journal, 1931, pp. 2265-6.

[25] Ibid., p. 2378.

of Italy, General de Division Claudel of France, the Earl of Lytton of Great Britain, Major General Ross McCoy of the United States of America, and Mr. Schnee of Germany. Lord Lytton was elected Chairman by the Commission. The parties had the right to nominate one assessor each to assist the Commission. The Secretary-General of the League of Nations designated a member of his staff to act as secretary-general of the Commission.

The Lytton Commission, as it was referred to, conducted a thorough examination of historical, ethnic, legal, economic and political interests.[26] The Chinese Government had stressed that it understood the Commission's first duty was to inquire into and report with its recommendations on the withdrawal of the Japanese forces.[27] The Lytton Commission's report indicated that the scope of the Commission's assignment had been much wider.[28]

The report of the Commission was submitted to the League Council, September 4, 1932. It consisted of 148 pages and was signed by all five members. The character of the dispute as indicated by the report was one of basic political difference, namely that China regarded Manchuria as an integral part of China while Japan regarded Manchuria as its first line of defense against Russia and of prime strategic importance.[29] According to the Commission's concept of its task, it was less interested in finding responsibility for past actions than on the necessity of finding means to avoid their repetition in the future. The report concluded with reflections and considerations upon the various issues with which the Council was confronted and with some suggestions regarding the lines on which it seemed possible to effect a durable solution of the conflict and the re-establishment of a good understanding between China and Japan.[30]

The Council, on November 26, 1932, decided to refer the Sino-Japanese dispute to the Assembly of the League in conformity with Article 15, paragraph 9, of the Covenant.[31] On December 9, the Assembly requested its Special Committee to study the report of the Council's Commission of Inquiry, the observations of the parties and the opinions and suggestions expressed in the Assembly, and to draw up and submit at the earliest possible moment, proposals with a view to settlement of the dispute. On February 24, 1933, attempts of the Special Committee to propose a procedure for settling the dispute having proved fruitless, the Assembly adopted a draft report prepared by the Committee in conformity with Article 15, paragraph 4, of the Covenant.[32]

B.  The Inter-American Peace System

The following instances of the application of the Treaty of Rio and the Pact of Bogotá comprise the experience in the use of fact-finding of the Inter-American Peace System.[33]

---

[26]L. of N., Doc. C.663.M.320, 1932. VII.

[27]L. of N., Official Journal, 1931, p. 2378.

[28]L. of N., Doc. C.663.M.320, 1932. VII.

[29]Ibid., pp. 38-39.

[30]Idem.

[31]L. of N., Official Journal, 1933, pp. 1900, 1910.

[32]L. of N., Official Journal, 1933, Special Supplement, No. 112, p. 24.

[33]Two studies by the United Nations Secretariat are: U. N. Doc. A/AC. 18/46 Analysis of Main Features of the Inter-American Peace System and U. N. Doc. A/AC. 18/SC.9L.6 Recent Inter-American Experience in the Field of Pacific Settlement.

Costa Rica and Nicaragua 1948-1949. Upon the submission by Costa Rica of a complaint that armed forces proceeding from Nicaragua had invaded its territory, the Council of the Organization of American States, meeting on December 14, 1948, adopted a resolution in which it constituted itself a provisional Organ of Consultation in accordance with Article 12 of the Inter-American Treaty of Reciprocal Assistance and appointed a committee "to investigate on-the-spot the facts denounced and their antecedents".

The members of the Committee, who were appointed by the Chairman of the Council, consisted of representatives of Brazil, Colombia, Mexico and of the United States of America, together with their military and civil advisers. The representative of Brazil was appointed Chairman of the Committee.

After meeting with groups, in San Jose and Managua, representing the two Governments as well as representatives of groups seeking to overthrow the Government of the other country, the Committee presented its report, December 24, 1948, in Washington, D. C., to the Provisional Organ of Consultation.

The Provisional Organ of Consultation, on the basis of the Committee's report, adopted a resolution, December 24, 1948, urging the two Governments to do their utmost to prevent a renewal of hostilities. In addition, an Inter-American Commission of Military Experts was dispatched to the area where the frontier incidents had occurred to insure fulfillment of the obligations laid down in the resolution. The two States signed a Pact of Amity and Friendship, on February 21, 1949, as a result of negotiations and the Council informed the Governments of member states that the incident was closed. [34]

Haiti and the Dominican Republic, 1950. After an earlier complaint by the Haitian Government had been referred to the Inter-American Peace Committee, the Haitian Government invoked the Inter-American Treaty of Reciprocal Assistance, on January 3, 1950, declaring that officials of the Dominican Republic were involved in an armed conspiracy which threatened the territorial integrity and political independence of Haiti. On January 6, 1950, at a meeting of the Council of the Organization of American States, the representative of the Dominican Republic denied the charges brought by Haiti and sought to invoke the Inter-American Treaty against Haiti which, he asserted, had supported activities hostile to the Dominican Government. The Council of the Organization of American States, on January 6, 1950, adopted a resolution constituting itself as Provisional Organ of Consultation under the Inter-American Treaty of Reciprocal Assistance and established a committee "to conduct an on-the-spot investigation of the facts and their antecedents". The Security Council of the United Nations was informed of the resolution and of all related activities.

The Committee consisted of the representatives of Bolivia, Colombia, Ecuador, The United States of America and Uruguay. The representative of Uruguay was elected Chairman.

After hearing evidence in Washington, the Committee interviewed citizens and officials of Haiti, the Dominican Republic, Cuba and Guatemala, as well as visiting Mexico. The Committee submitted its report March 13, 1950, to the Provisional Organ of Consultation. The report dealt in detail with the specific charges made by Haiti and the Dominican Republic and recorded the Committee's findings.

---

[34]Pan American Union, Applications of the Inter-American Treaty of Reciprocal Assistance 1948-1956, op. cit., pp. 19-57.

On April 8, 1950, the Provisional Organ of Consultation on the basis of the report, adopted a series of resolutions which had been proposed by the Committee. These resolutions, in addition to calling upon the governments concerned to take steps to prevent seditious movements and conspiracies against the other country, provided for the appointment of a special provisional committee (having the same composition as the original committee) to facilitate the observance of the resolutions by the parties.[35] The Special Provisional Committee submitted three reports to the Secretary-General of the Organization of American States, on June 30, 1950, October 31, 1950 and May 14, 1951.[36]

Costa Rica and Nicaragua, 1955. Meeting, on January 11, 1955, to consider a complaint by Costa Rica that its independence was being threatened by acts of the Government of Nicaragua, the Council constituted itself Provisional Organ of Consultation under the Inter-American Treaty of Reciprocal Assistance and established a committee "to conduct an on-the-spot investigation of the pertinent facts and submit a report thereon".

The Committee was composed of the representatives of Brazil, Ecuador, Paraguay, Mexico and the United States of America appointed by the Chairman of the Provisional Organ of Consultation, The representative of Mexico was elected Chairman of the Committee.

Subsequently, on January 12, 1955, the Council agreed to request those governments, which were in a position to do so, to place facilities and personnel at the disposal of the Committee in order to make in the name of the Committee and under its supervision pacific observation flights over the regions affected, after prior notification had been given to the governments over whose territories the flights would be made. The Governments of Ecuador, Mexico, the United States of America and Uruguay informed the Council they had placed aircraft at the disposal of the Committee. After examining the situation in Costa Rica, the Committee cabled urgent reports to the Council which, on January 14, 1955, requested the Committee "to send observers to all the airports in the region involved in the situation, as well as to any place that might be utilized for the transportation of military forces or material to Costa Rica, for the purpose of determining the origin of such forces and material." Following the purchase of four aircraft by Costa Rica from the United States of America, with the approval of the Council, on January 16, the Council resolved

> to request the Investigating Committee that, in accord-
> ance with the wishes expressed by the Governments of
> Nicaragua and Costa Rica, it proceed with utmost urgency
> to prepare in consultation with the said Governments and
> to put into effect through the military advisers of the Com-
> mission a plan for effective surveillance of the common
> frontier of the two countries, reporting as frequently as
> necessary to the Council, acting provisionally as Organ of
> Consultation, regarding the fulfillment of its mission."[37]

After setting up security zones with air and boundary patrols, the Committee returned to Washington, and submitted its report, on February 18, 1955. The Committee recommended that a bilateral commission of investigation and conciliation should be established under the terms of the Pact of Bogotá (to which both States had adhered) to provide a permanent Guarantee of the settlement of any future difficulties.

The Council, in a resolution, adopted on February 24, 1955, called on the two Governments to appoint their respective members of the Commission of Investigation and Conciliation. At the same time, the Council

---

[35]Ibid., pp. 69-149.
[36]Ibid., pp. 135-148.
[37]Ibid., p. 170.

terminated the activities of the Investigating Committee and established a Special Committee of the Council to continue the functions of the military observers and to cooperate with the two Governments, in obtaining fulfillment of the terms of the resolution. The military observation was terminated on February 25, 1955.[38]

Request of the Government of Ecuador, 1955. The Government of Ecuador requested, on September 8, 1955, that the Council call a meeting of the Ministers of Foreign Affairs, under the Inter-American Treaty of Reciprocal Assistance, to consider the threat to the territorial integrity of Ecuador posed by the concentration of Peruvian troops on the Ecuador-Peruvian border.

The Council took no action because, under a treaty of 1942 between Ecuador and Peru, the border had been guaranteed by Argentina, Brazil, Chile, and the United States of America. These four states appointed a commission of military observers composed of their military attaches stationed at Lima and Quito which conducted an on-the-spot investigation by means of air and land reconnaissance. Upon the issuance of the report, on September 26, 1955, that all was normal, Ecuador withdrew its complaint to the Council.[39]

Honduras and Nicaragua, 1957. In the controversy between Honduras and Nicaragua, the Council of the Organization of American States held a special meeting, May, 1957, to consider a note from the Government of Honduras invoking the Inter-American Treaty of Reciprocal Assistance for application in the conflict that had arisen between Honduras and Nicaragua. The note stated that Nicaragua had invaded Honduran territory with military forces by crossing the boundary line of the Coco or Segovia River, established by the arbitral award of December 23, 1906. At a meeting, held on May 2, the Council also examined a counter-complaint from Nicaragua charging Honduras with aggression and stating that Honduras had no right to claim the territory in question was Honduran, since Nicaragua had been entitled to reject the 1906 arbitral award of the King of Spain, granting the territory to Honduras.

At a meeting of May 2, the Council constituted itself as Provisional Organ of Consultation under the Inter-American Treaty of Reciprocal Assistance and authorized the Chairman of the Council to appoint a committee which could carry out an on-the-spot investigation of the pertinent facts and their antecedents and submit a report thereon. The Chairman selected the representatives of Argentina, Bolivia, Mexico, Panama and the United States of America to serve on the Committee. The representative of Panama was selected as Chairman.

The Committee proceeded to the area and succeeded in bringing about a cease-fire which went into effect May 5. Both parties agreed to abstain from taking further steps which might aggravate the situation and to allow plans to be drawn up for the withdrawal of troops. The Committee established a military advisory committee and, at its request, the Council asked member States to place officers of Colonel's rank and below at the Committee's disposal.

In its report of May 16, the Committee stated, however, that owing to the uncertain state of the boundary lines and the reservations made by Honduras and Nicaragua when adhering to the Inter-American Treaty of Reciprocal Assistance, it was unable to determine where responsibility for the aggression lay.

Terminating the activities of the Committee, the Council set up an ad hoc committee, on May 17, 1957, charged with the task of finding a peaceful and final solution. The Ad Hoc Committee succeeded in persuading the Governments of Honduras and Nicaragua to place the question

---

[38]Ibid., pp. 157-223.
[39]Ibid., pp. 225-237.

before the International Court of Justice in accordance with the Pact of Bogota. On June 27, 1957, the Council terminated its status as Provisional Organ of Consultation. The International Court of Justice rendered judgment in 1960 in favor of Honduras, holding that Nicaragua was obliged to accept the terms of the 1906 arbitral award.[40]

Situation in Panama, 1959. The Government of Panama submitted a complaint, on April 27, 1959, that its territory had been invaded by foreign elements seeking the overthrow of its Government. The Council, meeting on April 28, 1959, in special session, resolved to constitute itself a Provisional Organ of Consultation under the Inter-American Treaty of Reciprocal Assistance and authorized the Chairman to appoint an investigating committee. The representatives of Argentina, Brazil, Costa Rica, the United States of America and Paraguay were appointed members of the Committee. The purposes of the Committee were to verify the presence of foreign forces in Panamanian territory and to examine the possibility of others arriving by sea.

After visiting Panama and interviewing representatives of the opposing groups, the Committee, in conjunction with the Council of the Organization of American States, organized air and naval patrols to provide surveillance in the event of the arrival of additional foreign troops. After receiving a report from the Committee, June 9, 1959, that Panama had been the victim of an invasion of foreign elements, organized abroad and coming from Cuban ports, the Council adopted a series of resolutions, on June 18, 1959, calling on the governments of member states to observe the terms of the 1928 Havana Convention and the 1957 Protocol on the rights and duties of States in the event of civil strife.[41]

Situation in Nicaragua, 1959. The Government of Nicaragua, on June 2, 1959, submitted a complaint that it had been the victim of an armed attack by revolutionary forces of various nationalities who had flown from Costa Rica. The Council constituted itself as a Provisional Organ of Consultation and established an investigating committee consisting of the representatives of Brazil, Mexico, The United States of America and Uruguay.

The Committee visited Honduras, Nicaragua and Costa Rica and held talks with the Presidents and Foreign Ministers of the three Republics. In Nicaragua, the Committee interviewed certain persons in prison, no local officials being present during the interviews. The three Governments provided the Committee with documentary material and with information regarding the arms which had been seized.

Upon receiving the Committee's report that the invading forces had been organized by revolutionary elements in both neighboring countries, acting without participation of the Governments concerned, the Council, on July 28, 1959, took note of the Committee's report and adopted a resolution recommending that member States should strengthen their measures to maintain peace and should continue to observe the principles of non-intervention.[42]

Request of the Government of Venezuela, 1960. The Government of Venezuela requested a meeting of the Organ of Consultation of the Organization of American States to consider the acts of intervention and aggression by the Government of the Dominican Republic against the Government of Venezuela, which culminated in an attempt on the life of the Venezuelan Chief of State. On July 8, the Council of the Organization of American

[40]Organization of American States, Annual Report of the Secretary-General, 1956-1957, pp. 6-17. Also I.C.J. Reports, 1960, p. 192.

[41]Union Panamericana, Applicaciones del Tratado Interamericano de Assistencia Recíproca 1948-1960, op. cit., pp. 293-337.

[42]Ibid., pp. 339-383.

States, constituting itself as the Provisional Organ of Consultation, authorized its Chairman to appoint a committee to investigate the charges. The Chairman appointed the representatives of Argentina, Mexico, Panama, the United States of America and Uruguay with the representative of Panama acting as Chairman.

In preparing its report, the Committee heard the views of and studied documents presented by the representatives of both countries. It requested the Inter-American Peace Committee to provide information that, in the latter's judgment, might be useful to it in carrying out its mandate. The Committee visited Caracas and interviewed various members of the Venezuelan Government and also prison inmates, without the presence of Venezuelan authorities. The Committee also examined the bomb mechanism and visited the scene of the attempted assassination. Upon the invitation of the Government of the Dominican Republic, the Committee dispatched a sub-committee to Ciudad Trujillo where it met the Minister of Foreign Affairs.

When the foreign ministers of the twenty-one Member States of the Organization of American States met as the Organ of Consultation at San Jose, Costa Rica, on August 17, 1960, they had at hand the report of the five member Committee of Investigation which had been named by the Organization's Council to investigate the acts denounced and their antecedents.[43] As a result of the deliberations of the Organ of Consultation on the report of the Investigating Committee, a resolution was adopted [44] which emphatically condemned the Government of the Dominican Republic and, in application of the Inter-American Treaty of Reciprocal Assistance, called for breaking of diplomatic relations with the Dominican Republic and the instituting of a partial interruption of economic relations with that country by all member States. [45]

Dominican Republic and Haiti, 1963-1965. At a special meeting, held on April 28, 1963, the Council of the Organization of American States was requested by the Representative of Costa Rica to convoke a meeting of consultation and to constitute itself and act provisionally as Organ of Consultation for the purpose of studying the situation involving the Dominican Republic and Haiti.[46] The Council, on the same day, acting provisionally as Organ of Consultation authorized its Chairman to appoint a five member committee to make an on-the-spot study of the events, denounced by the Dominican Republic.

The Committee was composed of Columbia, Bolivia, Chile, Ecuador and El Salvador. The representative of Columbia was selected as Chairman. The Presidents of the Dominican Republic and Haiti, in reply to the request of the Chairman of the Council, announced their willingness to cooperate with the Committee of Investigation. The Committee visited Haiti and the Dominican Republic and interviewed high officials of both governments.

On May 8, 1963, the Council acting provisionally as Organ of Consultation approved a resolution assigning to the Investigating Committee the additional task of making an on-the-spot study of the situation existing between Haiti and the Dominican Republic and to offer the parties its services for the purpose of finding a prompt solution to the conflict and to ward off the threats to the peace and security of the area.

In its report, submitted to the Council on July 18, 1963, the Committee related the investigations and interviews it had carried on, presented

---

[43]Organization de Estados Americanos/Ser. F/11. 6/Doc. 5.

[44]Ibid. , Ser. C/11. 6.

[45]Organization of American States, Annual Report of the Secretary-General, 1960, pp. 7-9.

[46]Pan American Union, Inter-American Treaty of Reciprocal Assistance, Applications, Volume 2, Washington: 1964, pp. 163-164.

an account of the facts denounced by each of the parties to the dispute and formulated a series of conclusions. These conclusions provided the basis for a resolution which was adopted, on the same day, by the Provisional Organ of Consultation. The resolution called for both Governments to refrain from hostile acts and to observe their obligations under certain treaties and conventions.

The Committee continued its investigation at the request of the Council acting as Provisional Organ of Consultation. As a result of these investigations, the Committee submitted reports on August 15, 1963 and October 24, 1963. The Provisional Organ of Consultation did not meet until November 30, 1964. During this period the Committee continued its efforts to promote direct negotiations between the parties. On December 15, 1964, the Committee announced that preliminary negotiations between the parties had been fruitful and that the parties had agreed to begin formal negotiations on January 2, 1965, under the auspices of the Committee, at the headquarters of the Pan American Union. [47]

Panama and The United States of America, 1964.[48] The Government of Panama, invoking the Rio Treaty, requested the Council of the Organization of American States to convoke the Organ of Consultation. At a meeting held on February 4, 1964, the Council decided to convoke the Organ of Consultation and to constitute itself and act provisionally as Organ of Consultation. In this capacity, on February 7, 1964, the Council established a General Committee to investigate fully and at once the acts that had occurred in Panama on January 9 and 10 and thereafter and to submit a report to the Organ of Consultation on the matter. The General Committee was also to propose to the parties procedures to avoid further disturbances and to assist the parties in their search for a fair solution.

The General Committee, under the resolution, was authorized to create special committees that it deemed necessary for the fulfillment of its task. In accordance with this provision of the resolution, the General Committee established a Delegation composed of Brazil, Costa Rica, Mexico, Paraguay and Uruguay which was dispatched to Panama. The purpose of the Delegation was to investigate the facts as well as to assist the parties to find a just solution of the controversy between them. The resulting Joint Declaration issued by the parties - and signed in the presence of other members of the Council by the representatives of the two Governments - was an important step toward promoting better relations between the two parties.

Cuba and Venezuela, 1963-1964.[49] The Government of Venezuela, in a letter dated November 29, 1963, requested the convocation of the Organ of Consultation to consider the measures to be taken to deal with the acts of intervention and aggression on the part of the Government of Cuba which affected the territorial integrity and the sovereignty of Venezuela. On December 3, 1936, the Council of the Organization of American States acting provisionally as Organ of Consultation, after convoking the Organ of Consultation, appointed a committee to investigate the facts denounced by Venezuela. The Investigating Committee consisted of Argentina, Colombia, Costa Rica, the United States and Uruguay.

Upon its return from Venezuela, the Committee presented an extensive, well-documented report which the Organ of Consultation decided to transmit to the governments. The Committee, in the course of its activities communicated to the Cuban Government a request for its views on any points it wished to comment upon in writing. The Cuban Government

---

[47]OEA/Ser. G/V, C-d-128.

[48]Pan American Union, Inter-American Treaty of Reciprocal Assistance Applications, Volume 2, Washington: 1964, pp. 226-227.

[49]Ibid., pp. 182-183.

cabled on February 3, 1964 that it "neither recognizes, admits, nor accepts the jurisdiction of the Organization of American States." [50]

The conclusion of the Committee was that since 1959, the present Government of Cuba had carried on, supported, and directed in various ways a policy of intervention in the hemisphere and that this policy of political aggression had had positive application in the Republic of Venezuela.

The Organ of Consultation, meeting at Washington, D. C., from July 21 to 26, 1964, noting the report of the Investigating Committee and the conclusions contained in that report, adopted a resolution calling for the termination of diplomatic relations with the Government of Cuba and the imposition of economic sanctions in accordance with Articles 6 and 8 of Inter-American Treaty of Reciprocal Assistance (Treaty of Rio).

The Inter-American Peace Committee. As was pointed out earlier, the Inter-American Peace Committee is primarily a conciliatory body. It has, however, from time to time been called upon to conduct investigations.

On August 15, 1959, the Government of Haiti lodged a complaint with the Fifth Meeting of Consultation, that invading forces had sailed from a Cuban port and that the authorities of Cuba had said that they had been unable to prevent their departure.[51] On August 31, the Representative of Haiti on the Council of the Organization of American States, in a note addressed to the Chairman of the Committee, requested the Inter-American Peace Committee to make a thorough investigation of the events that had taken place. The Committee, considering its functions under Resolution IV, appointed a sub-committee which visited Haiti in October 1959. The Committee submitted a report based upon the report of its Sub-Committee to the Seventh Meeting of Consultation held in San Jose, Costa Rica a year later.[52]

The Committee conducted a more limited investigation as a result of the request of the Venezuelan Government addressed to the Chairman of the Committee on November 25, 1959. The Government of Venezuela complained that on the night of November 19, 1959, an aircraft of United States registry, manned by two Cuban citizens, had erroneously dropped leaflets over the island of Curacao, inciting the army of Venezuela to rebel against the legally constituted authorities of that country. The intention had been to drop the leaflets over a Venezuelan city. The aircraft and crew were seized by Dutch authorities after making a forced landing on the island of Aruba.

The Committee obtained full information from the Governments of the United States of America, Venezuela and the Netherlands. On the basis of its study of the case and in the light of the statements made by the persons directly involved, the Committee concluded that the necessary arrangements for the flight from Ciudad Trujillo to Aruba, as well as the loading of the leaflets in Ciudad Trujillo, could not have been carried out without the connivance of the Dominican authorities.[53]

Another case in which the Inter-American Peace Committee was requested to conduct an investigation under Resolution IV resulted from a complaint lodged by Venezuela, in a note, dated February 17, 1960, to the

---

[50]Ibid., p. 109.

[51]Quinta Reunión de Consulta de Ministros de Relaciones Exteriores, Actas y Documentos, OEA/Ser. F./III. 5, Washington, D. C., 1961, pp. 145-147.

[52]Report of the Inter-American Peace Committee to the Seventh Meeting of Consultation of Ministers of Foreign Affairs, OEA/Ser. F/II. 7/Doc. 6, August 5, 1960, p. 3.

[53]Ibid., p. 5.

Committee requesting the Committee to investigate "the flagrant violations of human rights by the Government of the Dominican Republic, which are aggravating the tensions in the Caribbean".

In response to the request of the Committee for permission to visit the Dominican Republic, that Government, exercising its option under Resolution IV, (2), refused the request. The Committee, nevertheless proceeded with its investigation requesting information from other American governments, receiving testimony from Dominican exiles and from nationals of other countries who had recently been in the Dominican Republic. In addition, the Committee examined extensive and reliable press material as well as valuable information provided it by certain representatives of member states.

On the basis of the evidence, the Committee submitted a report, on June 6, 1960, to the Council of the Organization of American States containing the conclusion that international tensions in the Caribbean region had been aggravated by flagrant and widespread violations of human rights which had been and were continuing to be committed in the Dominican Republic.[54]

The use of the Inter-American Peace Committee to dispel false charges is illustrated in the request by the Government of Mexico, on July 2, 1961 that the Committee "proceed immediately to make a thorough investigation in Mexican territory as it deems necessary in order to establish whether, as the Government of Mexico assures, the imputation is false."[55] The indignation of the Mexican Government rose from the transmittal by the Minister of Foreign Affairs of Guatemala to the Secretary-General of the Organization of American States of information that in Mexican territory, adjacent to the Guatemalan border "communist troops are being trained for an invasion into Guatemalan territory in the immediate future".

As a result of the subsequent denial of the Guatemalan Government that its message to the Secretary-General contained any accusation, direct or implied, against the Government of Mexico, the Committee considered that it was not necessary for it to visit Mexican territory and make the requested investigation under Resolution IV of the Fifth Meeting of Consultation.

The Inter-American Peace Committee had occasion to act once more under the provisions of Resolution IV at the request of the Government of Peru, contained in a note presented to the Committee on November 24, 1961. The Council of the Organization of American States, on November 22, 1961, had decided that the Committee was the appropriate organ in accordance with Resolution IV to deal with the f acts denounced which referred to the threat to the security of the region posed by the activities of the Cuban Government.

The Government of Cuba refused to send a representative, in response to the request of the Committee, to appear before it to state the view of his government. A second request for permission for the Committee to visit the Republic of Cuba to carry out its investigations was also rejected. Nevertheless, the Committee obtained information from the publications of the Cuban Government, documentation from many trustworthy sources, and valuable data received from governments of member states. In addition, it received the testimony of persons who had recently left Cuba.

---

[54]Ibid., Appendix D.

[55]Report of the Inter-American Peace Committee to the Eighth Meeting of Consultation of Ministers of Foreign Affairs 1962, OEA/Ser. L/III/CIP/I/62, January 14, 1962, pp. 18-21.

The Eighth Meeting of Consultation, held at Punta del Este, Uruguay, from January 22 to 31, 1962, adopted two resolutions excluding the present Cuban Government from participation in the inter-American system and calling for the partial suspension of trade with Cuba.[56] The conclusions contained in the report of the Inter-American Peace Committee were noted in the two resolutions adopted at the Eighth Meeting of Consultation and provided the factual basis for the action called for by the resolutions.

## C. The United Nations

The fact-finding experience of the United Nations can be divided into efforts at investigating engaged in by the Security Council, the General Assembly and the Secretary-General. Several instances of fact-finding by these organs do not fall strictly within the category of "international disputes". Some have dealt with violations of human rights and some with investigations into the deaths of politically prominent persons. Also, there have been instances in which the emphasis has been on military observation rather than on investigation.

It has been decided for the purpose of this study to describe briefly all of these efforts in order to present a full and complete picture of the experience of the United Nations in fact-finding. The headings have been selected to indicate the question rather than the particular commission of investigation or the organ which established it. This has been done in order to preserve somewhat a continuity of action where more than one commission or organ has been involved in dealing with a specific dispute or situation.

The Spanish Question. Upon the notification by Poland that a situation in Spain which constituted a threat to world peace existed, the Security Council, on April 29, 1946, adopted a proposal advanced by Australia, establishing a sub-committee to conduct further studies regarding the question.[57]

The Security Council Sub-Committee on the Spanish Question was composed of the representatives of Australia, Brazil, China, France and Poland. The representative of Australia was appointed Chairman of the Sub-Committee.

The Council resolution of April 29, 1946 provided that

. . . the Security Council . . .
Hereby resolves: to make further studies in order to determine whether the situation in Spain has led to international friction and does endanger international peace and security, and if it so finds, then to determine what practical measures the United Nations may take.

For this end, the Security Council appoints a Sub-Committee of five of its members and instructs this Sub-Committee to examine the statements made before the Security Council concerning Spain, to receive further statements and documents, and to conduct such inquiries as it may deem necessary, and to report to the Security Council before the end of May.[58]

The Sub-Committee met at United Nations Headquarters and adopted its own rules of procedure. A questionnaire was sent to Member States regarding specific issues. In response to a public announcement that the Sub-Committee would welcome information from any source, an extensive submission was made by the Spanish Republican Government. The Sub-

[56]Pan American Union Inter-American Treaty of Reciprocal Assistance Applications, Volume 2, Washington: 1964, pp. 69-70.

[57]U. N. Security Council, Official Records, First Year, First Series, Supplement No. 2, Annexes 3a and 3b, pp. 54-55, 244.

[58]Ibid., pp. 244-245.

Committee's examination of facts was based mainly on documents received from Member States and international agencies such as the United Nations War Crimes Commission in London, in response to questionnaires sent to them.

In a unanimous report, dated June 1, 1946 the Sub-Committee set out its findings and recommendations.[59] The Soviet Union vetoed proposals supported by the majority of members of the Security Council. The question was then transferred to the General Assembly which adopted, on December 12, 1946, resolution 39(I) reiterating the findings of the Sub-Committee.

The Sub-Committee had recommended that the Council endorse a condemnation of the Franco regime and recommend to the Assembly that unless the regime was withdrawn and certain other conditions obtained in Spain, the Assembly should recommend that "diplomatic relations with the Franco regime be terminated" by the Members of the United Nations. The Assembly merely recommended the recall of ambassadors and ministers plenipotentiary from Spain. The Assembly resolution also included other provisions concerning relations of Spain with the United Nations.[60]

The Greek Question. Among the first disputes confronting the United Nations in 1946 was the interference in the internal affairs of Greece by the Governments of the neighboring countries, Albania, Bulgaria and Yugoslavia. The first attempt to bring the Greek question before the Council was that of the Ukranian Soviet Socialist Republic. The draft resolution introduced by the United States of America made reference to investigating border incidents along the frontier between Greece, on one hand, and Albania, Yugoslavia and Bulgaria, on the other. The Soviet Union objected to the wording of the draft resolution in including Yugoslavia, Bulgaria and Albania on the grounds that reference to these countries was tantamount to accusation. The discussion was declared closed.[61]

A second attempt occurred when, in a letter, dated December 3, 1946, to the Secretary-General, the Greek delegation stated that a situation existed which was leading to friction owing to the support given by Albania, Bulgaria and Yugoslavia to guerrilla forces operating in Greece, in the form of training, weapons, supplies and bases, and which was likely to endanger international peace and security. The letter pointed out that Greece, under Articles 34 and 35 of the United Nations Charter desired to draw the attention of the Security Council to the urgent need for an investigation to be undertaken on the spot.[62]

A Security Council resolution, which was adopted unanimously, established a commission of investigation to "ascertain the facts relating to the alleged border violations along the frontier between Greece on one hand and Albania, Bulgaria and Yugoslavia on the other".[63] The Commission under the resolution, was to be "composed of a representative of each of the members of the Security Council as it will be constituted in 1947". The Commission consisted, accordingly, of representatives of Australia, Belgium, Brazil, China, Colombia, France, Poland, Syria, the United Kingdom, the Union of Soviet Socialist Republics and the United States of America.

---

[59]U. N. Security Council, Official Records, First Year, First Series, Special Supplement, "Report of the Sub-Committee on the Spanish Question".

[60]U. N. General Assembly, Resolution 39(I) December 12, 1946.

[61]U. N. Security Council, Official Records, First Year, Second Series, No. 16, pp. 396-400.

[62]U. N. Doc. S/203 (December 4, 1946).

[63]U. N. Security Council Official Records, First Year, Second Series, No. 28, pp. 700-701.

The resolution gave the Commission wide latitude to conduct its investigation "in order to determine the causes and nature of the above mentioned border violations and disturbances".[64]

The Commission was authorized

to conduct its investigation in northern Greece and in such parts of Greece, in Albania, Bulgaria and Yugoslavia as the Commission considers should be included in its investigation in order to elucidate the causes and nature of the . . . border violations and disturbances.[65]

It was empowered

to call upon the Governments, officials and nationals of those countries as well as such other sources as the Commission deems necessary.[66]

In addition to its powers of investigation, the Commission was also invited to make any proposals that it might deem wise for averting a repetition of border violations and disturbances in the areas where investigations were to be conducted.

The initial phase of the Commission's work took place in Athens and was largely confined to hearing the liaison representatives of the Greek, Albanian, Bulgarian and Yugoslav Governments. The Commission then proceeded to organize into investigating teams which conducted a total of thirty three field investigations. The Commission then went to Geneva to prepare its report.

During the period the Commission was preparing its report,[67] the Security Council adopted a resolution, on April 18, 1947, establishing a subsidiary group of the Commission composed of a representative of each of the members of the Commission. The Subsidiary Group was authorized to investigate only such incidents as were brought to its attention which occurred after March 22, 1947 and was specifically instructed not to hear evidence which was or could have been submitted to the Main Commission.[68]

The Commission of Investigation concerning Greek Frontier Incidents was able to carry out its task in spite of a certain amount of friction. When the Subsidiary Group was established, however, Albania, Bulgaria and Yugoslavia refused to cooperate and investigations could be conducted only on the Greek side of the frontier.

The report of the Commission contained its conclusions that the three northern neighbors of Greece, Albania, Bulgaria and Yugoslavia, had encouraged, assisted, trained and supplied Greek guerrillas in their activities against the Greek Government. After two draft resolutions based upon the Commission's report had been vetoed by the Soviet Union, the United States, in a procedural step, on September 15, 1947, through a resolution adopted by the Council, obtained removal of the item from the Security Council agenda. The Commission thereupon ceased to exist.

The removal of the Greek Question from the agenda of the Security Council led to consideration of the question by the General Assembly.[69] The United Nations Special Committee on the Balkans was subsequently set up by the General Assembly under a resolution adopted October 21, 1947.[70] The resolution called on the Governments of Albania, Bulgaria

---

64Idem.

65Idem.

66Idem.

67U. N. Doc. S/360 (May 23, 1947).

68U. N. Doc. S/AC.4/SG (April 29, 1947).

69U. N. Security Council Official Records, Second Year, No. 89, p. 2405; U. N. General Assembly Official Records, Second Session, Plenary Meetings, p. 300.

70U. N. General Assembly Resolution 109 II, October 21, 1947. Also U. N. General Assembly, Official Records, Second Session, Plenary Meetings, p. 462.

52

and Yugoslavia, on the one hand, and Greece, on the other, to co-operate in the settlement of their disputes by peaceful means.

The Special Committee consisted of representatives of Australia, Brazil, China, France, Mexico, the Netherlands, Pakistan, the United Kingdom, and the United States of America with seats held open for Poland and the Union of Soviet Socialist Republics. The latter two States declined to assume membership. Observers were provided by the States represented on the Committee.

The purposes of the Special Committee, under the terms of the Assembly resolution were to observe compliance by the four Governments with the Assembly's recommendations and to be available to assist the four Governments concerned in the implementation of such recommendations. The Special Committee also undertook certain functions in the nature of investigations and inquiries in accordance with the requirement that it report to the General Assembly and make such recommendations to the General Assembly as it saw fit.

In line with its task, therefore, besides making efforts to undertake political negotiations, the Special Committee conducted area surveys in Greek territory and made a number of investigations regarding guerilla activities, frontier incidents, refugees and similar matters affecting good relations between the Governments concerned. The Governments of Albania, Bulgaria and Yugoslavia refused to recognize the legality of the Special Committee under the provisions of the Charter and declined to admit it into their territorities.

The Special Committee submitted a number of reports to the General Assembly at its third session. On November 27, 1948, the General Assembly, in its resolution 193 (III), approved the reports and continued the Special Committee in being with the functions conferred on it by its earlier resolution 109 (II).[71] After submitting a further series of reports, the Special Committee was discontinued by resolution 508 (VI), adopted by the General Assembly on December 7, 1951, and its functions turned over to the Peace Observation Commission.[72]

Corfu Channel Incidents. The United Kingdom on January 10, 1947, acting under Article 35 of the Charter, called to the attention of the Security Council its dispute with Albania regarding an incident in which two British ships had been damaged by mines in the Corfu Channel on October 22, 1946.[73] The Albanian Government denied responsibility and contended that British warships had subsequently violated Albanian sovereignty by sweeping its territorial waters for other mines.[74] On February 27, 1947, the Security Council adopted a resolution establishing a sub-committee to investigate the facts in the case.

The Sub-Committee was composed of Australia, Poland and Colombia. Under the terms of the resolution of the Council, the Sub-Committee was requested to examine all the evidence concerning the incidents in question and to report to the Security Council on the facts of the case as disclosed by the evidence.

---

[71]United Nations, Interim Committee of the General Assembly. Organization and Procedure of United Nations Commissions VI The United Nations Special Committee on The Balkans.

[72]U. N. General Assembly Resolutions 508A (VI) and 508B (VI) (December 7, 1951).

[73]U. N. Security Council, Official Records, Second Year, Supplement No. 3, annex 8.

[74]Ibid., annex 9.

The Sub-Committee held ten meetings in all, the first meetings being devoted to interrogations of representatives of Albania, the United Kingdom and of Greece.  The remaining meetings were concerned with the study of the allegations and evidence presented by the two parties.

The report of the Sub-Committee stated that the first question was whether the Security Council considered itself competent to pronounce on the questions of whether the mine field existed and whether it had been laid by Albania or with its connivance.[75]  On April 3, 1947, the Security Council adopted a resolution, introduced by the representative of the United Kingdom, recommending that the two Governments should refer the dispute to the International Court of Justice.  The latter, after sending a commission of inquiry to the spot to gather information, delivered judgment in favor of the United Kingdom, holding Albania liable for the damage to the British warships.[76]

The Indonesian Question.  The Ukranian Soviet Socialist Republic by a letter, dated January 21, 1946, drew the attention of the Security Council, invoking Article 35, to the threat to the maintenance of international peace and security contained in the military activities of the British and Japanese forces in Indonesia and requested an investigation under Article 34 of the Charter.[77]  As all proposals put forward were rejected, the matter was considered closed.[78]

The Indonesian question was again raised in the Security Council by a letter, dated July 30, 1947, to the Secretary-General, in which the acting representative of Australia requested the Security Council to take immediate steps to restore international peace and security insofar as his Government considered that hostilities in progress in Java and Sumatra constituted a breach of the peace under Article 39 of the Charter.[79]  The Government of India at the same time addressed a letter to the Secretary-General drawing the attention of the Council under Article 35, paragraph 1, to the situation in Indonesia.[80]

On August 1, 1947, the Security Council rejecting Australia's complaint that called for action under Article 39, adopted a resolution calling on Indonesia and the Netherlands to cease hostilities and to settle their disputes by arbitration or other peaceful means.[81]  The initial fact-finding effort in the Indonesian situation was the Security Council Consular Commission at Batavia which was set up under a resolution adopted by the Security Council on August 25, 1947.[82]

The Consular Commission consisted of the career consular representatives in Batavia of Australia, Belgium, China, France, the United Kingdom and the United States of America.  The Commission obtained a number of military observers from the Governments of its members to assist it in observing the cease-fire orders of the Security Council.

Under its original terms of reference, the Consular Commission was required

> to prepare jointly for the information and guidance of the Security Council reports on the situation in the Republic of Indonesia following the resolution of the Council of 1 August 1947, such reports to cover the observance of the

---

[75]Ibid., Supplement No. 3, (S/300).

[76]I.C.J. Reports 1949, p. 250.

[77]U. N. Security Council, Official Records, First Year, First Series, Supplement No. 1, annex 4, p. 76.

[78]Ibid., pp. 256-263.

[79]U. N. Doc. S/449 (July 30, 1947).

[80]U. N. Doc. S/447 (July 30, 1947).

[81]U. N. Doc. S/459 (August 1, 1947).

[82]U. N. Doc. S/525 (August 25, 1947).

'cease-fire' orders and conditions prevailing in areas under
military occupation or from which armed forces now in
occupation may be withdrawn by agreement between the
parties.[83]

On October 21, 1947, the Commission submitted its report to the Council.[84]

Because of difficulties arising from the overlapping of functions of
the Consular Commission and the Committee of Good Offices, a resolution adopted by the Security Council, January 28, 1949, directed the Consular Commission

to facilitate the work of the United Nations Commission for
Indonesia (previously called the Committee of Good Offices
on the Indonesian Question) by providing military observers
and other staff and facilities to enable the Commission to
carry out its duties.[85]

In accordance with the Council resolution, the Committee was composed of three members consisting of Belgium, selected by the Netherlands, Australia, selected by Indonesia and the United States of America
selected by agreement between Belgium and Australia.

Although the Committee was established to assist the parties in the
pacific settlement of their dispute, the Council added to its tasks in subsequent resolutions. In a resolution adopted November 1, 1947, the
Council requested the Committee "to assist the parties in reaching an
arrangement which will ensure the observance of the cease-fire resolution".[86] In two subsequent resolutions adopted on February 28, 1948, the
Committee was asked to report to the Security Council on various political developments in the area.

In a resolution adopted on July 6, 1948, the Security Council requested a report on the existence of restrictions on the domestic and international trade of Indonesia and the reasons for the delay in the implementation of Article 6 of the Truce Agreement.[87] The Committee was requested in a resolution adopted on December 28, 1948 to report urgently
regarding a subsequent outbreak of fighting.[88]

The Committee carried out investigations, in accordance with the
resolutions adopted by the Security Council, by means of military assis-
tants or by military observers made available by the Security Council
Consular Commission at Batavia. The Committee also addressed a series
of questions to the parties and set up a drafting sub-committee to meet
with the representatives of the parties in an effort to reconcile any factual
discrepancies in their answers.[89]

Through its reports, the Committee kept the Council informed of the
progress of negotiations and of the political developments of the area
forming a background for the negotiations. Finally, on January 28, 1949,
the Security Council adopted a resolution renaming the Committee, the
United Nations Commission for Indonesia with the task of assisting in the
transfer of sovereignty from the Netherlands to Indonesia.[90]

---

[83]Idem.

[84]U. N. Doc. S/586 (October 21, 1947).

[85]U. N. Doc. S/1234 (January 28, 1949). The Committee of Good
Offices had been established by a resolution of the Security Council, adopted August 25, 1947, to assist the parties in the pacific settlement of their
dispute.

[86]U. N. Doc. S/597 (November 1, 1947).

[87]U. N. Security Council, Official Records, Third Year, No. 92, p. 15.

[88]U. N. Doc. S/1165 (December 28, 1948).

[89]U. N. Doc. S/1212 (January 14, 1949).

[90]U. N. Doc. S/1234 (January 28, 1949).

Dispute between India and Pakistan over Kashmir. In a letter, dated January 1, 1948, to the President of the Security Council, the representative of India to the United Nations, invoking Article 35 of the Charter, stated that a situation continuation of which was likely to endanger international peace and security existed between India and Pakistan. The Indian representative claimed that such situation resulted from aid Pakistan was giving to invaders from Pakistan and tribesmen from areas adjacent to the northwest frontier of Pakistan who were engaged in operations against the State of Jammu and Kashmir. If Pakistan did not desist, the Indian representative asserted India might be compelled to enter Pakistan territory. The Government of India therefore requested the Security Council to call on the Government of Pakistan immediately to stop giving such assistance.[91] The Government of Pakistan replied in a letter, dated January 15, 1948, from its foreign minister, charging India with unlawful occupation of the State of Junagadh and other states by Indian armed forces, mass destruction of Muslims and failure to implement agreements between the territories. [92]

The Security Council, on January 20, 1948, adopted a resolution setting up a commission with the dual function of (1) investigating under Article 34 of the Charter and (2) of exercising a mediatory function.[93] The Commission was to consist of three members, one to be selected by India and one by Pakistan. By a subsequent resolution of April 21, 1948, the membership was enlarged to five. India selected Czechoslovakia and Pakistan selected Argentina with the Security Council nominating Belgium and Colombia. In accordance with the terms of the resolution of April 21, 1948, the President of the Security Council then designated the United States as the fifth member.

Before the Commission began to operate, however, the Council, in view of the agreement of the parties as to the seriousness of the matter, adopted a resolution containing a finding that "the continuation of the dispute" was "likely to endanger international peace and security".[94] This in effect eliminated the first function of the Commission. The Commission did pursue its second function of exercising its good offices with a view to the restoration of peace and order and the holding of a plebiscite in order to determine whether the State of Jammu and Kashmir should accede to India or to Pakistan.

In pursuance of this latter function, the Commission, in addition to directing its attention towards obtaining a cease-fire in Kashmir, also endeavored to ascertain the attitudes of the two States, as well as the views of the Government of the State of Kashmir and of the Azad leaders, concerning a plebiscite. It became necessary for the Commission, in order to achieve this purpose, to conduct an inquiry. It invited submission of written or oral statements by representatives of Governments, organizations or private individuals. It submitted questionnaires to the representatives and military leaders of the two States.

In addition, the Commission sent a sub-committee to report on the political and economic conditions in the State of Jammu and Kashmir. This Sub-Committee also reported to the Commission on the administration in the territory controlled by the Azad leaders as well as on the refugee situation in western Kashmir.

The Commission was successful in arranging a cease fire.[95] In its third interim report, dated December 5, 1949, the Commission noted, in its conclusions, that

---

[91]U. N. Doc. S/628 (January 1, 1948).

[92]U. N. Doc. S/646 (January 15, 1948).

[93]U. N. Security Council Official Records, Third Year No. 1-15, p. 143; (S/654, January 20, 1948).

[94]U. N. Doc. S/726 (April 22, 1948).
[95]U. N. Doc. S/1196 (January 10, 1949).

The function of investigating the facts with which the Commission was invested by the Security Council has also been completed. The protracted negotiations of the past have provided thorough knowledge of the facts of the case. This is a positive achievement. The main issues which have prevented the Governments of India and Pakistan from progressing more rapidly toward a settlement of their dispute over Kashmir, and the conditions which they believe should regulate the putting into effect of their commitments, are now in sharp focus. The Commission trusts that United Nations action in the future should prove more effective with the foundation which this investigation provides. [96]

With a view to further mediatory action, the Commission proposed that the Security Council should designate a single representative to replace the Commission. The Commission was accordingly terminated by a decision of the Security Council on March 14, 1950. [97]

The Question of Palestine. On April 2, 1947, a request was addressed to the Secretary-General from the representative of the United Kingdom to convene a special session of the General Assembly for the purpose of constituting and instructing a special committee to prepare for the consideration of the question of Palestine by the Assembly at its next regular session. [98] In response to this request, the Secretary-General summoned the first special session of the General Assembly on April 28, 1947. The sole item on the agenda was the request of the United Kingdom which was submitted to the First Committee. The General Assembly, upon the recommendation of the First Committee, adopted resolution 106 (S-1) on May 15, 1947 constituting and instructing the United Nations Special Committee on Palestine. [99]

Under the terms of the resolution, the Special Committee was composed of the representatives of Australia, Canada, Czechoslovakia, Guatemala, India, Iran, the Netherlands, Peru, Sweden, Uruguay and Yugoslavia.

The task of the Special Committee was to submit to the General Assembly recommendations on the Palestine question concerning the future government of Palestine. [100] Paragraph 4 of the Assembly resolution provided that the Special Committee might

. . . conduct investigations in Palestine and wherever it may deem useful, receive and examine written or oral testimony, whichever it may consider appropriate in each case, from the mandatory Power, or from representatives of the population of Palestine, from Governments and from such organizations and individuals as it may deem necessary. [101]

The Special Committee attempted to arrive at an understanding of the issues involved in the Palestine problem by conducting a preliminary survey of the land, its peoples and their aspirations, and of the social, economic and religious systems. The Special Committee also conducted hearings in Palestine, visited the surrounding Arab States and sent a subcommittee to visit a number of displaced persons' camps in Germany and Austria. The Arab Higher Committee abstained from collaborating in the work of the Special Committee.

The report of the Special Committee contained a majority plan, supported by seven members, containing the principle of partition with econo-

---

[96]U. N. Doc. S/1430 (December 5, 1949).

[97]U. N. Doc. S/1469 (March 14, 1950).

[98]U. N. Doc. A/286 (April 2, 1947).

[99]U. N. Doc. A/307 (May 15, 1947).

[100]Idem.

[101]Idem.

mic union, and a minority plan, supported by three members, favoring a federal state. One member abstained from voting on both plans. Agreement was reached on twelve basic recommendations, eleven of which were adopted unanimously and the twelfth, with two dissenting votes. The factual chapters of the report were prepared by the secretariat and the approved text of the report was signed on August 31, 1947 and presented to the Secretary-General.[102] The Special Committee thereupon considered its function completed.

This report was submitted to an Ad Hoc Committee by the General Assembly. The Ad Hoc Committee, after studying the report of the Special Committee on Palestine, recommended adoption of the plan for partition with economic union and the creation of a commission of five members to implement the plan.[103]

The General Assembly, accepting the report of its Ad Hoc Committee in toto, adopted resolution 181 (II) which, among other things, established the commission which came to be known as "The United Nations Palestine Commission" to implement the General Assembly's resolution providing for partition with economic union.[104]

The United Nations Palestine Commission, after studying all the information submitted to it, reached the inescapable conclusion that, in view of the situation which had developed in Palestine, it was necessary to refer to the Security Council the problem of providing that armed assistance which alone would enable the Commission to discharge its responsibilities on the termination of the Mandate.[105]

The General Assembly appointed a United Nations Mediator,[106] in its resolution of May 14, 1948, whose function of mediation and conciliation were to be eventually absorbed by the Palestine Conciliation Commission.[107] The Security Council, had previously created a Truce Commission, by its resolution of April 23, 1948, to supervise implementation of its resolution of April 17, 1948 on the Palestine Question.

After the conclusion of the Armistice Agreements between Israel and Egypt, Jordan, Lebanon and Syria respectively, mixed armistice commissions charged with the responsibility of investigating complaints were set up. In each case, the Mixed Armistice Commission was composed of five members except in the Israeli-Egyptian Agreement where the Mixed Armistice Commission contained seven members. Where the Mixed Armistice Commission consisted of five members, two were designated by each of the parties and where the Mixed Armistice Commission consisted of seven members, three were designated by each of the parties. The remaining member and Chairman of each Commission was the United Nations Chief of Staff of the Truce Supervision Organization or a senior officer designated by him, following consultations with both parties to the Armistice Agreement.[108]

The Matter of Free Elections in Korea. The United Nations Temporary Commission on Korea was established by a resolution adopted by the General Assembly on November 14, 1947.[109] The Temporary Commission was composed of five representatives from countries interested in the Pacific area - Australia, Canada, China, India and the Philippines with one each from special geographic areas. Thus France was selected from

[102]U. N. Doc. A/364 (September 3, 1947).

[103]U. N. Doc. A/516 (November 25, 1947).

[104]Idem.

[105]U. N. Doc. A/532 (April 10, 1948).

[106]U. N. General Assembly Resolution 186 (S-2) (May 14, 1948).

[107]U. N. General Assembly Resolution 194 (III), December 11, 1948.

[108]U. N. Doc. A/5694 (May 1, 1964), pp. 113-115.

[109]U. N. General Assembly Resolution 112 (II), November 14, 1947.

Western Europe, the Ukranian Soviet Socialist Republic from Eastern Europe, El Salvador from Latin America and Syria from the Middle East. The Ukranian Soviet Socialist Republic declined to assume its seat on the Commission.[110]

The purpose of the Temporary Commission was to observe free elections which were to be held throughout Korea in order that duly elected representatives of the Korean people might participate in consideration before the General Assembly of the Question of the Freedom and Independence of Korea.[111] The inability of the Temporary Commission and its successor, the United Nations Commission on Korea, to gain access to the northern territory occupied by the forces of the Union of Soviet Socialist Republics prevented attainment of the purposes of the General Assembly.[112]

Nevertheless, the Temporary Commission proceeded to conduct hearings which it divided among three sub-committees. In Sub-Committee 1, which dealt with the free atmosphere for elections, responsible authorities were heard on the interpretation and application of the pertinent laws and regulations in force in Korea. Sub-Committee 2 heard Korean political leaders and representatives of various organizations whose views might be helpful to the Commission, in particular as regards the problems of separate elections in South Korea. Written communications were also received. Sub-Committee 3 examined the electoral laws of North and South Korea and acquainted itself with the views of Korean officials and experts as well as those of the occupying Governments. The authorities of the Union of Soviet Socialist Republics in North Korea refused to accept any communication addressed to them by the Commission.

The subsequent elections in South Korea were observed by means of a Main Committee, functioning as a committee of the whole, which maintained continuous liaison with the National Election Committee. Supervision of the elections took place by means of field observer groups of the Main Committee.[113]

Fortnightly information reports were prepared by the secretariat of the Temporary Commission under the supervision of the Chairman and the heads of the sub-committees. The report of the Temporary Commission to the General Assembly was published in two parts. The first part, consisting of three volumes, was issued at Seoul on July 21, 1948. The second part, in two volumes, was issued in New York on October 15, 1948.[114]

One aspect of the Temporary Commission's task had been that of military observer to "arrange with the occupying powers for the complete withdrawal from Korea of their armed forces . . ."[115] The resolution of the General Assembly setting up the subsequent United Nations Commission on Korea continued this function. In addition, the tasks of lending "its good offices to bring about the unification of Korea and the integration of all Korean security forces in accordance with principles laid down by the General Assembly" and to "seek to facilitate the removal of barriers to economic, social and other friendly intercourse caused by the division of Korea" were assigned to the United Nations Commission on Korea.[116]

---

[110]Idem.

[111]Idem.

[112]U. N. Doc. A/575 (July 21, 1948). Report of the United Nations Temporary Commission on Korea and U. N. Doc. A/936 (July 28, 1949) Report of The United Nations Commission on Korea.

[113]U. N. Doc. A/575 (July 21, 1948) and A/575, Add. 3 (October 15, 1948).

[114]Idem.

[115]Idem.

[116]U. N. General Assembly Resolution 195 (II), December 12, 1948.

In its report, adopted at Seoul on July 28, 1949, the United Nations Commission on Korea noted, among other things, the effect of the cold war on the problem of Korean unification and the danger to open military conflict.[117] By cablegram, dated June 25, 1950, the Commission was able to notify the Secretary-General of the outbreak of hostilities.[118] A subsequent report of the Commission provided the Security Council with a basis for recommending to its members that they furnish armed assistance to the Republic of Korea.[119]

The Matter of Eritrea. The Governments of France, U.S.S.R., United Kingdom and the United States notified the Secretary-General, on September 15, 1948, that the question of the disposal of the former Italian Colonies had been referred that day to the General Assembly in accordance with Article 23, paragraph 3, Annex XI of the Treaty of Peace with Italy.[120]

A commission was formed to ascertain more fully the wishes and the best means of promoting the welfare of the inhabitants of Eritrea, to examine the question of the disposal of Eritrea, and to prepare a report for the General Assembly, together with such proposal or proposals as it might deem appropriate for the solution of the problem of Eritrea.[121] The Commission was composed of representatives of Burma, Norway, the Union of South Africa, Guatemala and Pakistan.

The report of the United Nations Commission for Eritrea, was transmitted to the Secretary-General, by letter, dated June 8, 1950.[122] The Commission was split in its final report but the General Assembly, on December 2, 1950, accepting one recommendation, recommended "that Eritrea be constituted as an autonomous unit federated with Ethiopia under the sovereignty of the Ethiopian Crown".[123]

Free Elections in Germany. Acting on a proposal made by the Chancellor of the Federal Republic of Germany, the Governments of France, Great Britain and the United States presented to the General Assembly at its sixth session a request for the appointment of an international commission to carry out investigations in Germany in order to determine whether conditions existing there would make it possible to hold free elections.[124] The General Assembly adopted on December 20, 1951, resolution 510 (VI) providing for the appointment of such a commission.

The Commission was composed of representatives of Brazil, Iceland, the Netherlands, Pakistan and Poland. The task of the Commission under the Assembly resolution, was to conduct

a simultaneous investigation in the Federal Republic of Germany, in Berlin, and in the Soviet Zone of Germany to ascertain and report whether conditions in these areas are such as to make possible the holding of geniunely free and secret elections throughout these areas . . . .[125]

---

[117]U. N. Doc. A/936 (July 28, 1949).

[118]U. N. Doc. S/1496 (June 25, 1950).

[119]U. N. Doc. S/1511 (June 27, 1950).

[120]U. N. Doc. A/645 (September 15, 1948).

[121]U. N. General Assembly Resolution 289 (IV), November 21, 1949.

[122]U. N. Doc. A/1285 (June 8, 1950).

[123]U. N. General Assembly Resolution 390 (V), December 2, 1950.

[124]U. N. Doc. A/1938 (November 5, 1951).

[125]U. N. General Assembly, Official Records, Sixth Session, Resolutions, pp. 10-11.

The Commission was further directed by the General Assembly to report at the earliest practicable date to the Secretary-General, for the consideration of the four Powers and for the information of the other Members of the United Nations, on the results of its efforts to make the necessary arrangements with all the parties concerned to enable it to undertake its work . . .[126]

If the Commission was unable forthwith to make the necessary arrangements, the Assembly resolution directed it

to make a further attempt to carry out its task at such time as it is satisfied that the German authorities in the Federal Republic, in Berlin, and in the Soviet Zone will admit the Commission, . . .[127]

The Commission submitted a unanimous report to the Secretary-General on April 30, 1952.[128] In its report, the Commission stated that it considered the directive given to it, under the Assembly resolution, to make the necessary arrangements with the parties took precedence. The necessary arrangements included the grant of normal diplomatic facilities for the Commission and its staff; the right to travel freely throughout Germany and the right of free access to such persons, places and relevant documents as the Commission might consider necessary. It also included the right to communicate freely with the people of Germany; immunity for its communications from censorship, delay or suppression and the right to summon witnesses.

The report stated that the Commission was able to conclude satisfactory arrangements with the Allied High Commission for Germany, the Government of the Federal Republic of Germany, the Allied Command in Berlin with respect to the French, British and American Zones and the Government of the western sector of Berlin. The report went on to state that the Commission was unable to establish contact with the authorities in the Soviet Zone of Germany or in the eastern sector of Berlin and thus was unable to make the necessary arrangements with them. The Commission concluded in its report that in view of the latter fact, it saw little prospect at that time of its being able to pursue its task.

The Commission submitted a supplementary report covering the period from May to August 1952 and then, in view of its inability to carry out its task beyond the extent to which it had been able to do in the preliminary period, adjourned sine die.[129]

Apartheid in South Africa. The number of states requesting that the question of racial conflict resulting from the policies of apartheid of the Government of the then Union of South Africa be included on the agenda of the seventh session of the General Assembly gave impetus to the ensuing discussion and to the proposal for an investigation.[130]

On December 5, 1952, the General Assembly adopted resolution 616 A (VII) establishing a commission to study the racial situation in South Africa. In accordance with the terms of the resolution, the Commission was to consist of three persons. Upon the proposal of the President, the Assembly selected Ralph Bunche, Herman Santa Cruz and Jaime Torres Bodet. Mr. Bunche and Mr. Torres Bodet being unable to serve, the Assembly appointed Dantes Sellegarde and Henri Laugier. Mr. Santa Cruz was elected Chairman.

---

[126]Idem.

[127]Idem.

[128]U. N. Doc. A/2122 and Add. 1 (August 11, 1952).

[129]U. N. Doc. A/2122 (August 11, 1952).

[130]U. N. Doc. A/2183 (September 12, 1952).

The Government of the then Union of South Africa objected to the investigation on the grounds that it violated Article 2 (7) of the Charter.[131] However, in its report, the Commission of Investigation noted that, under the Charter, the Assembly is empowered to undertake any investigations and to make any recommendations to the member states that it deems desirable concerning the application and enforcement of the purposes and principles of the Charter.[132]

The report of the Commission, under the circumstances, were therefore based largely on an analysis of the relevant legislation in force in South Africa, on a study of other written materials regarding the situation in South Africa and on oral and written statements made by non-governmental organizations and private individuals. In addition, the Commission examined memoranda submitted by certain Member States. The major section of the Commission's report dealt with the substantive aspects of the racial situation in South Africa.

After submitting its unanimous report, which held that the apartheid policy was contrary to the principles of the Charter,[133] to the eighth session of the General Assembly, the Commission was authorized, under resolution 721 (VIII), to continue its work and to report to the General Assembly at its ninth session.[134] The Commission was subsequently authorized by the General Assembly at its ninth session to continue its work and submit a further report.[135] The Commission submitted its final report to the tenth session of the General Assembly which noted the report and commended the Commission for its work.[136]

The question of apartheid in South Africa arose again on November 1, 1962, when the Special Political Committee adopted a draft resolution presented by thirty-four African and Asian States, which, in a series of proposals concerning the policies of apartheid of the Government of South Africa, recommended that a Special Committee should be established to keep the racial policies of the South African Government under review when the General Assembly was not in session. The draft resolution was incorporated in resolution 1761 (XVII), adopted by the General Assembly on November 6, 1962.

The President of the General Assembly, in accordance with the terms of resolution 1761 (XVII), announced on February 18, 1963, the appointment of Algeria, Costa Rica, the Federation of Malaya, Ghana, Guinea, Haiti, Hungary, Nepal, Nigeria, the Philippines and Somalia as members of the Special Committee.

The Special Committee determined that, in view of the conclusions reached by the Security Council and General Assembly, its task was not simply to review the relevant information regarding the policies of the South African Government but to provide a basis for further efforts by Member States to secure a speedy and effective solution of the grave situation in South Africa.

The Government of South Africa categorically refused to co-operate or assist the Special Committee, claiming the adoption of resolution 1761 (XVII) including the establishment of the Special Committee was contrary to the provisions of the Charter.[137] The Committee proceeded to review official documentary sources, press reports, memoranda received from organizations and individuals and granted hearings to persons and repre-

---

[131]U. N. General Assembly Official Records, Seventh Session, Plenary Meetings, pp. 331-332.

[132]U. N. General Assembly Official Records, Eighth Session, Supplement No. 16, (A/2505), p. 34.

[133]Ibid., p. 118.

[134]U. N. General Assembly Resolution 721 (VIII), December 8, 1953.

[135]U. N. General Assembly Resolution 820 (IX), December 14, 1954.

[136]U. N. General Assembly Resolution 917 (IX), December 6, 1955.

[137]U. N. Doc. A/AC.115/L.4 (April 18, 1963).

sentatives of organizations.

On September 16, 1963, the Committee submitted its first major report. The report was taken note by the General Assembly in resolution 1881 (XVIII), adopted October 11, 1963, and resolution 1978 (XVIII), adopted December 16, 1963.[138] In the latter resolution, the General Assembly requested the Special Committee to continue its work and "to submit reports to the General Assembly and to the Security Council whenever necessary".[139]

Hungary. As a result of the outbreak of fighting in Hungary, in October 1956, the General Assembly adopted resolution 1004 (ES-III), on November 4, 1956, at its second emergency session. In that resolution, it requested the Secretary-General to investigate the situation in Hungary. The Secretary-General formed a committee of three consisting of Oscar Sundersen of Norway, Arthur Lall of India and Alberto Lleras of Colombia, to assist him in his investigation.[140] After examining all the material available to the Secretariat, the Secretary-General noted that

Until it is possible to open up further sources of reliable material through observation on the spot in Hungary and by the cooperation of the Governments directly concerned, there would be little purpose in our attempting an assessment of the recent situation or of recent events.[141]

It was suggested by the Secretary-General that the Assembly might work to establish an ad hoc committee to take over the activities of his investigatory group under broader terms of reference. The General Assembly adopted this suggestion in resolution 1132 (XI), on January 10, 1957, establishing a Special Committee on the Problem of Hungary, composed of representatives of Australia, Ceylon, Denmark, Tunisia, and Uruguay.[142]

The Committee was established, according to the resolution, for the purpose of ensuring that the General Assembly and all Member States should "be in possession of the fullest and best available information" regarding the situation in Hungary" as well as regarding developments relating to the recommendations of the General Assembly on this subject.[143]

The Committee made a preliminary survey of the immediately available information in order to establish a basis for the examination of witnesses and to ascertain what additional information of other types would be necessary. It received information from certain Member States and expressed its desire that Member States having diplomatic representatives in Budapest at the time of the events in question transmit any special knowledge in their possession to the Committee. The Committee was not successful in obtaining the permission of the Hungarian Government to enter its territory.[144]

After submitting interim reports on February 20, and June 12, 1957, the Special Committee submitted its unanimous report[145] which the General

---

138[U]. N. Doc. A/5497 (September 16, 1963).

139The Special Committee continued its review of events in the Republic of South Africa in two additional reports: U. N. Docs. A/5692 (March 25, 1964) and A/5707 (May 25, 1964).

140[U]. N. Doc. A/3359 (November 4, 1956).

141[U]. N. Doc. A/3485 (January 8, 1957).

142[U]. N. Doc. A/3546 (January 10, 1957).

143Idem.

144[U]. N. General Assembly, Official Records, Eleventh Session, Supplement No. 18 (A/3592).

145Idem.

Assembly endorsed in resolution 1133 (XI), adopted September 14, 1957.[146] Among the conclusions of the Committee, contained in its report, were that consideration of the question by the United Nations was legally proper, and that what took place in Hungary was a spontaneous national uprising.[147]

In paragraph 9 of the Assembly's resolution, the President of the General Assembly, Prince Wan Waithayakon, was requested, as the General Assembly's Special representative on the Hungarian problem, to take such steps as he deemed appropriate, in view of the Committee's findings, to achieve the objectives of the United Nations.[148] The final report of the Special Committee, dated July 14, 1958, was endorsed by the General Assembly in its resolution 1312 (XIII), which was adopted on December 12, 1958.[149]

The post of Special Representative was filled by Sir Leslie Munro in 1958. The post was discontinued by the General Assembly in its resolution 1857 (VII), adopted on December 20, 1962.

Laos. The Secretary-General, on September 5, 1959 asked the President of the Security Council to convene the Council urgently in order to consider a communication from the Foreign Minister of Laos. The Foreign Minister requested that an emergency force be dispatched to Laos as soon as possible in order to halt acts of aggression which were being committed along the north-eastern frontier of Laos by elements from the Democratic Republic of Viet-Nam.[150]

In a resolution adopted on September 7, 1959, the Security Council appointed a sub-committee to examine the question further.[151] The Sub-Committee, under the terms of the resolution, consisted of representatives of Argentina, Italy, Japan and Tunisia.

After holding initial meetings in New York and examining the statements made before the Security Council and the documents available at United Nations Headquarters, the Sub-Committee, at the invitation of the Laotian Government, visited Laos from September 15 to October 13, 1959. During that time, the Sub-Committee met members of the Government and held consultations with the Liaison Committee, set up by the Government, from which it received various documents and clarifications. Two working parties of the Sub-Committee visited different areas of Laos.

The Sub-Committee returned to New York after leaving two alternate representatives in Laos, with an appropriate secretariat, to collect any additional information that might be required. It submitted a unanimous report giving an account of its operations and findings to the Security Council on November 3, 1959.[152]

The report contained the Sub-Committee's conclusion that although there had been guerrilla activity, there was insufficient evidence to prove the charges that crossings of the Laotian frontier by regular troops of the Democratic Republic of North Vietnam had occurred.[153]

Death of Mr. Lumumba. On February 21, 1961, as a result of the killing of the Congolese leaders, Patrice Lumumba, Maurice Mpolo and Joseph Okito, the Security Council adopted a resolution, Part A, paragraph 4 of which provided for an immediate and impartial investigation

---

[146]U. N. Doc. A/3572/Add 1 (September 14, 1957).

[147]Idem.

[148]Idem.

[149]U. N. General Assembly, Official Records, Thirteenth Session, Annexes, Agenda item 69, (A/3849).

[150]U. N. Docs. S/4212 (September 4, 1959) and S/4213 (September 5, 1959).

[151]U. N. Doc. S/4216 (September 7, 1959).

[152]U. N. Doc. S/4236 (November 3, 1959).
[153]Ibid., p. 31

into the circumstances of the death of these leaders. The Advisory Committee on the Congo, to which the question had been referred by the Secretary-General, recommended that a commission should be established to carry out the investigation composed of members to be nominated by the Governments of Burma, Ethiopa, Mexico and Togo.[154] The General Assembly established the Commission by resolution 1601 (XV), adopted April 15, 1961.

The Commission examined documentary material furnished by the Secretary-General. Member States, were requested to forward any relevant information in their possession. A number of witnesses, in the course of hearings conducted in Belgium and Geneva, furnished statements to the Commission. The Commission did not visit the Congo upon the advice of officials connected with the United Nations Operation in the Congo that it would be unwise to do so at that time.

The Commission submitted its report November 11, 1961.[155] The report contained the conclusions of the Commission that the responsibility for the murder of Mr. Lumumba, Mr. Okito and Mr. Mpolo must be shared by the authorities of the Congolese Government and Katanga Province.[156]

The Commission expressed the hope that its findings could serve as a basis for further investigation and also in judicial proceedings which it hoped would be instituted as soon as possible.[157]

Assassination of the Prime Minister of Burundi. On October 23, 1961, the General Assembly adopted unanimously resolution 1627 (XVI) which requested the United Nations Commission for Ruanda Urundi to conduct an on-the-spot investigation into the circumstances of the Prime Minister of Burundi's death and to submit a preliminary report to the General Assembly as soon as possible.

The Commission received the Assembly's request while in Geneva where it was engaged in preparing its report on the legislative elections in Ruanda Urundi and the referendum which had been held in Ruanda.

The report of the Commission contained a statement of the facts and circumstances surrounding the Prime Minister's death as revealed by the official statements made to the Commission. It appeared that the crime had been committed by a Greek national born in Ruanda Urundi who had made a full confession. The report also presented the main trends of opinion circulating in Burundi regarding the reason for the crime.[158]

Death of Mr. Hammarskjold. The General Assembly, on October 26, 1961 adopted resolution 1628 (XVI) which provided for a commission of "five eminent persons" to carry out an investigation into the circumstances surrounding the death of Mr. Hammarskjold and the persons who died with him in the service of the United Nations.

Upon the recommendation of the President of the Assembly, and in accordance with the terms of the resolution, five individuals were chosen who were nationals respectively of Sierra Leone, Argentina, Sweden, Nepal and Yugoslavia.

---

[154]U. N. Security Council, Official Records, Sixteenth Year, Supplement for January, February and March 1961, (S/4771 and Add. 1-3).

[155]U. N. Security Council, Official Records, Sixteenth Year, Supplement for October, November and December 1961, (A/4964, S/4976, November 11, 1961).

[156]Idem.

[157]Idem.

[158]U. N. General Assembly, Official Records, Sixteenth Session, Annexes, agenda item 49 (A/5086).

The Commission proceeded to Leopoldville, after an organizational meeting held in New York. It also met in Salisbury and in Geneva. It examined reports and proceedings of the Rhodesian Board of Investigation and the Rhodesian Commission of Inquiry, as well as all exhibits submitted to the latter. Tests were made on the wreckage of the plane. The Commission heard ninety witnesses who it thought might yield new information or whose appearance was essential for the purpose of forming a judgment.

The report of the Commission was submitted to the President of the General Assembly[159] which took note of the report in resolution 1759 (XVII), adopted on October 26, 1962.

The Question of Angola. The Security Council was convened March 10, 1961, to consider "the crisis in Angola", brought to its attention by the representative of Liberia.[160]

As a result of the inability of the Security Council to adopt a resolution concerning the situation in Angola, the matter was referred to the General Assembly at the request of forty members of the United Nations.[161] A resolution was adopted by the General Assembly, on April 20, 1961, providing, among other things, for the appointment of a sub-committee to

examine the statements made before the Assembly concerning Angola, to receive further statements and documents, to conduct such inquiries as it may deem necessary and to report to the Assembly as soon as possible.[162]

The Security Council, on June 9, 1961, reaffirmed the resolution of the General Assembly and requested the Sub-Committee appointed under the General Assembly resolution to implement its mandate without delay.[163]

The President of the General Assembly appointed Bolivia, Dahomey, Malaya, Finland and the Sudan as members of the Committee. The representatives of Bolivia and Finland were elected Chairman and Vice-Chairman respectively.[164]

The Sub-Committee failed to obtain the consent of the Portuguese Government to permit the Sub-Committee to visit Angola. The Portuguese Government did, however, invite the Chairman of the Sub-Committee to visit Lisbon in order to hold talks with various members of the Portuguese Government. As a result of this visit, the Portuguese Government submitted documentary information relating to Angola to the Sub-Committee.

Upon the invitation of the Congolese Government (Leopoldville), the Vice-Chairman and the representatives on the Sub-Committee of Dahomey and the Sudan, visited the Republic of the Congo (Leopoldville), between August 9 and 18, 1961 and gave hearings to representatives of seven Angola groups and to Angolan refugees in Leopoldville and in other places in the Congo. The Sub-Committee also received information from the Inter-

---

[159]U. N. General Assembly, Official Records, Seventeenth Session, Annexes, agenda item 22 (A/5069 and Add. 1), April 24, 1962. The report while not excluding any possibilities, could find no evidence which pointed to any particular cause for the crash of the plane carrying the United Nations personnel.

[160]U. N. Doc. S/4738 (February 20, 1961).

[161]U. N. Doc. A/4712 and Add. 1. (March 20, 1961).

[162]U. N. General Assembly Resolution 1603 (XV), April 20, 1961.

[163]U. N. Doc. S/4835 (June 9, 1961).

[164]U. N. General Assembly Resolution 1603 (XV), April 20, 1961.

national Labor Organization, from non-governmental organizations and from individuals with first-hand information on Angola. [165]

The Sub-Committee was thus enabled to submit a detailed report of the situation to the General Assembly at its sixteenth session. [166] The General Assembly, noting the work of the Sub-Committee, authorized it to continue in operation. [167] The Sub-Committee submitted a continuation report, covering the period from November 13, 1961 to November 8, 1962, to the General Assembly at its seventeenth session. [168] In the continuation report, the Sub-Committee, although sharply critical of Portugal's policies in Angola, felt that the primary responsibility for implementing the resolutions of the United Nations with regard to Angola lay with the Government of Portugal. [169]

South West Africa. From the inception of the United Nations, the problem of South West Africa has been before the General Assembly. Following the submission of a special report by the Committee on South West Africa, [170] the Special Committee on South West Africa was established by a resolution of the General Assembly adopted on December 19, 1961. [171] In accordance with resolution 1702 (XVI), the Committee was to consist of the representatives of seven Member States selected by the President of the General Assembly. Those appointed were Brazil, Mexico, Burma, Norway, Philippines, Somalia and Togo.

The tasks of the Special Committee, under resolution 1702 (XVI), included making a visit to South West Africa and the discharge of certain responsibilities which had been assigned to the Committee on South West Africa by the Assembly in sub-paragraphs (a), (b) and (c) of paragraph 12 of its resolution 749 (VIII) of November 28, 1953. The latter included examination, within the scope of the questionnaire adopted by the Permanent Mandates Commission of the League of Nations, of the information available with respect to the territory.

Although the Republic of South Africa, the mandatory Power under the League of Nations, objected to the jurisdiction of the Special Committee, it did permit the Chairman and Vice-Chairman of the Committee to visit the territory of South West Africa and to conduct an on-the-spot investigation, as well as to visit the Republic of South Africa in order to review the matter at issue with the Government on an informal basis.

The Chairman and Vice-Chairman, in their visit to South Africa, held discussions with the Prime Minister, the Minister of Foreign Affairs, other members of the Government, representatives of the Liberal Party, and with a joint deputation of the South African Indian Congress, the Coloured Congress and the Congress of Democrats. In their visit to South West Africa, which covered nine days, the Chairman and Vice-Chairman also met privately with a considerable number of individuals and with deputations who wished to present their views. Upon returning to South Africa, the Chairman and Vice-Chairman resumed their discussions with South African authorities.

The report of the Chairman and Vice-Chairman was subsequently incorporated into the report of the Special Committee on South West Africa

---

[165]U. N. Doc. A/4978 (Report of the Sub-Committee on the Situation in Angola, November 20, 1961).

[166]Idem.

[167]U. N. General Assembly Resolution 1742 (XVI), January 30, 1962.

[168]U. N. Doc. A/5286 (November 8, 1962).

[169]Ibid., p. 26.

[170]U. N. General Assembly, Official Records, Sixteenth Session, Supplement No. 12, (A/4926, October 26, 1961).

[171]U. N. General Assembly Resolution 1702 (XVI), December 19, 1961.

which was presented to the seventeenth session of the General Assembly.[172] The Special Committee reported the facts of its visits and the results of its investigations and concluded that its mission could not be accomplished without force and that the population desired immediate United Nations administration and eventual independence. After dissolving the Special Committee, the General Assembly adopted a resolution reaffirming the right of the people of South West Africa to independence.[173]

Violation of human rights in South Viet-Nam. In considering item 77 of the agenda of its eighteenth session, entitled "Violation of human rights in South Viet-Nam:, the President of the General Assembly read a letter from the head of the Special Mission of the Republic of Viet-Nam containing an invitation for the representatives of several Member States to visit Viet-Nam for the purpose of examining the relations between that Government and its Buddhist community.

Following the withdrawal of a draft resolution, the President of the Assembly, at its 1234th plenary meeting stated that, in the absence of objection, he presumed it was the wish of the Assembly that he should act in accordance with the letter. There being no objection, the President of the Assembly announced, at the 1239th plenary meeting of the Assembly, that he had appointed a mission to visit the Republic of Vietnam composed of the representatives of Afghanistan, Brazil, Ceylon, Costs Rica, Dahomey, Morocco and Nepal.

The Mission collected information from various sources such as the provisions of law in force in the Republic of Vietnam, information in the press, activities of organizations interested in the observance of human rights, on-the-spot investigations, petitions and the hearing of witnesses. The report of the Mission was submitted to the General Assembly at its eighteenth session.[174]

The Secretary-General's Special Representative to Oman. On December II, 1962, the representative of the United Kingdom transmitted to the Secretary-General an invitation from the Sultan of Muscat and Oman to send a representative on a personal basis to visit the Sultanate to obtain first-hand information as to the situation there. The Secretary-General appointed Mr. Herbert de Ribbing of Sweden as his Special Representative. The Secretary-General requested his Special Representative to report

on such questions as the presence of foreign troops in Oman, any evidence of oppression, instances of sabotage and fighting, the existence of a 'rebel movement', and the existence of any 'rebel forces' actually in control of a particular area.[175]

The Special Representative visited the Sultanate where he held discussions with the Sultan, interviewed Government officials, held meetings with sheikhs and notables throughout the country. After engaging in discussions with the British authorities in Bahrein, the Special Representative proceeded to Saudi Arabia where he talked to the Prime Minister, and to the Iman Ghalib ben Ali and his brother. After holding discussions with officials in London, the Special Representative returned to New

---

[172]U. N. General Assembly, Official Records, Seventeenth Session, Supplement No. 12, (A/5212, August 31, 1962).

[173]U. N. General Assembly Resolution 1805 (SVII), December 14, 1962.

[174]U. N. General Assembly, Official Records, Eighteenth Session, Annexes, Agenda item 77 (A/5630, December 7, 1963). At its 1280th plenary meeting, on December 13, 1963, the General Assembly decided not to continue consideration of the item. (Ibid., p. 93.).

[175]U. N. General Assembly, Official Records, Eighteenth Session, Annexes, agenda item 78 (A/5562, October 8, 1963).

York and submitted his report.[176]

The report of the Special Representative of the Secretary-General noted that the people of Oman were of the same ethnic descent and that the struggle between the interior tribes and the Sultan was of long duration.[177]

The Special Representative's report to the Secretary-General was made available to Member States. On December 11, 1963, in resolution 1948 (XVIII), the General Assembly, taking note of the report, established an Ad Hoc Committee, composed of five Member States appointed by the President of the General Assembly. The Ad Hoc Committee was to examine the question of Oman and report to the nineteenth session of the General Assembly.

The five members of the Ad Hoc Committee appointed by the President of the Assembly were Afghanistan, Costa Rica, Nepal, Nigeria and Senegal.[178] The Committee, after a thorough study, concluded that the question of Oman was a serious international problem requiring the attention of the General Assembly. The Committee also found that the problem arose from foreign intervention and that the General Assembly should call on all the parties concerned to facilitate a negotiated settlement.[179] The Ad Hoc Committee submitted its report to the General Assembly at its nineteenth session which noted that the report of the Committee had been received.[180]

The United Nations Malaysia Mission. By a communication addressed to the Secretary-General of the United Nations, August 5, 1963, the Foreign Ministers of the Federation of Malaya, the Republic of Indonesia and the Republic of the Philippines requested the Secretary-General to ascertain the wishes of the people of Sabah (North Borneo) and Sarawak in certain specified respects, prior to the establishment of the Federation of Malaysia.

Accepting the request in a reply dated August 8, 1963, the Secretary-General designated a representative and set up two working teams each composed of eight members of the Secretariat. In his letter of August 8, 1963, the Secretary-General emphasized that the acceptance of the request was dependent on the consent of the Government of the United Kingdom and of the Governments of Sabah (North Borneo) and Sarawak to the proposed mission.

Dividing into two teams of four officers each with administrative and secretarial staff, the Mission visited the area between August 16 and September 5, 1963. It interviewed, through the two teams, elected representatives, leaders and representatives of groups who also submitted their opinions in writing. The Mission studied election laws and other documentary material, including memoranda submitted by political parties.

Upon receiving a report from his Representative, the Secretary-General communicated his final conclusions to the Governments of the Federation of Malaya, the Republic of Indonesia, the Republic of the Philippines and the United Kingdom. The report of the Representative and the Secretary-General's final conclusions were circulated to the Member States.[181]

---

[176]U. N. Doc. A/5562 (October 8, 1963).

[177]Idem.

[178]U. N. Doc. A/5846 (January 22, 1965).

[179]Ibid., p. 222.

[180]U. N. General Assembly, Official Records, Nineteenth Session, Annexes, Volume 2, Annex No. 16, p. 97.

[181]U. N. General Assembly, Official Records, Nineteenth Session, Supplement No. 1. (A/5801). The Secretary-General's conclusions were that he had no doubt about the wishes of a sizable majority of the peoples of the territories to join in the Federation of Malaysia.

# CHAPTER IV

## OTHER EXAMPLES OF FACT FINDING IN INTERNATIONAL RELATIONS

The Hague Conventions of 1899 and 1907 initiated an approach to obtaining the facts in international disputes which was both novel and unique. In previous chapters the development of this concept in direct or modified form was examined as it was utilized under the Hague formula or by the League of Nations, the United Nations and the Organization of American States as well as in the employment of commissions of conciliation by whom inquiry may have been employed.

There are many other examples in international relations where fact-finding operates which do not fall within the format of the commissions of inquiry envisaged by the Hague Conventions. The position taken in this study is that an evaluation of the role and the development of the concept of the Hague Conventions relating to fact-finding cannot be truly arrived at without some consideration of these other examples of fact-finding in international relations. Such examples can be divided into three categories, viz., (1) International Tribunals, (2) Administrative Commissions, and (3) Specialized Treaties.

## A. International Tribunals

Both the Permanent Court of International Justice and the International Court of Justice have been authorized under their Statutes to establish commissions of inquiry.[1] In two cases, the Courts established commissions of inquiry. These were in the Chorzow Factory case by the Permanent Court of International Justice[2] and in the Corfu Channel case by the International Court of Justice.[3] The Permanent Court of International Justice refused to establish a commission of inquiry in two cases even when requested to do so by one of the parties.[4] In one case before the Permanent Court of International Justice concerning the diversion of

---

[1]Article 50 of the Statutes of the two Tribunals provides:
"The Court may, at any time, entrust any individual, body, bureau, commission or other organization that it may select, with the task of carrying out an inquiry or giving an expert opinion."
The rules of both Courts with respect to inquiry are also similar. For the texts see Permanent Court of International Justice, Series D, No. 1 (1936), pp. 39 ff and Yearbook of the United Nations 1946-1947, pp. 596-608.

[2]Permanent Court of International Justice, Series A, No. 17 (1928).

[3]International Court of Justice, The Corfu Channel Case, 5 vols. (1949, 1950).

[4]The Free Zones of Upper Savoy and The District of Gex case, Permanent Court of International Justice, Series A, No. 22 (1929) and The Oscar Chinn case, Permanent Court of International Justice, Series A/B, No. 63, (1934).

water from the Meuse River, because of the proximity of the site to the seat of the Court, the judges, themselves, conducted an on-the-spot inquiry.[5]    The Court may, under Article 50 of its Statute, make use of expert opinion as well as utilizing commissions of inquiry in order to arrive at a determination of the facts. [6]

There have been no instances of the use by the two international courts of investigating commissions in the preparation of an advisory opinion but the following statement issued by the Permanent Court of International Justice in the Western Carelia case outlines limitations which the Court recognized as applying to inquiry in cases requiring an advisory opinion:

> The Court does not say that there is an absolute rule that
> the request for an advisory opinion may not involve some
> inquiry as to facts, but, under ordinary circumstances, it
> is certainly expedient that the facts upon which the opinion
> of the Court is desired should not be in controversy, and it
> should not be left to the Court to ascertain what they are.[7]

While in only two cases before the Permanent Court of International Justice and the International Court of Justice have commissions of inquiry been ordered, the following brief examinations of the procedures followed and the circumstances surrounding these two examples of inquiry may be useful.

The Chorzow Factory case arose as a result of the failure of the Germans and Poles to agree on the value of the Chorzow factory property after a decision in the case of the German Interests in Upper Silesia was rendered in favor of Germany. As a result of the parties' failure to present adequate data bearing on the amount, the Court was compelled to establish a commission of inquiry and reserved decision on fixing the amount until the report of the commission could be issued.[8]

In the Corfu Channel case, a commission of inquiry was created to determine the answers to specific questions presented to it by the Court.[9] These questions concerned the type of mine that damaged the British destroyers, the methods, dates and purposes for which the mines had been laid, whether the Albanian authorities could have detected the mines being laid, how many mines could a particular minelayer carry and how long would it take to lay them.   Further questions directed to the commission concerned the means used to create the mine field and whether the mine field could have been laid without the knowledge of the Albanian authorities.[10]  The Commission was also directed that

> The experts shall bear in mind that their task is not to prepare a scientific or technical statement of the problems involved, but to give to the court a precise and concrete opinion upon the points submitted to them.

---

[5]Diversion of Water from the Meuse, Permanent Court of International Justice, Series A/B, No. 70 (1937).

[6]See Gillian M. White, The Use of Experts by International Tribunals, Syracuse: Syracuse University Press, 1965.

[7]Permanent Court of International Justice, Series B, Advisory Opinion Relating to the Status of Eastern Carelia, No. 5 (1923), p. 28.

[8]Permanent Court of International Justice, Series A, No. 17 (1928).

[9]See supra. for a description of the events leading up to submission of the case to the International Court of Justice.  Also International Court of Justice, Reports of Judgments, Advisory Opinions and Orders, (1949), pp. 4ff and 244 ff; International Court of Justice, The Corfu Channel Case, 5 vols. (1949-1950).

[10]International Court of Justice, Reports of Judgments, Advisory Opinions and Orders (1948), pp. 124-127.

The experts shall not limit themselves to stating their findings; they will also, as far as possible give the reasons for these findings in order to make their true significance apparent to the court. If need be, they will mention any doubts or differences of opinion amongst them.[11]

The Commission was directed to conduct an on-the-spot investigation after it was unable to present entirely conclusive answers in its first report.[12]

The composition of the Commission of Inquiry in the Corfu Channel case was arrived at by selection of three naval officers from the list of experts compiled by four governments in response to a request by the Court registrar before oral proceedings began.[13]

In both the cases in which Commissions of Inquiry have been used by the Court and also where it conducted an inquiry on-the-spot itself, the consent of all the parties concerned had been obtained. The co-operation of a third party, Yugoslavia, was obtained in the Corfu Channel Case in order to permit the development of a complete inquiry.[14]

The Court rules permit some latitude to commissions of inquiry. In the Chorzow Factory case, the Commission was directed to determine by a majority vote whether or not to conduct an on-the-spot investigation. One of the Court orders in the Corfu Channel case directed the Commission to conduct inquiries at Sibenik and Saranda and the surrounding land and waters. The Commission felt that these instructions permitted it to decide what other sites to visit. At the same time, the Court order provided that the parties could make suggestions to the Commission with respect to sites for investigation.

The Court orders in the Chorzow Factory case and the Corfu Channel case provided that the reports of the Commissions should be read at a public sitting. In the Corfu Channel inquiry, the Court ordered that the parties be allowed to submit written observations on the findings which were to be included in the report of the Commission.

The weight which the Court will give to the findings of a Commission of Inquiry is left open by the rules of the Court. In the Corfu Channel inquiry, the only one of the two which was actually completed, the Court held that it could not

fail to give great weight to the opinion of experts who examined the locality in a manner giving every guarantee of correct and impartial information.[15]

In addition to the Permanent Court of International Justice and the International Court of Justice, other international courts have been given authority to use commissions of inquiry. Among these have been the Central American Court of Justice which operated from 1907 to 1918[16] and the Central American Tribunal which was established in 1923 but

---

[11]Idem.

[12]Ibid., (1940), p. 21.

[13]A letter was sent to the governments of Denmark, Norway, the Netherlands and Sweden. (International Court of Justice, Corfu Channel Case, vol. 5, p. 170).

[14]Ibid., p. 264.

[15]International Court of Justice, Reports of Judgments, Advisory Opinions and Orders (1949), p. 21.

[16]For text of statute, see William M. Malloy, op. cit., vol. 2, pp. 2399, 2402-2404. For rules of the Court, see American Journal of International Law, Supplement, vol. 8, (1914), pp. 198-210.

which never functioned.[17] At the present time, the European Court of Human Rights, which came into existence in 1959, is authorized to employ commissions of inquiry.[18]

Of the present courts, special mention should be made of the court which is now the Court of Justice of the European Communities. Originally created in 1952, to insure observance of law and the interpretation and implementation of the Treaty establishing the European Coal and Steel Community,[19] the functions of the European Court of Justice were enlarged to carry out similar tasks with respect to the European Economic Community and the European Atomic Energy Community by the treaties setting up those entities in the spring of 1957.[20] The European Court of Justice, when seized of a matter, has the necessary authority to seek information regarding any facts in a dispute.

## B. Administrative Commissions

Investigative authority has been given to many international administrative commissions or agencies. Among these are (1) mixed commissions of a bilateral nature such as the International Joint Commission which the United States and Great Britain created in 1909 to deal with problems relating to the boundary between Canada and the United States;[21] (2) multi-lateral regional commissions such as the European Commission of Human Rights created in 1951;[22] and (3) specialized agencies of the United Nations and commissions created by such agencies for the purpose of insuring execution of internal agreements.

All of the administrative agencies mentioned above are authorized to collect information and to conduct inquiries in promoting the execution of the agreements under which each was established. For the most part, the function of fact-finding pursued by these agencies is of a statistical nature designed to accumulate sufficient information to permit the agency to make recommendations to its members in accordance with the purposes of the agreement. Such information is also used to measure the degree of adherence to the principles and purposes of the agreement by each of the parties.

It is to be assumed that any differences between the parties would be resolved through requests by the agency to the party at fault for further information on the steps it was taking to act in accordance with the provisions of the convention. Safeguards for the observance of regulatory measures are provided for only insofar as the States or Parties will find it difficult to participate in a cooperative climate in the activities covered by the agreement.

The use of fact gathering in such instances demonstrates a two-fold character. First, it indicates the importance of finding the facts as a

[17]For text of Treaty, see Max Habicht, op. cit., pp. 38ff. The Central American Tribunal was also authorized to use the results of commissions established under bilateral arrangements.

[18]For rules of procedure, see European Yearbook, vol. 8 (1960), pp. 383-407.

[19]United Nations, Treaty Series, vol. 261, p. 140 (Articles 31 through 45) and Ibid., vol. 261, p. 247 (Protocol on the Code of the Court of Justice).

[20]Infra.

[21]C. J. Chacko, The International Joint Commission between the United States of America and the Dominion of Canada. New York: Columbia University Press, (1932).

[22]Set up by Treaty of Rome. For text, see American Journal of International Law, Supplement, vol. 45 (1951) pp. 24-39. For commission's rules of procedure, see European Yearbook (1960), pp. 383-407.

guide to intelligent action and second, it indicates that the use of routine procedures for gathering the facts and processing the information thus obtained minimizes the possibility of the enlargement of international differences into international disputes in the areas in which such procedures have been established by treaty.

1. Mixed Commissions

International Joint Commission - United States of America and the Dominion of Canada.

In 1905, an International Waterways Commission was set up by the United States and Canada to investigate and report on the conditions and uses of the waters crossing the common boundary of the two states.[23] As a result of the recommendations made by the International Waterways Commission that a body with more extensive powers to deal with border problems be created, the International Joint Commission was formed in 1909 by the United States and Canada.[24]

The six member Commission is composed of three members selected by each party. When the Commission meets in Canada, the Canadian members select a chairman and when the Commission holds its meetings in the United States, the United States members select one of their group as presiding officer.[25] The Commission is invested by Article 9 of the Treaty establishing it with investigative and conciliatory duties. There is no obligation on the part of either government to submit a dispute to the Commission. If one party requests the Commission to consider a matter, Article 9 has been construed as requiring the consent of both parties before the Commission can undertake an investigation.[26]

The function of the Commission in dealing with a matter under Article 9 is to investigate and to make recommendations.[27] Each government is left free with respect to the action it wishes to take on the recommendations of the Commission. As a bilateral mixed commission, the Joint Commission differed from the formula for constituting commissions of inquiry prescribed by the Hague Conventions. The authority to make recommendations was a further characteristic attributed to the Joint Commission distinguishing it from the commissions of inquiry envisaged by the Hague Conventions.

While many inquiries have been conducted by the Commission as a whole, the tendency in recent years has been to utilize boards or experts. On-the-spot investigations have been conducted where the Commission found such a procedure was required. The Commission has at times been specifically directed to utilize data gathered by national agencies of the parties.

Both parties have adopted legislation giving the Commission power to issue subpoenas to witnesses.[28] The regular sessions of the Commission are held twice annually in Washington and Ottowa and special meetings may be called by the chairmen. While a majority may conduct hearings, all commissioners must be present for the preparation of the report. Permanent offices are maintained by the Commission in both States. Each government pays the salaries and the expenses of its commissioners and joint expenses are equally shared.

The Commission has dealt with almost two dozen matters requiring

[23] C. J. Chacko, op. cit., pp. 74-75.

[24] Ibid., pp. 75-76. For text of the treaty establishing the commission, see United States, Treaty Series, No. 548.

[25] For text of the rules of procedure, adopted by the commission in 1912, see C. J. Chacko, op. cit., pp. 395-404.

[26] Ibid., pp. 241-245.

[27] Ibid., p. 242.

[28] For text of legislation of both parties, see C. J. Chacko, op. cit., pp. 406-408.

investigation with the substance of the recommendations of the commission in nearly all of the cases receiving the approval of both parties.[29] The experience of the Commission has covered a wide range of subjects relating to water apportionment, usage and pollution as well as to navigational problems and to air pollution.[30] The Commission has prepared draft treaties as well as recommending in its reports courses of action to the two parties such as the creation of special boards to handle special problems. Many of the investigations conducted by the Joint Commission have taken a considerable time to complete, the Columbia River Basin Case, for example, requiring an investigation that covered sixteen years.[31]

2. Multilateral Regional Commissions

The regional commissions established under several international agreements designed to provide for the regulation of fishing in specific areas are empowered to collect statistical information, to conduct and coordinate research and to make recommendations on the basis of the information obtained. The Commission established in 1950 by the Northwest Atlantic Fisheries Convention may obtain such information in collaboration with governmental or other agencies or by acting independently.[32] It is also empowered to conduct hearings.[33] Under the Convention for the High Seas Fisheries of the North Pacific Ocean, the International North Pacific Fisheries Commission has similar powers.[34] As an aid to the investigatory powers of the International North Pacific Fisheries Commission, the officials of any Party to the Convention may board a vessel to inspect its equipment, books, documents and other articles and may question the persons on board where a fishing vessel of a contracting party is found in waters in which that State has agreed to abstain from exploitation.[35] The North-East Atlantic Fisheries Commission, established under the North-East Atlantic Fisheries Convention, which came into force June 27, 1963, is assisted in its work by regional committees which are responsible for particular areas.[36] The main task of the Commission is to keep under review the fisheries in the area, to consider, in the light of available technical information, what conservation measures are required and to make appropriate recommendations to the contracting parties.[37]

Similar in the statistical and fact-gathering nature of its activities is the International Whaling Commission established under a 1946 convention.[38]

Each agency created by members of the European Community has been empowered by the treaty under which it has been established to collect information relating to compliance with decisions taken under the treaty. The committees and special committees established within the framework of the Benelux Economic Union are required to observe within their particular fields of competence, the execution by national administrations of the decisions taken.[39]

[29]L. M. Bloomfield and Gerald F. Fitzgerald, Boundary Water Problems of Canada and the United States, Toronto: Carswell, 1958, p. 60.

[30]For a summary of the commission's docket through 72 see Ibid., pp. 65-205.

[31]William S. Kenworthy, "Joint Development of International Waters", American Journal of International Law, vol. 54 (1960), p. 600.

[32]United Nations, Treaty Series, vol. 157, p. 157.

[33]Idem.

[34]United Nations, Treaty Series, vol. 205, p. 65.

[35]Idem.

[36]United Nations, Treaty Series, vol. 486, p. 157.

[37]Idem.

[38]United Nations, Treaty Series, vol. 161, p. 72.

[39]United Nations, Treaty Series, vol. 381. p. 165.

Methods of fact-finding are also employed by the Council of Europe.[40]
Such methods are divided according to whether the subject matter con-
cerns a situation which may affect the aims of the Council, as defined in
article 1 of its Statute or arises with reference to a convention concluded
under the auspices or within the framework of the Council of Europe. In
the former instance, any of the statutory organs of the Council of Europe,
viz., the Committee of Ministers or the Consultative Assembly, may engage in fact-finding efforts. In the past, the Consultative Assembly has
acted as a fact-finding body in two matters. A working group of the
Political Committee of the Assembly drew up proposals for the settlement
of the issue of the Saar which arose between France and the Federal Republic of Germany. In a second instance, another working group of the
Political Committee examined the difficulties that had arisen between
Austria and Italy over the status of the German speaking minority in
Northern Italy. In both cases, the working group attempted to find the
facts by means of reports from governments, reports prepared by members of the Consultative Assembly and by direct contacts between the
chairmen and rapporteurs of the working groups and the governments
concerned.

The major conventions concluded under the auspices of or within the
framework of the Council of Europe, which incorporate fact-finding procedures, are the Convention for the Protection of Human Rights and
Fundamental Freedoms,[41] the treaty establishing the European Atomic
Energy Agency,[42] the treaty establishing the European Economic Community,[43] and the treaty establishing the European Coal and Steel Community.[44]

The fact-finding procedures of the executive agencies established
under these various treaties may be categorized as of a statistical or
reporting nature or in the nature of quasi-judicial inquiry. The statistical or reporting activities designed to gather information may be on a
periodic basis or upon specific request and are basically similar in essence. With reference to the fact-gathering activities of these agencies
in the nature of quasi-judicial inquiry various differences may be noted.

Under the Convention for the Protection of Human Rights and Fundamental Freedoms, two organs have been established to insure compliance:
The European Court of Human Rights and the European Commission of
Human Rights. All complaints concerning breaches of the Convention
must be addressed to the Commission which, if it declares the case ad-
missible, must proceed to ascertain the facts. The Commission may
carry out any investigation, the Contracting States being under obligation
to furnish all the facilities necessary to make the investigation effective.
From the time of its inception in 1954, the Commission has heard witnesses, and taken evidence on a few occasions, delegating a sub-commission
in 1958, in one case, to conduct an on-the-spot investigation. The rules
of the Court provide for various forms of inquiry and other measures for
obtaining information. A final binding decision can be taken by the
European Court of Human Rights or by the Committee of Ministers after
the Commission has submitted its report. Neither the Court nor the
Committee of Ministers has engaged in an inquiry before rendering a
decision with respect to any case submitted to it.

The Commission established under the treaty creating the European
Atomic Energy Community is given power, under Article 187 of the Treaty,
to collect information and to verify relevant matters under conditions laid

---

[40]Ibid., vol. 87, p. 103.
[41]Ibid., vol. 213, p. 221.
[42]Ibid., vol. 298, p. 176.
[43]Ibid., vol. 298, p. 11.
[44]Ibid., vol. 261, p. 140.

down by the Council of Ministers.  Thus far this article has not been implemented because other provisions of the treaty have enabled the Commission to secure all the information it required without requiring authorization by the Council of Ministers.  The main method, under these other provisions, used by the Commission for the direct ascertainment of the facts has been the dispatch of inspectors to the site in question.

The High Authority of the European Coal & Steel Community has the necessary powers of investigation to ensure that the obligations are observed regulating agreements and combinations in restraint of trade.  Inspectors are employed where necessary by the High Authority.  These inspectors have direct access to firms to ensure adherence to agreed upon price levels.  A great use is made of consultative arrangements in gathering information for the purpose of determining future policy and forecasts.

Under Article 213 of the Treaty creating the European Economic Community, the Commission established under the treaty, in order to accomplish the tasks entrusted to it, is empowered to collect all information and seek appropriate verification within the limits and subject to the conditions set by the Council of Ministers in conformity with the provisions of the Treaty.  The Commission receives its information from the Contracting States who are under obligation to furnish all necessary information.  Where the Commission, having been informed by these means, considers that a Member State has failed to observe its obligations under the Treaty, it may invite the State concerned to present its observations.  If these observations do not succeed in modifying the opinion of the Commission, it renders its final opinion.  Under Article 169 of the Treaty, the Commission may refer the matter to the European Court of Justice if the Member State does not comply with the opinion within a reasonable time.

A Member State may refer a matter to the European Court of Justice under Article 170 of the Treaty, but before doing so must first refer the matter to the High Commission of the European Economic Community.  The Commission must render a reasoned opinion after the states concerned have submitted their comments in written and oral procedings.

Within the framework of its powers of investigation, the Commission may collect all necessary information from Governments or from the competent authorities of Member States, as well as from commercial enterprises and associations.  It can request the authorities of Member States to verify the information so provided.  The Commission can itself seek necessary verification regarding firms and associations.  The agents of the Commission in order to achieve this purpose are empowered to inspect correspondence and other relevant documents; to make copies or to take extracts from such material; to conduct oral inquiries on the spot and to have access to all premises, sites and means of transport of commercial enterprises.  If an enterprise opposes verification, the Member State concerned must provide the agents of the Commission with the necessary assistance.

3.  Specialized Agencies of the United Nations

The Council of the International Civil Aviation Organization is entrusted by the Treaty establishing the organization with, among other functions, that of conducting inquiries into the pertinent facts to ascertain whether States are observing the particular regulations concerned.[45]  Further functions relating to inquiry are assigned to the Council by the International Air Services Transit Agreement.[46]  The procedure of inquiry ordinarily consists of the submission of documents by the complaining and respondent States although the introduction of oral evidence is not excluded.

---

[45]Ibid., vol. 15, p. 296.

[46]United States, Statutes, vol. 59, p. 1693.

With respect to the maintenance of air navigation facilities, Article 69 of the Convention on International Civil Aviation provides a special procedure for investigating airports or other air navigation facilities of a contracting state which are in the opinion of the International Civil Aviation Organization Council not reasonably adequate for the safe, regular, economical and efficient operation of international air services. In this connection, the Council may consult with the State directly concerned and the other States affected with a view to determining what steps are necessary to remedy the situation. A special body, called the Implementation Panel, was also created under a resolution adopted by the International Civil Aviation Organization Assembly in 1956. The Implementation Panel is composed of persons serving in their independent capacity. Their function is to consider whether the plans approved for different regions with respect to air and navigation services are being adequately implemented by the Member States and to consult with States, where necessary, in order to assist and encourage them to meet their responsibilities under Article 28 of the Convention relating to the maintenance of certain standards of air and navigation facilities and services. The Implementation Panel or its members in performance of their function undertake missions to various areas and submit reports and recommendations to the International Civil Aviation Organization Council.

The International Labor Organization, since its creation in 1919, has developed many procedures for measuring the extent of observance of the conventions and recommendations adopted by the organization.[47] The procedure used may be divided into two groups according to whether they relate to the system of periodic reporting by the Member States or to the methods followed upon the receipt of particular complaints alleging non-observance of an International Labor Organization convention or recommendation.

A system of periodic reporting is based on Article 22 of the Constitution of the International Labor Organization which provides that States which have ratified conventions are required to make an annual report on the measures taken to give effect to such conventions. The reports are required to supply detailed information on relevant national laws and regulations and on the procedures taken to ensure the application of the particular convention. Copies of these annual reports must be given by each Member State to the representative organizations of employers and workers in its country. These organizations may make observations on the application of the provisions of the convention and the States are then requested to supply information in their reports with respect to any observations which had been received.

Fact-finding is employed by the International Atomic Energy Agency to determine whether there has been compliance with the operations of the Agency's safeguards systems and with the measures set by the Agency for the maintenance of health and safety. The first objective relates to the authority of the Agency to

establish and administer safeguards designed to ensure that special fissionable and other material, services, equipment, facilities and information made available by the Agency or at

---

[47] See report of the International Labor Organization submitted to the Economic and Social Council in United Nations Doc. E/4144 (December 29, 1965) for a fuller review of that organization's procedure for securing the implementation of the International Labor Organization's conventions and recommendations. Also see E. A. Landy, The Effectiveness of International Supervision: Thirty Years of I. L. O. Experience, Dobbs Ferry, New York: Oceana Publications, Inc., 1966.

its request or under its supervision are not used in such a way as to further any military purpose. [48]

The duties of the Agency in safeguarding any project for which it is responsible include the right to review the design of principal nuclear facilities and to arrange for the keeping of records and the submission of records. In addition, the Agency may send inspectors into the territory of recipient States, with broad rights of access,

as necessary to account for the source and special fissionable materials supplied and fissionable products and to determine whether there is compliance with the undertaking against use in the furtherance of any military purpose... and with any other condition prescribed in the agreement between the Agency and the State or States concerned. [49]

The Agency has set forth detailed guidelines to aid in implementing these provisions of its Statute in a document entitled "The Agency's Safeguards System." [50]Several agreements have been concluded with States incorporating these guidelines. Inspections under the safeguards system may be routine, initial or special. Routine inspections include the audit of records and reports; the physical verification of nuclear inventories, measurement and sampling and the examination of principal nuclear facilities. Initial inspections are intended to verify conformity of construction of safeguarded nuclear facilities to the designs submitted to the Agency. Special investigations may be conducted where any report or other source of information may require further clarification.

The inspectors are part of the staff of the Agency. Prior to an inspection, the State in which the material or installation is located is informed of the designation of an inspector and of the place and approximate time of his arrival. [51]Under the Agency's safeguards system inspectors must be granted rights of access to and inspection of all relevant records and facilities.

Inspection is also provided for with regard to health and safety standards and measures under the Statute of the International Atomic Energy Agency [52]and in a document entitled "The Agency's Health and Safety Measures". [53] The latter document is referred to in all relevant project agreements concluded between the Agency and Member States. The fact gathering includes action by the States concerned such as filing of annual reports, listing cases of radiation exposure of persons in excess of applied safety standards, the types and amounts of radio-active waste disposed of, and the mode of disposal. Each such State is also required to conduct supervisory examinations and to notify the Agency in the event of a major incident. The Agency may require such States to supply it with information necessary to evaluate potential radiation hazards, details of the design and operation of facilities and of the proposed system of administration. The Agency's inspectors may evaluate operations to ensure that satisfactory radiation levels are maintained; such inspections as are conducted deal mainly with tests of radiation sources, examination of facilities where radiation sources are stored and the evaluation of the radiation exposure of persons.

---

[48]Statute of International Atomic Energy Agency Article IIIA.5.

[49]Ibid., Article XII.A.

[50]International Atomic Energy Agency Document INFCIRC/66, dated December 3, 1965.

[51]See The Agency's Inspectorate (International Atomic Energy Agency Document GC(V) INF/39, dated August 28, 1961) for details of the methods of designation and notification.

[52]Statute of International Atomic Energy Agency, Articles III.A.6 and XII.A.2 and A.6.

[53]International Atomic Energy Agency Document INFCIRC/18, dated May 31, 1960.

An example of fact-finding by the World Health Organization is found in the implementation of the International Sanitary Regulations.[54] Member States are required under certain provisions of these regulations, to provide information in order for the World Health Organization to be able to determine whether the measures taken conform to the regulations. On the basis of the information furnished by the States, the World Health Organization prepares an annual report of the functioning of the regulations and on their effect on international traffic. This report is reviewed by the Committee on International Quarantine and by the World Health Organization in order to measure the degree of compliance with the regulations by the Member States.

Information concerning the compliance of a State with the regulations is also provided to the World Health Organization by other States, by international carriers and by travellers proceeding from the state under investigation. A special investigation may be made, ordinarily by correspondence with the State concerned, to obtain clarification of the situation and to effect elimination of measures not in conformance with the regulations.

4. Fact-Finding under Conventions adopted by Conferences under the Auspices of the United Nations Cultural Organization. The Convention for the Protection of Cultural Property in the Event of Armed Conflict. [55]

The execution of the provisions relating to fact-finding of the Convention for the Protection of Cultural Property in the Event of Armed Conflict is assigned to the protecting Powers of the parties to a conflict. Delegates of the protecting Powers are empowered to investigate, with the approval of the party to which they are accredited, the circumstances in which violations of the Convention have occurred. The Commissioner-General for cultural property, appointed by agreement between the party to which he will be accredited and the protecting Powers acting in behalf of the opposing parties, has the right, with the agreement of the party to which he is accredited, to order an investigation or to conduct one himself. Whenever he considers it necessary, the Commissioner-General may propose for the approval of the party to which he is accredited an Inspector of Cultural Property to be charged with a specific fact-finding mission. Experts may also be appointed for the same purpose.

The Convention against Discrimination in Education

The Protocol to the Convention against Discrimination in Education[56] established a Conciliation and Good Office Commission which is responsible for seeking a settlement of any disputes which may arise between the parties to the convention. The Commission may call upon the States concerned to supply any relevant information and, after obtaining all the information it thinks necessary, ascertain the facts and make available its good offices to the States concerned.

C. Specialized Treaties

The foremost example of a specialized treaty which provides for fact-finding is the Antarctica Treaty which was signed at Washington on December 1, 1959.[57] The Antarctica Treaty is unique in its fact-finding approach insofar as it resorts to the use of unilateral direct observation. Because of its unique approach, Article 7 of the Treaty, which provides for the inspection and information gathering procedure is reproduced in full below:

---

[54]United Nations, Treaty Series, vol. 175, p. 215. Adopted by the Fourth World Health Assembly in 1951 in accordance with Article 21 of the Constitution of the World Health Organization.

[55]United Nations, Treaty Series, vol. 249, p. 215.

[56]United Nations Educational Scientific and Cultural Organization General Conference at Paris, adopted December 10, 1962.

[57]Ibid., vol. 402, p. 71. For an extensive treatment, see article by James Simsarian "Inspection Experiences under the Antarctic Treaty and the International Atomic Agency," American Journal of International Law, vol. 60 (1966), pp. 502-510

1. In order to promote the objectives and ensure the observance of the provisions of the present Treaty, each Contracting Party whose representatives are entitled to participate in the meetings referred to in Article 9 of the Treaty shall have the right to designate observers to carry out any inspection provided for by the present Article. Observers shall be nationals of the Contracting Parties which designate them The names of observers shall be communicated to every other Contracting Party having the right to designate observers and like notice shall be given of the termination of their appointment.
2. Each observer designated in accordance with the provisions of paragraph 1 of this Article shall have complete freedom of access at any time to any or all areas of Antarctica.
3. All areas of Antarctica, including all stations, installations and equipment within those areas, and all ships and aircraft at points of discharging or embarking cargoes or personnel in Antarctica, shall be open at all times to inspection by any observers designated in accordance with paragraph 1 of this article.
4. Aerial observation may be carried out at any time over any or all areas of Antarctica by any of the Contracting Parties having the right to designate observers.
5. Each Contracting Party, shall, at the time when the present Treaty enters into force for it, inform the other Contracting Parties, and thereafter shall give them notice on advance, of

(a) All expeditions to and within Antarctica, on the part of its ships or nationals and all expeditions to Antarctica organized in or proceeding from its territory;

(b) All stations in Antarctica occupied by its nationals; and

(c) Any military personnel or equipment intended to be introduced by it into Antarctica subject to the conditions prescribed in paragraph 2 of Article 1 of the present Treaty.

Article 9 of the Treaty provides that representatives of the Contracting States shall meet

at suitable intervals and places for the purpose of exchanging information, consulting together on matters of common interest pertaining to Antarctica, and formulating and considering, and recommending to their Governments, measures in furtherance of the principles and objectives of the Treaty.[58]

Article XI of the Antarctic Treaty is of interest because it answers the question as to what procedures will be resorted to in the event that a dispute may arise which the routine procedures of the Treaty cannot resolve. In such case, under Article XI, the Treaty provides that if any dispute arises between two or more of the Contracting Parties concerning the interpretation or application of the Treaty, those Contracting Parties shall consult among themselves with a view to having the dispute resolved by negotiation, inquiry, mediation, conciliation, arbitration, judicial settlement or other peaceful means of their own choice.

It is also provided in Article XI that if a dispute of such character is not so resolved, the dispute shall, with the consent, in each case, of all the parties to the dispute, be referred to the International Court of Justice for settlement.

---

[58]The "measures" referred to include "facilitation of the exercise of the rights of inspection". Three meetings of governmental representatives have been held for the purpose of arriving at recommendations concerning the operation of the Treaty; in Canberra in 1961, in Buenos Aires in 1962 and in Brussels in 1964. For a reproduction of these recommendations, see 88th Congress, 2nd Session, House Document No. 358, pp. 32-41, Message from the President of the United States Transmitting a Special Report on the United States Policy and International Co-operation in Antarctica.

The assumption underlying the use of a provision such as Article XI is that the Contracting Parties will adhere to the provisions of the Treaty. The use of observer teams to observe compliance is a necessary control in line with the basic assumption. However, where compliance is lacking, the provisions of Article XI recognize that such failure to comply may be the result of differing interpretations as to the letter or the application of the Treaty. The distinction between the supervisory fact-finding of inspection under a treaty in order to prevent disputes and the use of a commission of inquiry to elucidate the facts in resolving a dispute is also clearly emphasized by a provision such as Article XI of the Antarctic Treaty.

# CHAPTER V

## INITIATING FACT-FINDING

As was pointed out in Chapter II earlier, the League of Nations Covenant provided ample authority in clear language for the initiation of investigations by the League Council or Assembly. Under Article 5, paragraph 2, the appointment of a committee to investigate particular matters by the Assembly or by the Council was considered a matter of procedure and to be decided by a majority vote.

The authority of the Assembly or Council of the League was never called, directly, into question. Even in the Polish-Lithuanian dispute over Vilna in 1920, the Lithuanian Government did not object to the creation of a commission of investigation to set up a line of demarcation in the neutral zone upon any lack of authority on the part of the Council. Lithuania's opposition to the investigation was based, instead, on the grounds that Lithuania had not accepted the principle underlying the Council's original proposal.[1] In the Manchurian dispute, Japan, after its attack upon the Chinese forces in Manchuria, through its representative to the League Council, M. Yoshizawa, proposed sending a commission of enquiry to the spot.[2]

An investigation was also considered at the time of the Italian invasion of Ethiopia. After being invaded by Italian troops, Ethiopia had requested the dispatch of impartial observers to establish the facts in regard to any aggression or other incident that might occur in order to fix the responsibility therefore.[3] The investigation was not undertaken not because of lack of authority but, as was stated in the Council Committee's report, because the circumstances had changed thereby eliminating the necessity for an investigation.[4]

The Council of the Organization of American States acting as a Provisional Organ of Consultation, the Organ of Consultation and the Inter-American Peace Committee have similarly encountered little opposition to their initiating investigations. In all cases, however, the consent of the parties was obtained before proceeding to an on-the-spot investigation. Although the Charter of the Organization of American States and the Inter-American Treaty of Reciprocal Assistance contain no specific provisions authorizing investigations, such power on the part of the above mentioned organs to investigate has never been considered as open to question.

A. Investigatory Powers of Political Organs of The United Nations
   The authority of the Security Council, the General Assembly and the

---

[1] L. of N. Official Journal, (1922), 6, (PII), p. 551.

[2] L. of N. Official Journal, (1931), p. 2365.

[3] L. of N. Official Journal, (1935), p. 1602.

[4] Ibid., p. 1618. Report of the Council under Article 15 (4) as submitted by the Committee of the Council (Committee of Thirteen) on October 5 and adopted by the Council on October 7, 1935.

Secretary-General to initiate investigations is contained both expressly and impliedly in the United Nations Charter. In exercising its authority, the Security Council has encountered obstacles to such investigations arising out of voting arrangements concerning the necessity for the affirmative votes of all five permanent members on substantive issues.

The following discussion is concerned with the exercise by the Security Council, the General Assembly and the Secretary-General of the authority given them under the Charter to initiate investigations of fact.

1. The Security Council.

The exercise of its power of investigation has evoked much discussion in the Security Council - a discussion which has revolved, essentially, around the exercise of the veto by the Soviet Union.[5] The issue of the proper exercise by the Security Council of the authority given it under the United Nations Charter to investigate, centers about Articles 24, 25, 27, 29, 34, 36, 37, 38, 39 and 40 of the Charter.

Articles 25, 27 and 29, deal with the obligation of members of the United Nations, voting procedures, and the power of the Security Council to establish subsidiary organs, respectively. Article 36 gives the Security Council the power to recommend appropriate procedures or methods of adjustment. Article 37 gives the power to recommend terms of settlement. Article 38 provides that the Security Council, at the request of the parties to a dispute, may make recommendations with a view to pacific settlement. Article 39 provides for determination by the Security Council of the existence of a threat to the peace. Article 40 states that the Security Council shall duly take account of failure to comply with provisional measures. Articles 36, 37, 38, 39 and 40 imply that the Security Council must have available to its sufficient information upon which to base any course of action it may decide to undertake.

The primary source of the investigatory power of the Security Council is Article 24 in which the power to investigate is implied in the primary responsibility which the members confer on the Security Council for the maintenance of international peace and security.

More specific authorization, apparently, is given to the Security Council to investigate by Article 34 which states:

The Security Council may investigate any dispute or any situation which might lead to international friction or give rise to a dispute, in order to determine whether the continuance of the dispute or situation is likely to endanger the maintenance of international peace and security.

Article 27 has focused attention on the limitations imposed by political realities upon the exercise by the Security Council of its powers of investigation. At the same time, the discussions on Article 27 at San Francisco and during the course of Security Council debate have illuminated many aspects of the investigatory power of the Security Council.[6]

The differences on the question of voting procedures in the Security Council which were unresolved at the opening of the San Francisco Con-

---

[5]For an argument for a narrow interpretation of the United Nations Charter with respect to the investigatory power of the Security Council, see Leo Gross, "The Question of Laos and the Double Veto in the Security Council," American Journal of International Law, vol. 54 (January, 1960), pp. 118-131. For a broader interpretation, see Ernest L. Kerley, "The Powers of Investigation of the United Nations Security Council", American Journal of International Law, vol. 55 (October, 1961) pp. 892-918. Also, see Wellington Koo Jr., op. cit., for an excellent discussion of the voting procedures of the Security Council.

[6]For a discussion of Article 27 and its history, see Goodrich and Hambro, op. cit., pp. 213-227.

ference on International Organization resulted in the issuance of a Statement by the Four Sponsoring Powers, joined later by France.[7] The Four Power Statement provided that it was the understanding of the Four Sponsoring Powers that a decision of the Security Council to undertake an investigation would require the affirmative votes of the Four Sponsoring Powers (and subsequently, France).

With respect to investigation, the Four Power Statement on voting procedures in the Security Council explained

> . . . decisions and actions by the Security Council may well have major political consequences and may even initiate a chain of events which might, in the end, require the Council under its responsibilities to invoke measures of enforcement under Section B, Chapter VIII. This chain of events begins when the Council decides to make an investigation, or determines that the time has come to call upon states to settle their differences, or make recommendations to the parties. It is to such decisions and actions that unanimity of the permanent members applies, with the important proviso, referred to above for abstention from voting by parties to a dispute.
> 5. To illustrate: in ordering an investigation, the Council has to consider whether the investigation - which may involve calling for reports, hearing witnesses, dispatching a commission of inquiry, or other means - might not further aggravate the situation. After investigation, the Council must determine whether the continuance of the situation or dispute would be likely to endanger international peace and security. If it so determines, the Council would be under obligation to take further steps. Similarly, the decision to make recommendations even when all parties request it to do so, or to call upon parties to a dispute to fulfill their obligations under the Charter, might be the first step on a course of action from which the Security Council could withdraw only at the risk of failing to discharge its responsibilities.[8]

At San Francisco much of the sentiment against the so-called veto was channelled into the area of pacific settlement. Although the view was supported that the permanent members should have the veto power in decisions which might require them to make material sacrifices, those decisions relating to pacific settlement, it was urged, did not require sacrifices from anyone except the parties to the dispute.[9] The Four Power Statement was designed to explain why the requirement of the affirmative vote of all four Sponsoring Powers was necessary in the area of pacific settlement as well as in decisions on enforcement measures.

The application of the Four Power Statement to Security Council voting has at times, in practice, restricted the Security Council in the exercise of its powers to investigate. Unfortunately, the distinctions between a substantive investigation under Articles 24, 39 or 40, an investigation for the purpose of making recommendations under Articles 36, 37 and 38

---

[7] The United Nations Information Organizations Documents of the United Nations Conference on International Organization, San Francisco, 1945 (London and New York: 1945) Vol. II, pp. 710-714.

[8] Idem.

[9] Ibid., Summary Report of the Ninth Meeting of Committee III/1, May 17, 1945, Doc. 417, III/1/19 (1), (Documents, Vol. II), pp. 305, 309.

and a procedural type of investigation under Article 34 to permit the Security Council to determine its competence were disregarded by the Four Power Statement. However, considering the flexibility of fact-finding bodies in United Nations practice, it would be unfair to criticize the Four Sponsoring Powers' voting formula with respect to its failure to distinguish between investigations for different purposes.

The manner in which the Security Council dealt with the matter of the Franco Regime in Spain is illustrative of this flexibility. A draft resolution, offered by the Polish representatives, stating that

The existence and activities of the Franco regime in Spain have led to international friction and endangered international peace and security

and calling on the members to sever their diplomatic relations with Spain under Articles 39 and 41, was introduced at the 34th meeting of the Security Council.[10] The draft resolution, proposed by Australia, at the 35th meeting of the Council, provided that the Council would decide to investigate the situation in Spain "in accordance with Article 34," and to appoint a committee to ascertain whether the situation in Spain was one essentially within the domestic jurisdiction of that state, whether that situation was one which might lead to international friction or give rise to a dispute, and, if so, whether the continuance of that situation was likely to endanger the maintenance of international peace and security.[11]

Inasmuch as the adoption of this resolution would have required the affirmative vote of the Soviet Union which had already expressed its opposition to the delay which would result from an investigation,[12] the Australian representative, at the 37th meeting, revised his resolution to eliminate the reference to Article 34.[13] This resolution, which was subsequently adopted at the 39th meeting by a vote of ten, with the Soviet Union abstaining, referred to the investigating body as a sub-committee rather than a committee, with the function of the committee altered so that the sub-committee was now authorized "to call for further statements, documents, and evidence and to conduct such inquiries as it may deem necessary."[14] The Australian delegate explained at the 37th meeting that the purpose of the deletion of the reference to Article 34 was "to enable the proposed body to be brought in under Article 29 as a subsidiary organ."[15] Immediately, before the vote taken at the 39th meeting, the Soviet representative asserted that he objected to the redraft, but that since his voting against the resolution would make its adoption impossible, he would abstain.[16]

The final resolution which was adopted did not limit the purpose of the investigation to the determination whether the situation was one likely to endanger the maintenance of international peace and security, but required the information whether the situation had led to international friction and did endanger the maintenance of peace. The resolution, as adopted, also contained as its purpose an inquiry into the question of what practical measures the United Nations might take regarding the situation.[17]

Inevitably, debate on initiating an investigation by the Security Council became a discussion of voting procedures under the Charter. Article 27 pertaining to voting in the Security Council, provides in paragraph 2

---

[10]U. N. Security Council Official Records, First Year, First Series, p. 167.

[11]Ibid., p. 198.

[12]Ibid., pp. 185-193.

[13]Ibid., p. 216.

[14]Ibid., pp. 244-245.

[15]Ibid., p. 216.

[16]Ibid., p. 243.

[17]Ibid., p. 244.

that "Decisions of the Security Council on procedural matters shall be
by an affirmative vote of seven members." Paragraph 3 of the same article states that

Decisions of the Security Council on all other matters shall be
made by an affirmative vote of seven members including the
concurring votes of the permanent members . . . .

The Statement of the Four Sponsoring Governments, referred to earlier
in this chapter, noted that a decision to conduct an investigation was to
be construed as a non-procedural matter requiring the concurring vote
of the permanent members. As if to eliminate any doubt with respect to
this matter, the Four Power Statement concluded with the following:

In this case, it will be unlikely that there will arise in
the future, any matters of great importance on which a
decision will have to be made as to whether a procedural
vote would apply. Should, however, such a matter arise,
the decision regarding the preliminary question as to
whether or not such a matter is procedural must be taken
by a vote of seven members of the Security Council, including the concurring votes of the permanent members. [18]

The history of attempts to initiate investigations by the Security Council revolves, in many cases, about successful, and also unsuccessful,
attempts to surmount the obstacle presented by the so-called "double
veto." [19]

Professor Gross has pointed out, that according to the arrangement
under Article 27, ". . . the majority of seven applies to matters which
incontrovertibly are 'procedural' by agreement or precedent." He goes
on to say very unequivocally "The qualified majority which embraces 'all
other matters' includes by necessary implication the question whether
a matter is procedural." [20]

The attempts in the Security Council to initiate investigations have,
accordingly, taken one of two paths. The first such path was to meet
with a veto, the second path was to establish a sub-committee of inquiry
under Article 29.

The Czechoslovak case is an example of the application of a veto. The
matter had been brought before the Council by the representative of Chile,
under Article 35, requesting that the Security Council investigate the situation in Czechoslovakia in accordance with Article 34. Subsequently,
the Chilean delegate offered a draft resolution which, as amended on the
proposal of the Argentinian delegate, was put to a vote at the 303rd meeting, on May 24, 1948, and failed to be accepted due to a veto by the Soviet
Union. [21]

The resolution avoided any reference to authorization under Article
34. It specifically stated that the committee would hear evidence, statements and testimonials "without prejudice to any decisions which may be
taken in accordance with Article 34 of the Charter." [22] According to the
Belgian representative, the draft resolution entailed no judgment on substance; its purpose was to elucidate the facts (which were sufficiently well
known to the Council) inasmuch as that elucidation of facts was important
to the determination whether the Council was competent to deal with the
matter. [23]

---

[18]UNCIO, Vol. 11, p. 714.

[19]For a discussion of the double veto, see Leo Gross, op. cit., pp.
118-131.

[20]Leo Gross, op. cit.

[21]U. N. Security Council Official Records, Third Year, pp. 28-29.

[22]Ibid., p. 2.

[23]Ibid., p. 18.

Mr. Gromyko, the Soviet representative, on the other hand, stated that he believed it was a matter of substance and therefore proposed that the question as to whether it was substantive or procedural be put to a vote.[24] The United States delegate asserted that the decision of the Security Council to establish a sub-committee was clearly procedural under Article 29.[25] This position was supported by the Canadian representative who argued that "The Canadian delegation is firmly convinced that this represents a convenient way of carrying on the further inquiries of the Security Council . . . ."[26]

In ruling on the preliminary question, The President, commenting on the term "investigation" as used in the Four Power Statement, said:

I had wondered whether . . . the word "investigation" could not be interpreted as applying to the sending of a commission to conduct an inquiry on the spot and whether, therefore, a distinction might not be drawn between that and an investigation to be carried out directly by a subsidiary organ of the Security Council.

However, if we refer to paragraph 5 of Part I of the Declaration, we find the following: 'To illustrate: in ordering an investigation, the Council has to consider whether the investigation - which may involve calling for reports, hearing witnesses, dispatching a commission of inquiry, or other means - might not further aggravate the situation.'

In those circumstances, I consider that the word 'investigation' which appears in the first line of that paragraph, is used in its widest meaning, and I think it applies to the situation now before us.[27]

The Corfu Channel case is an example of the creation of a sub-committee under Article 29.[28] An Australian resolution had been introduced calling for the appointment of a sub-committee, "as a preliminary step in the consideration of the incidents of the Corfu Channel," whose function it would be "to examine all available evidence concerning the above mentioned incidents and to make a report to the Security Council on the facts of the case as disclosed by such evidence."[29]

The question of voting procedure was placed squarely before the Council by the United Kingdom delegate who questioned whether he was entitled to vote on the resolution, pointing out that, if the appointment of the sub-committee was non-procedural, he, as a party to the dispute, was barred by Article 27 (3) from voting, whereas, if the appointment was procedural, no such limitation applied.[30] The President in ruling that the United Kingdom delegate might participate in the voting stated

We have to establish a purely advisory sub-committee whose only task will be to assist the Council in the submission of facts; this body will take no decisions; it will confine itself to formulating conclusions intended to help the Council in taking a decision. The sole function of the future sub-committee will be to facilitate the Council's work by classifying

---

[24]Ibid., p. 19.

[25]Ibid., pp. 19-20.

[26]Ibid., p. 21.

[27]Ibid., p. 20.

[28]U. N. Security Council Official Records, Second Year, Supplement No. 3, Annex 8.

[29]U. N. Security Council Official Records, Second Year, p. 432.

[30]Ibid., p. 425.

information submitted to the council; there is no question in this case of undertaking an investigation.[31]

The representative of the United States supported this position and the resolution was adopted by eight affirmative votes with three abstentions on February 27, 1947.[32] The Sub-Committee, itself, proceeded on the principle that it was neither a commission of investigation or a fact-finding committee in the strict sense of the word, holding in its report that "The main duty in this case was to examine the statements and evidence already submitted to the Security Council and to ascertain whether additional evidence existed."[33]

The attempt to avoid the conception of investigation contained in the Four Power Statement - and elimination of the possibility of a Soviet veto - received the most intense discussion in the case of the appeal of the Laotian Government in 1959 regarding aggression by North Vietnam.[34] The Secretary-General, in addressing the 847th meeting of the Council on September 7, 1959, concerning the appeal of Laos, emphasized that his request to do so was not based on Article 99 of the Charter, explaining that

It would have meant the inscription by the Secretary-General of a substantive issue on the agenda. In this latter respect it would necessarily also have involved as to facts for which, in the present situation, I have not a sufficient basis.[35]

The United States delegate introduced a draft resolution,[36] which was adopted with ten votes in favor and one against ( the U.S.S.R.), calling on the Council to appoint a sub-committee

to examine the statements made before the Security Council concerning Laos, to receive further statements and documents and to conduct such inquiries as it may determine to be necessary and to report to the Security Council as soon as possible.[37]

The French representative, appearing to follow the political basis of interpretation used by the President of the Council in the Czechoslovak case, in reverse, pointed out that

The decision taken is based on Article 29 of the Charter; it is an answer to a request made by a sovereign state, a Member of the United Nations, in connection with events which have taken place in its territory, it affects only members of the Council and provides those members with appropriate means, under the present circumstances, to cast further light on the situation.[38]

The United Kingdom delegate asserted that paragraph 2, and not paragraph 4 of the San Francisco Declaration, covering the establishing of subcommittees applied in the Laos Case.[39] He further stated that the second paragraph of Part I of the San Francisco Declaration was clearly intended to apply only when the Charter did not give guidance

where there was a genuine doubt as to whether a matter was procedural or substantive. In the present case, Article 29 of the Charter gives a clear indication . . .[40]

---

[31]Ibid., p. 426.

[32]Ibid., p. 432.

[33]U. N. Doc. S/300, p. 1 (March 12, 1947).

[34]U. N. Doc. S/4213 (September 7, 1959).

[35]U. N. Security Council Official Records, Fourteenth Year, p. 3.

[36]Ibid., p. 22.

[37]U. N. Doc. S/4216 (September 7, 1959).

[38]U. N. Security Council Official Records, Fourteenth Year, p. 15.

[39]Ibid., p. 18.

[40]Idem.

The Soviet representative argued that paragraphs 4 and 5 of the Four Power Declaration were applicable.[41] Mr. Sobolev asserted that

When paragraph 2 of the declaration, like Article 29 of the Charter, says that the Security Council will "establish" such bodies or agencies as it may deem necessary for the performance of its functions, it is referring to bodies . . . which have no connection with questions of peace and security.[42]

The Soviet representative also referred to bodies which are "procedural in nature."[43]

In its report of November 3, 1959, the Sub-Committee stated that in view of the expressions of opinion in the Council regarding the origin and nature of the situation in Laos, it had decided to accept the invitation of the Government of Laos to visit that country.[44]

The representative of Italy on the Sub-Committee in referring to such visit, indicated the confusion surrounding the matter when he attempted to distinguish between an inquiry and an investigation. He said that the Sub-Committee had to confine itself strictly to an inquiry which meant "fact-finding." That implied, he continued, that it must receive information on the facts from the Government concerned rather than seek facts on its own initiative.

He went on, in the report of the Sub-Committee, to say

It was not within competence of the Sub-Committee to concern itself with the substance of the issues involved in the situation which had given rise to the appeal of the Laotian Government, nor to take any steps designed to influence the course of events to which the Laotian Government had referred.

As interpreted by the Sub-Committee, its mandate from the Security Council was not a request to investigate the charge of aggression made in the vote of September 4 or to come to any conclusions or judgment concerning its validity. Its task was rather that of assisting the Security Council in bringing together a factual account of these events . . .[45]

A most vigorous criticism of the action of the Security Council in the Laos case came from Professor Gross who said

In the Laos case it was not merely the (Four Powers) Statement but the Charter itself that suffered a setback. It is not by disregarding the law of the Charter that the Security Council will promote the rule of law in international relations.[46]

The distinction between an inquiry under Article 29 and an investigation under Article 34, which has been referred to above, leads to the query of what other distinctions exist as to investigations conducted by the Security Council. One such distinction has been posed by the question, how long does an investigation initiated under Article 34 continue?[47] Does the investigation cease once it has served the purpose of enabling the Security Council to determine whether the continuance of the dispute or situation is likely to endanger the maintenance of international peace

---

[41]Idem.

[42]Ibid., p. 28.

[43]Idem.

[44]U. N. Doc. S/4236 (November 3, 1959).

[45]Idem.

[46]Leo Gross, op cit., p. 131.

[47]For a discussion of this point, see Eduardo Jimenez de Arechaga, Voting and The Handling of Disputes in The Security Council, New York: Carnegie Endowment For International Peace, 1950, pp. 83-85.

and security? Or can the investigating body remain in existence until the Security Council specifically decides to terminate its functions? This point was the subject of discussion in the Security Council on the duration of the Commission of Investigation Concerning Greek Frontier Incidents.

In answer to the objection that the power of investigation under Article 34 had already been exercised by establishment of a commission whose report was before the Council, Mr. Parodi, the French representative, stated:

> I feel that if the Security Council has had the power to initiate an investigation for the purpose of obtaining information, and of ascertaining whether a situation endangering peace exists, it is reasonable to suppose it can continue its investigation when the situation itself seems likely to continue.[48]

It has been proposed that the definition of an investigation pursuant to Article 34 should cover not only those investigations whose purpose it is to determine whether a danger to peace exists, but also those which are continued in order to verify whether the existing dispute or situation might eventually become a threat to the peace which would call for enforcement action under Chapter VII.[49]

> A much more limited view is taken by one writer who states that The practice of the Council, while affirming the existence of two separate bases of fact-finding activities, has not been clear regarding the distinction between them. It has been submitted that the only valid and persuasive distinctions are the limited purpose for which Article 34 investigation may be ordered, and the obligation of Members to cooperate in an investigation having as its purpose the determination of the Security Council of its own competence.[50]

The position taken by the United States representative in the discussions before the Council on the duration of the Commission of Investigation Concerning Greek Frontier Incidents is probably the best expression of interpretation of the Charter provisions. The United States representative said

> . . . it is inherent in the powers conferred by Article 34, and conferred by other provisions of the Charter relating to the duties and functions of the Security Council, that it may continue to make such investigations as long as it thinks that that situation exists.[51]

The final point in this discussion of the authority of the Security Council to investigate is whether the Security Council must investigate

The competence of the Security Council to act under Chapter VI of the Charter appears to be closely tied in with the wording of Article 34.

---

[48]U. N. Security Council, Official Records, Second Year, No. 61, p. 1426. The President of the Security Council believed the duration of the Commission should extend "as long as no resolution in connection with its report is adopted" (U. N. Security Council, Official Records, Second Year, No. 71, p. 1798).

[49]Eduardo Jimenez de Arechaga, op. cit., pp. 84-85.

[50]Ernest L. Kerley, op. cit., p. 918. Two proponents for a more liberal interpretation of the Charter are Professors McDougal and Gardner. See Myres Smith McDougal and Richard N. Gardner, "The Veto and the Charter; An Interpretation for Survival", Yale Law Journal, Volume 60 (February, 1951), pp. 258-292.

[51]Security Council, Official Records, Second Year, No. 61, p. 1425.

With the exception of Article 38, Articles 33, 35, 36, and 37 of the United Nations Charter deal specifically with a dispute "the continuance of which is likely to endanger the maintenance of international peace and security . . . ." This is in the specific wording of Article 33. Article 35 refers to "any dispute, or any situation of the nature referred to in Article 34 i.e., "any dispute, or any situation which might lead to international friction or give rise to a dispute, . . ." and Articles 36 and 37 refer to a "dispute of the nature referred to in Article 33."

The competence of the Security Council to take action under Chapter VI is clearly based, with the exception of Article 38,[52] on the existence of a specific type of dispute i.e., a dispute "the continuance of which is likely to endanger the maintenance of international peace and security." The question that arises, therefore, is whether it is obligatory on the part of the Security Council to conduct an investigation under Article 34 in order to determine its competence to act under Chapter VI of the Charter. The wording of Article 34 is definitely not obligatory. The phrasing is "may investigate." The drafting history, at no stage indicates usage of an obligatory term. The phrase "should be empowered to investigate" appeared in Paragraph 1, Chapter VIII of the Dumbarton Oaks Proposals.[53] At its 34th meeting, the wording was changed by the Coordinating Committee from "is empowered to investigate" to "may investigate."[54]

The Council, in practice, has considered an investigation under Article 34 as not prerequisite to a determination by it that a dispute is likely to endanger international peace and security. Nor is it necessary for the Council to make an explicit determination. In any case, if an explicit determination is believed necessary, it can be made not as a separate and previous decision but as a consideration in the preamble of a resolution containing recommendations. [55]

It would appear that as a matter of practicality, the Security Council would find it necessary to order an investigation only where there is doubt or discrepancy as to whether the continuance of a dispute or situation is likely to endanger peace and security.[56]

In practice, the Security Council, has considered itself competent, under Article 34, to conduct a broad investigation of the facts of any dispute or situation brought before it. In addition to conducting such investigation, for the purpose of determining the serious nature of the dispute or situation, the investigation may also be used for the purpose of establishing the factual bases for recommendations under Articles 33, 36 and 37. The inherent and implied power of the Security Council, under Article 24, to investigate in fulfilling its responsibility for the maintenance of international peace and security provides adequate support for this approach.

The distinction between the power of the Security Council and its ability to exercise that power - in this case in conducting investigations - has been underlined by the lack of agreement between the permanent members of the Council. Some inquiries have been initiated under Article 29 but for the most part action in the Security Council has been

---

[52]Article 38 states "without prejudice to the provisions of Articles 33 to 37, the Security Council may, if all the parties to any dispute so request, make recommendations to the parties with a view to a pacific settlement of the dispute."

[53]UNCIO, Vol. 3, p. 12.

[54]Ibid., Vol. 17, p. 268.

[55]Eduardo Jimenez de Arechaga, op. cit., p. 86. See discussion on pp. 85-88 of the same work.

[56]Ibid., p. 87.

blocked at crucial times by the negative vote of one of its permanent members.

One result of the impasse in the Security Council has been to shift greater responsibility for the maintenance of peace and security to the General Assembly. This has resulted, in turn, in greater use by the General Assembly of its powers of investigation under the Charter which will be discussed next.

2. The General Assembly

The authority of the General Assembly to conduct investigations in the interests of maintaining international peace and security is implied by Articles 10, 11, 14 and 22 of the United Nations Charter.

Article 10 states:

The General Assembly may discuss any question or any matters within the scope of the present Charter or relating to the powers and functions of any organs provided for in the present Charter and, except as provided in Article 12, may make recommendations to the Members of the United Nations or to the Security Council or to both on any such matters.

Article 11 further provides in paragraph 2

The General Assembly may discuss any questions relating to the maintenance of international peace and security brought before it by any Member of the United Nations, or by the Security Council, or by a state which is not a Member of the United Nations in accordance with Article 35, paragraph 2 and, except as provided in Article 12, may make recommendations with regards to any such questions to the state or states concerned or to the Security Council or to both. Any such question on which action is necessary shall be referred to the Security Council by the General Assembly either before or after discussion.

Article 14 emphasizes the power of the General Assembly to recommend, subject to Article 12,

measures for the peaceful adjustment of any situation, regardless of origin, which it deems likely to impair the general welfare or friendly relations among nations, including situations resulting from a violation of the provision of the present Charter setting forth the Purposes and Principles of the United Nations.

And, finally, Article 22 provides

The General Assembly may establish such subsidiary organs as it may deem necessary for the performance of its functions.

At the second session of the General Assembly, Article 22 was thoroughly discussed in connection with the proposal of the United States to establish an Interim Committee as a subsidiary organ of the General Assembly.[57] The United States proposal set forth the function of the Interim Committee as aiding the General Assembly in the discharge of its responsibilities in the maintenance of international peace and security (Articles 11 and 35), the promotion of international cooperation in the political field (Article 13) and the peaceful adjustment of any situations likely to impair the general welfare or friendly relations among nations (Article 14).[58] Of interest to this study is the conferral upon the Interim Committee, in order to enable it to discharge its functions, of the power

---

[57]U. N. Doc. A/AC/1/SR74.
[58]Idem.

of investigation, and the ensuing discussion concerning the power of the General Assembly itself to conduct investigations.[59]

The experience of the General Assembly in discharging its responsibilities in the maintenance of international peace and security indicates wide support for the General Assembly's power to conduct investigations and to appoint commissions of enquiry. Pertinent to the General Assembly's experience in initiating and conducting investigations is the "Uniting for Peace" Resolution.

Uniting for Peace Resolution

The "Uniting for"Peace" Resolution 377 (V), adopted by the General Assembly on November 3, 1950, was designed to consolidate and extend the Assembly's power in situations constituting a threat to the peace where the Security Council was unable to act because of a great power veto. What is of primary interest here are the provisions of the "Uniting for Peace" Resolution establishing a Peace Observation Commission. Paragraph 3 of Resolution A states that the General Assembly

Establishes a Peace Observation Commission, which for the calendar years 1951 and 1952 shall be composed of fourteen members, namely: China, Colombia, Czechoslovakia, France, India, Iraq, Israel, New Zealand, Pakistan, Sweden, the Union of Soviet Socialist Republics, the United Kingdom of Great Britain and Northern Ireland, the United States of America and Uruguay, and which could observe and report on the situation in any area where there exists international tension, the continuance of which is likely to endanger the maintenance of international peace and security.[60]

The resolution goes on to provide that upon the invitation or with the consent of the state into whose territory the Commission would go, the General Assembly, or the Interim Committee when the General Assembly is not in session, may utilize the Commission if the Security Council is not exercising the functions assigned to it by the Charter with respect to the matter in question. Decisions to utilize the Commission would be made on the affirmative vote of two-thirds of the members present and voting.

The legality of the Uniting for Peace Resolution is supported by Professor Stone who prefers to base such legality on Article 51 with respect to the collective measures provisions, although he advances arguments of a different nature with regard to the Peace Observation Commission.[61]

---

[59]The Interim Committee's authority to conduct investigations was authorized by G. A. resolution III (II) paragraph 2 (e) (U. N. General Assembly Resolutions 2nd Session, September 16 - November 29, 1947, p. 16), which states that the Interim Committee has power to conduct in-investigations and appoint commissions of enquiry within the scope of its duties, as it may deem useful and necessary, provided that decisions to conduct such investigations or enquiries shall be made by a two-thirds majority of the members present and voting. An investigation or enquiry elsewhere than at the Headquarters of the United Nations shall not be conducted without the consent of the state or states in whose territory it is to take place.

[60]U. N. General Assembly Official Records, Fifth Session, Supplement No. 20, pp. 10-12.

[61]Julius Stone Legal Controls of International Conflict (New York: 1954) pp. 266-281. The almost unanimous adoption by the General Assembly of the "Uniting for Peace" resolution is regarded as based upon an interpretation of the Charter which furthers its general and major purposes, according to McDougal and Gardner, op. cit.

For example, in answer to the objections that Article 39 entrusts the determination that there is a threat to the peace, breach of the peace, or act of aggression only to the Security Council, Professor Stone replies that there is no conflict. Not only does the Commission not "determine", being merely able to "report on the situation" but the General Assembly itself is neither able nor likely to make such determination. Any recommendation the General Assembly would make under Resolution A, would not have any legal binding force for members, unlike the constitutional consequences of a Security Council "determination" under Article 39.

In addition, according to Professor Stone, paragraph 2 of Article 11 in providing that any question relating to the maintenance of international peace and security on which action is necessary shall be referred to the Security Council implies that the General Assembly must have the power to make the determination that the question requires Security Council action. Again, while this does not entail the legal implications of a determination by the Security Council under Article 39, it attributes, by implication, to the General Assembly, the power to conduct an investigation of fact where necessary.

On the power of the General Assembly under the "Uniting for Peace" Resolution, Professor Goodrich has declared that the Charter contains only two legal limitations to prevent the Assembly's "encroachment" on the primary responsibility of the Security Council: one was the provision contained in Article 12, para. 1 that the General Assembly should not make a recommendation with regard to any dispute or situation at the same time that the Security Council was exercising its Charter functions in this same respect: the second limitation was that contained in the Article 11, paragraph 2, requiring the General Assembly to refer any question concerning "action" to the Security Council either before or after discussion.[62]

The power of the General Assembly to conduct investigations is implied in the functions assigned to the Assembly by the United Nations Charter. The establishment of the Peace Observation Commission under the "Uniting for Peace" Resolution would appear to be an exercise by the General Assembly of such implied power and more specifically, of its powers under Article 11, paragraph 2.

The "Uniting for Peace" Resolution has been discussed here as pertinent to the use by the General Assembly of its power to investigate. However, the question of the legality of the "Uniting for Peace" Resolution does not have any bearing on the power of the General Assembly to investigate but only on the special circumstances created by the resolution surrounding the exercise of that power. For that reason, although touching on the subject of the "Uniting for Peace" Resolution no attempt has been made herein to discuss it in any detail.

3. The Secretary General

The authority of the Secretary-General to conduct investigations in the maintenance of international peace and security is implied in the powers given the Secretary-General under Article 99 of the United Nations Charter which provides that

The Secretary-General may bring to the attention of the Security Council any matter which, in his opinion, may threaten the maintenance of international peace and security.

The independent power of the Secretary-General to observe and to conduct investigations would, of course, be limited, as is the General

---

[62]Leland M. Goodrich "Development of the General Assembly" International Conciliation, (May, 1951, No. 478), p. 262. For a detailed discussion of the legality of the "Uniting for Peace" resolution, see Tae Ho Yoo, The Korean War and The United Nations: A Legal and Diplomatic Historical Study, Louvain: Librairie Desbarax, 1965, pp. 122-140.

Assembly's power by Article 2 (7). Moreover, the independent power of the Secretary-General to obtain information is to be distinguished from his acting to obtain information as an agent of the Security Council or of the General Assembly.

An example of the latter is the Iranian Question. The United States representative suggested to the Council, on March 29, 1946, with all present concurring, that the President of the Council request the Secretary General to ascertain at once from the U.S.S.R. and Iranian Governments through their representatives, and report to the Council at its meeting on April 3rd, the existing status of the negotiations between the two Governments and, particularly, to ascertain from the representatives of those two Governments and report whether or not the reported withdrawal of troops was conditioned upon the conclusion of agreement between the two Governments on other subjects.[63]

In a more formal designation of the Secretary-General as its agent, the Security Council, on April 4, 1946, adopted a resolution on the Iranian Question, requesting the Secretary-General to receive reports concerning the withdrawal of Soviet troops from Iran.[64]

In support of an independent power to investigate, the Secretary-General made the following statement before a vote was taken on a United States draft resolution, during consideration of the Greek Question by the Security Council, in September 1946:

Should the proposal, of the United States representative not be carried, I hope that the Council will understand that the Secretary-General must reserve his right to make such enquiries or investigations as he may think necessary in order to determine whether or not he should consider bringing any aspect of this matter to the attention of the Council under the provisions of the Charter.[65]

A feature of United Nations commissions has been the appointment to some of them of a personal representative of the Secretary-General. That was done in the cases of the Special Committee on Palestine[66] and the Commission for India and Pakistan.[67]

In the matter of the Secretary-General providing preliminary information on a question before the General Assembly or Security Council, the practices of the League of Nations and the United Nations have differed. The practice of the Secretary-General of the League was to present a report considering the factual situation in connection with questions brought to the attention of the Council and the Assembly of the League.[68] The Secretary-General of the United Nations has collected information in such preliminary fashion only in the Palestine question, in which instance, a special library was established and five special volumes covering factual background material were prepared. A similar function was performed for the United Nations Temporary Commission on Korea.

---

[63]U. N. Security Council Official Records First Year, Second Series p. 82.

[64]Ibid., pp. 88-89. Also, under this concept, see the Rules of Procedure of the Security Council giving the Secretary-General the power to make either oral or written statements to the Security Council or its committees, concerning any question under consideration, or to act as rapporteur for a specified question before the Council. (U.N. Doc. A/96, Rev. 3, Rules 22 and 23, p. 7).

[65]U. N. Security Council Official Records, First Year, Second Series, p. 404.

[66]U. N. Doc. A/364, Vol. 1, p. 3 (September 3, 1947).

[67]U. N. Doc. S/1100, p. 8 (November 9, 1948).

[68]F. P. Walters, op. cit., Vol. 1, p. 87.

In this connection, a feature of the League of Nations Covenant and of League practice, must be recalled, which differs from that of the United Nations. Under article 15, paragraph 1, the Secretary-General of the League of Nations was obliged after having received notice of the existence of a dispute from a party to "make all necessary arrangements for a full investigation and consideration thereof."

The Secretary-General of the League made a rather extensive use of these powers in 1932 when he, on receiving the Chinese Government's appeal under Article 15, requested certain members of the Council having representatives on the spot to authorize these representatives to constitute a committee for the purpose of inquiring into the causes and developments of the situation at Shanghai and in the neighborhood.

The Secretary-General addressed a similar request to the Government of the United States of America and that Government instructed its Consul-General at Shanghai to cooperate with the Committee in its work.[69] The Secretary-General, on January 29, and 30, 1932, in two statements before the Council noted his "arrangements for a prompt investigation" in order to obtain impartial and speedy information for the Council's consideration.

In the establishing of the Shanghai Committee, no decision of the Council was taken because the Secretary-General did not make his proposals to the Council as a whole but only to those members who had representatives at Shanghai.[70] Thus the Secretary-General initiated a fact-finding body without a formal decision of the Council and preparatory to the consideration of the merits by Council.

The exercise of the United Nations Secretary-General's implied power, which is less obligatory, under Article 99, to obtain information, independently, is perhaps best illustrated by the situation in Jordan at the time the Lebanese question was before the General Assembly. At that time, the Secretary-General announced that Jordan had agreed to the stationing in Jordan of a special representative of the Secretary-General to keep under review the adherence of all to the principles set out in Part 1 of the General Assembly resolution on the Lebanon and Jordan questions before the Assembly.[71]

The Secretary-General pointed out that

The reports to the Secretary-General from the representatives stationed in Amman would not be public documents unless the situation was found to call for their circulation as official documents of the United Nations. Such circumstances which might serve as a basis for action by the General Assembly or the Security Council, represents obviously an alternative line of action open to the Secretary-General in such cases as would seem to him to call for stronger measures than diplomatic demarches.[72]

A similar case is that in which the Secretary-General dispatched a special representative to Cambodia and Thailand.[73] The representative of Thailand, in replying to the charges of the Cambodian representative, stated that Thailand was prepared to welcome any United Nations' representatives to observe the situation in the border area and if the Secretary-General should consider the case as falling within the purview of Article 99 of the Charter, the Government of Thailand would be happy to welcome the representative of the Secretary-General and give him every facility to inspect the border area.[74]

[69]L. of N. Doc. A (Extra), 3, 1932 VII, p. 1.

[70]L. of N. Official Journal, (1932) pp. 341-344, 349.

[71]U. N. Doc. A/3934, Rev. 1 (September 29, 1958).

[72]U. N. General Assembly Official Records, Third Emergency Special Session, Supplement No. 1, p. II.

[73]U. N. Doc. S/4121. (December 2, 1958).

[74]U. N. Doc. S/4126. (December 8, 1958).

A more recent case in which the power of the Secretary-General to investigate was demonstrated was the situation, in Yemen, in which the Secretary-General sent his personal representative, Dr. Bunche, into the area on a fact-finding mission.[75] Subsequently, the Secretary-General reported that he had appointed General Horn, as his representative, to visit the area with a view to setting up an observer group to observe the implementation of the disengagement agreement.[76] What is interesting is that the Secretary-General was acting in Yemen, initially, without specific authorization from either the Security Council or the General Assembly.[77]

In yet another case, the matter of ascertaining the wishes of the Population of North Borneo and Sarawak, the Secretary-General was approached, directly, by the Governments of the Federation of Malaysia, the Philippines, and Indonesia for that purpose.[78] Again, the matter was neither before the Security Council nor the General Assembly.

In the Cyprus situation, also, although the matter had been brought to the attention of the Security Council on December 26, 1963,[79] a request was addressed by the Governments of Cyprus, Greece, Turkey and the United Kingdom directly to the Secretary-General to send a personal representative to Cyprus.[80]

The exercise of the powers of investigation, given him under Article 99, by the Secretary-General is governed by the political nature of the dispute and, consequently, the Western and Soviet bloc positions and attitudes. The extent to which the Secretary-General is willing and able to exercise his power to conduct investigations depends upon his personality and the support which he may expect to receive.

4. Obligation of Parties to Accept Investigation

Under Article 25 of the United Nations Charter, "the Members of the United Nations agree to accept and carry out the decisions of the Security Council." Whether this obligation extends to a decision of the Security Council to conduct an investigation was the subject of an extended debate during consideration of a United States proposal, on June 27, 1947[81] to set up a commission to aid in the implementation of the recommendations made by the Security Council's Commission of Investigation Concerning Greek Frontier Incidents.

The establishment of the Commission under the United States proposal was attacked by the representatives of the Soviet Union, Albania, Bulgaria and Yugoslavia on the grounds that it was proposed to give the Commission power in excess of that permitted by Article 34. In addition, these representatives argued, the Commission was to have the power to enter into the territory of states and summon witnesses whereas under Chapter VI the Security Council merely had the power of recommendation.

As the Soviet representative pointed out, a decision to investigate under Article 34 is in the nature of a recommendation to the States affected. "All decisions taken under Chapter VI," he said, "including decisions to conduct an investigation are in the nature of recommendations".[82] He went on to note that "the idea that Security Council decisions to conduct an in-

---

[75]U. N. Doc. S/5298 (April 29, 1963).

[76]U. N. Doc. S/5321 (May 27, 1963).

[77]U. N. Doc. S/5331 (June 11, 1963).

[78]U. N. General Assembly Official Records, Nineteenth Session, Supplement No. 1 (A/5801).

[79]U. N. Doc. S/5488 (December 26, 1963).

[80]U. N. Doc. S/5514 (January 13, 1964).

[81]U. N. Security Council, Official Records Second Year, No. 51, pp. 1124-6.

[82]Ibid., No. 64, p. 1541.

vestigation are obligatory is contrary to Chapter VI of the Charter".[83] A country which does not fulfill even the recommendations bears a certain moral responsibility but no more than a moral responsibility."[84] He continued with the argument that if such recommendations are treated as compulsory, failure of a State to fulfill such recommendations would require other measures, namely compulsory measures, to be applied to it. If this were so, then Chapter VI regarding the pacific settlement of disputes would vanish leaving only Chapter VII which provides for compulsory decisions.[85]

In reply to the Soviet representative, the French delegate drew a distinction between a decision to investigate under Article 34 and a recommendation under Articles 36, 37 and 38. The representative of France stressed that it was only with respect to Article 34 that states were under an obligation to cooperate with a commission of investigation. In explaining why the Council possessed greater powers under Article 34 than it had under subsequent articles of Chapter VI, the French representative noted that Article 34 refers only to an investigation for the sole purpose of providing the Security Council with information. Being preliminary and a simple measure of enquiry, the Security Council, he felt, should have greater power and should be able to decide, and not merely to recommend, that an investigation be made.[86]

The United States representative, in his reply to the Soviet statement, took a different approach. Noting that the Council must have "certain operating powers" in order to fulfill its "role as a conciliator and also as a guardian of the peace", he contended that Article 34 gave the Council the "right to investigate any dispute whether or not the State investigated approves or likes it". Acknowledging that the Charter does not "confer on the Security Council, operating under Chapter VI, any power of sanction or enforcement," the United States representative stated that it is nevertheless "the duty of the Members of the United Nations to conform to" the decisions of the Security Council.[87] Failure to do so, he continued,

. . . does lay non-complying States open to serious charges, which may be brought before the Security Council and acted upon, charges of non-compliance with their own obligations under the Charter to cooperate with the Security Council in its decisions.[88]

In his reply to the Soviet argument that all decisions taken under Chapter VI are in the nature of recommendations, the Australian representative pointed out that "Article 27 specifically refers to 'decisions under Chapter VI.'"[89]

The legal obligation of a Member State to allow an investigating team, established under Article 34, to enter its territory was supported in the Security Council discussions noted above by the representatives of Australia, Belgium, France, the United Kingdom and the United States. At the same time, the existence of such obligation was vigorously contested by the representative of the Soviet Union. Little support for the extension of such an obligation to investigations for the purpose of making recommendations under Articles 36, 37 and 38 was evidenced.

The position has been taken that once a decision to investigate has

[83]Ibid., p. 1537.
[84]Ibid., p. 1542.
[85]Idem.
[86]Ibid., No. 65, p. 1553. This view is also supported by Ernest L. Kerley (op. cit., p. 918).
[87]Ibid., No. 65, p. 1553.
[88]Ibid., No. 64, p. 1541.
[89]Ibid., No. 64, p. 1544.

been taken under Article 34, the affected States must cooperate with it.[90] The difficulty lies not in the Charter which would support such an interpretation but in the application of that interpretation. As will be seen from the following discussion of the terms of reference of United Nations commissions of investigation, restriction to an investigation solely for the limited purpose expressed in Article 34 has not been the experience of the Security Council.

Since the practice of the Security Council in establishing commissions of investigation allows for such wide latitude in function, it is doubtful if the obligation under the Charter to accept an investigation in accordance with the provisions of Article 34 could be realistically insisted upon. It would therefore appear that "suggestions to spell out the obligation of Members to accept investigation by the United Nations . . . are not realistic."[91]

The reluctance on the part of states to arbitrarily impose limitations upon national sovereignty is basic to this realistic approach. Any such limitations must be clearly spelled out and as clearly capable of application. The practical aspect of this problem was recognized by the League of Nations. The League Covenant conferred a much stronger obligation upon the Members of the League to accept an investigation. Article 12, paragraph 1 of the Covenant specifically stated that Members of the League agreed that

if there should arise between them any dispute likely to lead
to a rupture, they will submit the matter either to arbitration,
or judicial settlement or to inquiry by the Council.

The League Covenant also provided that the decision to investigate was not subject to the unanimity rule. In all cases, nevertheless, the League undertook investigation only with the consent of the states concerned.

The Organization of American States with its sweeping powers for collective action under the Treaty of Rio and under its Charter has resorted to investigation many times. In no case, did the commission of investigation fail to address a request for permission from the parties concerned to enter their territories.

B. Terms of Reference

There has been little uniformity in the terms of reference of the fact-finding bodies of the United Nations Security Council and General Assembly. The distinguishing characteristic of the terms of reference of these investigating bodies has been the desire of the Security Council and General Assembly to afford them the greatest latitude in order to achieve their general purpose--the maintenance of international peace. As a matter of practice, the terms of reference of several committees were continually clarified and defined by the Security Council and General Assembly, as the case might be, in the course of the work of the investigating body.

Basically, the power of the Security Council to investigate rests upon Article 24 of the United Nations Charter. The Security Council, however, may conduct an investigation for particular purposes which are not necessarily exclusive.

---

[90]Eduardo Jimenez de Arechaga, op. cit., p. 89.

[91]Leland M. Goodrich and Anne P. Simons The United Nations and The Maintenance of International Peace and Security, Washington, D. C., The Brookings Institution, 1957, p. 202. The Commission to Study the Organization of Peace maintains that members of the United Nations are obligated to cooperate with inquiries by virtue of Articles 104 and 105 of The Charter. (Commission to Study the Organization of Peace. Arthur N. Holcombe, Chairman, Strengthening the United Nations, New York: Harper, 1957).

Under Article 34, the Security Council, in determining its competence, "may investigate any dispute, or any situation . . . in order to determine whether the continuance of the dispute or situation is likely to endanger the maintenance of international peace and security".

Under Articles 36, 37 and 38, the Security Council may, in accordance with the principles of pacific settlement laid down in the Hague Conventions, elucidate the facts in order to facilitate a solution.[92]

Under Article 39, the Security Council "shall determine the existence of any threat to the peace, breach of the peace, or act of aggression and shall make recommendations, or decide what measures shall be taken in accordance with Articles 41 and 42 to maintain or restore international peace and security."

Article 40 of the Charter provides that the Security Council, after calling upon the parties "to comply with such provisional measures as it deems necessary or desirable", shall "duly take account of failure to comply with such provisional measures". The power of the Security Council to conduct such investigation as it deems necessary to determine whether there has been failure to comply must be inferred from Article 40.[93]

It has been the usual practice of the Security Council not to relate its resolutions establishing investigating bodies to any of these specific charter provisions. This, of course, makes for greater flexibility. There have been exceptions. The resolution establishing the Commission of Investigation concerning Greek Frontier Incidents referred to Article 34. The Commission for India and Pakistan was set up under a resolution referring to Article 34 but this aspect of the original dual function of investigation and mediation was later abandoned. In three other cases, those of the sub-committees in the matter of Franco Spain, in the Corfu Channel case and in the Laos case, reference was made to Article 29, but this reference did not limit, in itself, the task of the commission in any of these instances.

The terms of reference of commissions of investigation have varied, however, with relation to the nature and purpose of the investigation as the following examples show.

The Spanish Question was brought to the attention of the Security Council in letters, dated April 8 and 9, 1946, to the Secretary-General, from the representative of Poland, requesting the Council, under Articles 34 and 35, to place on its agenda the situation arising from the existence and activities of the Franco regime in Spain.[94]

The resolution proposed by the Australian representative, on April 29, 1946, which was adopted by a vote of 10 to 0 with one abstention -- the U.S.S.R., referred only to Article 35 and resolved

> to make further studies to determine whether the situation in Spain has led to international friction and does endanger international peace and security and if it so finds, to determine what practical measures the United Nations may take.[95]

The terms of reference were specific, namely to determine whether there was a situation in Spain which did endanger international peace and security and if the answer to it was found to be in the affirmative, to

---

[92]Eduardo Jimenez de Arechaga, op. cit., p. 80.

[93]Idem.

[94]U. N. Security Council Official Records, First Year, First Series, Supplement No. 2, Annexes 3a and 3b, pp. 54-55.

[95]U. N. Security Council Official Records, First Year, First Series, p. 244.

determine what practical measures the United Nations might take.

The Sub-Committee on the Spanish Question, within the scope of reference assigned to it as above outlined, found that the Security Council could not make the determination required under Article 39 for action under Chapter VII because no threat to the peace had been established.[96] However, the Sub-Committee did find that the situation in Spain was a situation under Article 34, the continuance of which was, in fact, likely to endanger the maintenance of international peace and security and as such, could be dealt with under Chapter VI, Article 36, under which the Security Council is empowered to recommend appropriate methods of adjustment in order to improve the situation.[97] The Sub-Committee concluded that the withdrawal of the Franco regime and the satisfaction of the other conditions of political freedom set out in the declaration by the Governments of the United Kingdom, the United States and France, dated March 4, 1946, were the recommendations that could be made by the Security Council under Articles 37 and 38.[98]

The terms of reference of the Commission investigating Greek Frontier Incidents apparently were of a more limited nature than those of the Spanish Sub-Committee. The Greek investigation was formally established by a Security Council resolution, under Article 34,

> to ascertain the facts relating to alleged border violations
> along the frontier between Greece on the one hand and
> Albania, Bulgaria, and Yugoslavia on the other hand.[99]

The resolution adopted by the Security Council went on to empower the Commission to conduct its investigation in such places as will enable it "to elucidate the causes and nature of the above mentioned border violations and disturbances."[100] The preamble to the above mentioned resolution was as inappropriate to an investigation under Article 34 as the above quoted portions from the body of the resolution. The preamble stated

> Whereas there have been presented to the Security Council
> oral and written statements by the Greek, Yugoslavian,
> Albanian, and Bulgarian Governments, relating to disturbed
> conditions in Northern Greece, along the frontier between
> Greece on the one hand and Albania, Bulgaria, and Yugoslavia
> on the other, which conditions, in the opinion of the Council,
> should be investigated before the Council attempts to reach
> any conclusion regarding the issues involved.[101]

The Commission, although its mandate included an elucidation of the causes and nature of the border disturbances noted, in its report, that it did not investigate charges with respect to territorial claims which it felt were better raised before appropriate international bodies.[102] The Commission did go into an investigation of guerrilla warfare and aid to the guerrillas as well as into the internal disturbances in Greece.[103]

The Security Council resolution, in the India-Pakistan dispute over Kashmir, setting up the United Nations Commission for India and Pakistan, specifically referred to Article 34 as the basis of action in investing the Commission with the dual function

---

[96]U. N. Doc. S/75, p. 10 (June 6, 1946).

[97]Idem.

[98]Idem.

[99]U. N. Security Council Official Records, First Year, Second Series, No. 28, pp. 700-1.

[100]Idem.

[101]Idem.

[102]U. N. Doc. S/360 (May 23, 1947), p. 182. Nevertheless, the Commission did devote a portion of Chapter VII Part II, and Section E in Part III to territorial claims. (Ibid., pp. 155-163; pp. 181-182.)

[103]Ibid., p. 178.

(1) To investigate the facts pursuant to Article 34 of the Charter;

(2) To exercise without interrupting the work of the Security Council, any mediatory influence likely to smooth away difficulties . . .[104]

The terms of reference of the Commission presented, initially, a problem. A letter, dated January 1, 1948, from the representative of India to the Secretary-General, had charged that the situation in the State of Jammu and Kashmir resulted from the aid that Pakistan was giving to invaders from Pakistan and tribesmen from areas adjacent to the north-west frontier of Pakistan who were engaged in operations against the State of Jammu and Kashmir.[105] In countering these charges, in a letter, dated January 15, 1948, the Foreign Minister of Pakistan, not only accused India of unlawful occupation of the State of Junagadh and other states by Indian armed forces, but also of mass destruction of Moslems.[106] As finally adopted by the Security Council, the resolution embodying the complaints of India and Pakistan joined issue on the situation in Kashmir and tabled the other claims of Pakistan.[107]

Before the Commission began to operate, the Council, in view of the agreement of the parties as to the seriousness of the matter, adopted a resolution containing a finding that "the continuation of the dispute" was "likely to endanger international peace and security".[108] The Commission therefore considered its first function as eliminated and pursued its second function.

On June 3, 1948, the Security Council adopted a resolution, apparently extending the terms of reference of the commission in the Kashmir Dispute, which read as follows:

The Security Council

Reaffirms its resolutions of 17 January 1948, 20 January 1948 and 21 April 1948;

Directs the Commission of Mediation to proceed without delay to the areas of dispute with a view to accomplishing in priority the duties assigned to it by the resolution of 21 April 1948; and Directs the Commission further to study and report to the Security Council when it considers it appropriate on the matters raised in the letter of the Foreign Minister of Pakistan, dated 15 January 1948, in the order outlined in Paragraph D of the resolution of the Council, dated 20 January 1948.[109]

The United Nations Special Committee on Palestine had as wide a scope of reference as possible. The Assembly resolution establishing it stated:

2. The Special Committee shall have the widest power to ascertain and record facts, and to investigate all questions and issues relevant to the problems of Palestine . . .

---

[104]U. N. Doc. S/654 (January 20, 1948).

[105]U. N. Doc. S/628 (January 1, 1948).

[106]U. N. Doc. S/646 (January 15, 1948).

[107]U. N. Doc. S/654 (January 20, 1948). See discussion on terms of reference in U. N. Security Council Official Records, Third Year, No. 74, pp. 2-21

[108]U. N. Doc. S/726 (April 22, 1948).

[109]U. N. Doc. S/819 (June 3, 1948). The resolution of April 21, 1948 had eliminated the functions of the commission under Article 34 and established its primary purpose as good offices and mediation.

3. The Special Committee shall conduct investigations in Palestine and wherever it may deem useful, receive and examine written or oral testimony, whichever it may consider appropriate in each case, from the Mandatory Power, from representatives of the population of Palestine, from Governments and from such organizations and individuals as it may deem necessary.[110]

Yet, limitations to its scope were evident in the case of three young Jews who were sentenced to death by the Military Court in Jerusalem, on June 16, 1947. Their execution was bound to result in wide disturbances. The Special Committee adopted, on June 22, 1947, a resolution to communicate to the mandatory power "the concern" of the majority of the Committee "as to the possible unfavorable repercussions that execution of the three death sentences might have upon the fulfillment of the task" of the Committee.[111] At the same time, the Special Committee agreed to send a letter to the relatives of the condemned persons stating that

it is beyond the scope of the Committee's instructions and functions to interfere with the judicial administration in Palestine; but having regard . . . to the task of the Committee, the matter is being brought to the attention of the proper authorities.[112]

The Governments of Palestine and of the United Kingdom took the position that the death sentences were still sub judice and that the General Assembly's resolution prescribing the task of the Committee was not relevant to the cases.

The opinion seems warranted that such "informal" requests for the postponement of execution or for the commutation of death sentences by commissions of inquiry are in order if they have reason to believe that the execution might in some way adversely affect their task.

The investigation in the matter of Eritrea was also an inquiry requiring a wide scope of reference. The pertinent portion of the General Assembly resolution establishing the scope of the commission of investigation stated that, in carrying out its responsibility to examine the question of the disposal of Eritrea, the Commission should ascertain all the relevant facts, including written or oral information from the present administering Power, from representatives of the population of the territory, including minorities, from governments and from such organizations and individuals as it may deem necessary.

In particular, the Commission was to take into account:
(a) The wishes and welfare of the inhabitants of Eritrea, including the views of the various racial, religious and political groups of the provinces of the territory and the capacity of the people for self-government;
(b) the interests of peace and security in East Africa;
(c) the rights and claims of Ethiopia based on geographical, historical, ethnic or economic reasons, including in particular Ethiopia's legitimate need for adequate access to the sea;
3. That in considering its proposals the Committee shall take into account . . . the various suggestions for the disposal of Eritrea submitted during the fourth regular session of the General Assembly . . . .[113]

---

[110] U. N. Doc. A/307, p. 8 (May 23, 1947).

[111] U. N. General Assembly Official Records, Second Session, Supplement No. 11, Vol. I, p. 6 and Vol. II, p. 13.

[112] Idem.

[113] U. N. General Assembly Resolutions 1st to 4th Session, 1946-1949, p. 1172. (Resolution 289IV).

Sometimes, a commission, set up for one purpose, has found authorization in its terms of reference in order to achieve another purpose. The United Nations Temporary Commission on Korea was such a commission. Its task was to implement Resolution 112 (II) in such parts of Korea as were accessible. Resolution 112 (II) provided for free elections in Korea for the purpose of achieving an independent United Korea. Events caused its successor, the United Nations Commission on Korea, to become an observer group on the situation in Korea with respect to the potential danger of an outbreak of hostilities.[114]

In one case, a misinterpretation of the terms of reference was helpful to the fact-finding body in performing its task. This occurred in the case of the Special Committee on South West Africa. The terms of reference of the Committee directed it to conduct an investigation in South West Africa with regard to implementation of the declaration on the right to independence of colonial countries and peoples.[115]

The Chairman and Vice Chairman of the Committee were invited to visit the Republic of South Africa and the Territory of South West Africa after discussion between the Chairman and Vice Chairman and the permanent representative of the Republic of South Africa to the United Nations. It was the understanding arrived at in these discussions that the purpose of the visit by the Chairman and Vice Chairman would be to determine how to reconcile the views of the United Nations and the Republic of South Africa. The Republic of South Africa interpreted this to mean - in narrower terms of reference - that it had only to demonstrate that there was neither tension nor other disturbance nor any arms buildup in South West Africa.

The report of the Chairman and Vice Chairman was based on the much broader terms of reference of the Committee's enabling resolution. This report, which was incorporated into the report of the Special Committee on South West Africa, was sharply critical of the apartheid policies pursued by the Government of the Republic of South Africa in its administration of South West Africa.[116]

The Commission formed to carry out an investigation in Germany in order to determine whether conditions existing there would make it possible to hold free elections[117] narrowed its scope of reference to conform to the situation. The Commission was directed by the General Assembly resolution to forthwith make the necessary arrangements for its investigation. Unable to establish contact with the authorities in the Soviet Zone of Germany or in the eastern sector of Berlin, the Commission adjourned sine die.[118] The Commission interpreted its terms of reference to give precedence to making the necessary arrangements with the parties.[119] When these could not be made, it considered its task completed.

As a rule, the terms of reference of commissions of inquiry have been wide in scope. Each situation has, in its own way, influenced the interpretations of the terms of reference. An inquiry like that in the Greek question which was actually designed to achieve a cessation of hostilities could not do so in the case of guerrilla warfare without "ascertaining the facts

---

[114]U. N. General Assembly Resolution 293 (IV), October 21, 1949. Under General Assembly Resolution 195 (III) December 12, 1948, the United Nations Commission on Korea was to
"(d) Observe the actual withdrawal of the occupying forces and verify the fact of withdrawal when such has occurred . . ."
[115]U. N. General Assembly Resolution 1702 XVI, December 19, 1961.
[116]U. N. Doc. A/5212 and U. N. Doc. A/5212/ Add. 1 & 2.
[117]U. N. Doc. A/938 (November 5, 1951).
[118]U. N. Doc. A/2122/Add. 2 (August 11, 1952).
[119]Idem.

relating to alleged border violations."[120]The inquiry was, therefore extensive in nature. Investigation in cases where a cease-fire is to be imposed on two clearly defined and responsible authorities lends itself to a more limited interpretation of the terms of reference.

The terms of reference may from the outset restrict the activities of a fact-finding body thereby rendering it ineffective. Fact-finding to be effective must be of a specific and discernible fact or facts. The case of Laos in which the problem was to determine whether North Vietnam regular troops had crossed the Laotian border is an example of a fact difficult to discern. The topographical obstacles posed by the jungle terrain made observation difficult. In addition, considering the common ethnic origin of the Laotian and North Vietnamese, a North Vietnamese soldier out of uniform was not easily discernible, nor distinguishable, from a Laotian.

The case of the claims and counterclaims in the dispute between Cambodia and Thailand over border violations is an illustration of lack of specific facts to observe. In this instance, the borders were not clearly marked - in fact, unmarked and in dispute. A decision of the International Court of Justice was required to determine if a temple was located in the territory of Thailand or Cambodia. Obviously, under such circumstances, the possibility of determining a specific fact - the violation of borders - was remote because the borders were unmarked and in dispute.

The terms of reference of commissions of investigation established under the Organization of American States have been general in nature and broadly interpreted by the commissions. However, the diversity in the United Nations has not and does not permit such practice. It should be noted that the instances in which commissions of investigation were used by the Organization of American States were confined to securing an end to hostilities or of a situation which might lend to open warfare. The Commission in each such instance was given the task of conducting an on-the-spot investigation. Sometimes reference was made to investigating "the facts and their antecedents" and sometimes to "the pertinent facts". In all such instances, the Commission of Investigation interpreted its terms of reference as liberally as was necessary in order for it to carry out its task of putting an end to the situation.

C. Composition of Fact-Finding Bodies
 1. Size
The number constituting a fact-finding body has varied from one, as in the case of a special representative of the Secretary-General of the United Nations, or a rapporteur, as in the practice of the League, to as many as eleven or fifteen (the full membership of the United Nations Security Council or the League of Nations Council respectively). Out of twenty-one important fact-finding committees, eleven were composed of three members, two were composed of four members and eight were composed of five members. A membership of three to five would appear to have been usual for committees of investigation of the League of Nations and the United Nations. The size of investigating bodies of the Organization of American States has usually been five.

However, the size of an investigating body should be dependent primarily on the requirements dictated by the task. The United Nations Special Committee on Palestine, although composed of eleven members, was able to complete its work more efficiently by dividing into teams which covered a wide area. In some cases, where the Commission has

_____
[120]U. N. Security Council Official Records, First Year, Second Series, No. 28, pp. 700-1.

also had the responsibility of mediation or conciliation, the need to represent all interests, equally, influenced the size of the commission as in the India-Pakistan Dispute. The use of alternates on commissions is also helpful in permitting expansion of the activities of the commission in the field by having the alternates serve on working teams. Provision for alternates is usually made in the resolution establishing the commission.

The size of the commission becomes less important when the addition of delegations, as well as alternates, to the commission is considered. Usually, as in the case of the Commission of Investigation Concerning Greek Frontier Incidents, the resolutions establishing commissions provide that each member is entitled to select the personnel necessary to assist him. In addition, the resolutions request the Secretary-General to provide such staff and assistance to the commission as it deems necessary for the prompt and effective fulfillment of its task.

The size of a commission should be related to its functions. Where truce and conciliation or mediation are chiefly involved, a small compact group can operate more effectively. Where commissions whose main task is investigation are concerned they may well be larger in order to (1) more fully reflect the composition of the principal organ, (2) permit the members themselves to take part in the investigating teams and (3) allow adequate representation of minority views.[121]

2. Membership Selection

The membership selection and the organization of committee of investigation of the League of Nations would appear to follow a different pattern from that of the United Nations.

In the League of Nations' practice, the president of the commission was only in a few cases appointed in advance. Usually, the nationality of its members was fixed and their qualifications, diplomatic, military or otherwise. Then the President of the Council together with the Secretary-General unofficially approached the governments of countries whose nationals were sought to propose suitable persons to serve on the commission. Usually at least two persons were proposed and the selection was made mostly by the Secretary-General who tried to balance the group in such a manner as to enable it to work smoothly and effectively as a team.

Thus, the role of national governments in the process of appointment of members of commissions of investigation was safeguarded but at the same time two important results could be achieved: (1) The individuals selected considered themselves as impartial and independent experts and not as representatives of governments of their nationality. (2) The commission was constituted and worked as a well-balanced team composed of men of different but mutually complementing experience and professional backgrounds best suited for the particular task entrusted to them.

This practice of appointing individuals, not governments, was abandoned from the very beginning by the United Nations. Almost all United Nations commissions of investigation and fact-finding sub-committees have been composed of states, i.e., of persons appointed by their respective governments and acting under instructions in their representative

---

[121]U. N. Doc. A/AC/18/SC.6/6, Interim Committee of the General Assembly Study of the Organization and Operation of United Nations Commissions, p. II.

and not in their individual capacity.[122] One exception was the Commission to Investigate the Racial Conflict Resulting from the Policies of Apartheid of the Government of South Africa. Members of fact-finding bodies of the Organization of American States have also been selected as representatives of states.

Whether or not individuals or governments are appointed, the expertise in the staff of a commission as provided by the Secretariat insures the functioning of the commission. The stature and diplomatic experience of the members of the commission are important, however, in promoting better relations with the parties concerned, an important factor in the operation of the commission. Certainly, one factor in the method of selecting members of a commission should be concerned with the aura of impartiality and objectivity which should surround any fact-finding endeavor.

In an effort to achieve the objective of a commission of individual experts, the creation of a panel for inquiry and conciliation was provided for by resolution 268 (III), adopted by the General Assembly on April 28, 1949.[123] According to the resolution, the panel would consist of persons designated by the Members and would be available to "any States involved in controversies: and "to the General Assembly, the Security Council and their subsidiary organs, when exercising their respective functions in relation to disputes and situations." Each Member State would designate from one to five persons, "who by reason of their training, experience, character and standing are deemed to be well fitted to serve as members of commissions of inquiry."[124] The resolution also provided that the method of selecting members of a commission of inquiry of conciliation shall be determined in each case by the organ appointing the commission.[125]

The practice of the Organization of American States, as mentioned earlier, has been to designate states as members of its commissions of investigation. Representatives of the States so designated sitting on the Council of the Organization are then assigned to the commission of investigation. In this way, the ambassadorial rank of the members, the close relationship to the major organ and the support of their governments

---

[122]The League of Nations' tradition was voiced by Mr. Stettinius of the United States, on February 11, 1946, who, opposing a Ukranian motion to send a commission of inquiry to Indonesia, said "The United States believes that, as a general rule, any fact-finding or investigating commission ordered by the Council should be composed of impartial persons chosen for their competence, who would represent, not their individual countries, but the Security Council." (U. N. Security Council Official Records, First Year, First Series, No. 1, p. 235). The United States maintained this position in presenting, on September 20, 1946, a draft resolution, in the second Greek case, proposing that "The Security Council . . . establish a commission of three individuals to be nominated by the Secretary-General . . . on the basis of their competence and impartiality and to be confirmed by the Security Council." (U. N. Security Council Official Records, First Year, Second Series, No. 16, p. 396). However, on December 18, 1946, in the third Greek Case, the first proposal submitted by the United States for an investigation provided for "a commission . . . composed of a representative of each of the permanent members of the Council and of Brazil and Poland." (U. N. Security Council Official Records, First Year, Second Series, No. 27, p. 630).

[123]U. N. General Assembly Resolution 268D (III), April 28, 1949.

[124]Idem.

[125]See Appendix C infra for text of Resolution 268D (III).

adds prestige to the commission and enhances its position as an organ for conciliation.

3. Impartiality

In the practice of the United Nations, it would appear that impartiality would be more difficult to achieve insofar as selection of member states rather than individuals is the basis in the constitution of committees of investigation.[126] The problem would center on finding disinterested states by which is meant not only states without material interests involved in the dispute, or a political alliance with one of the parties, but states without any strong cultural or economic ties with one of the parties. That this is difficult to attain is shown by the following: The Spanish Sub-Committee included France and Poland; the Corfu Channel Sub-Committee contained Poland and Australia; the Greek Commission included the U.S. S.R., Poland, the United Kingdom and, after March 12, 1947, the United States of America; the Eritrean Commission had as a member Norway (allied with Britain), Guatemala (with Italian leanings) and Pakistan (a Moslem nation).

A certain kind of impartiality may be achieved by balancing evenly the the members biased in favor of the two opposing parties and selecting a detached and neutral country as chairman, coupled with taking decisions, at least on fact-finding matters, by a majority. Such a composition is more suitable, however, for commissions charged with conciliation and mediation, in addition to investigation.

One example, of this way of aiming for impartiality occurred in the Kashmir case where each party selected one country: India selected Czechoslovakia and Pakistan selected Argentina with the Security Council appointing reasonably neutral states, Belgium and Colombia, while the President of the Security Council appointed the United States as the impartial umpire.[127]

The interests of States cannot be discounted. Where states serve as members, the question naturally arises whether or not the representatives of the States serving on the commission act under instructions from their governments. It would be highly naive to assume that interested governments will leave to their representatives complete discretion and freedom of action. As one delegate pointed out, the absence of instructions may likely occur only where completely disinterested countries serve on the commission. That was what Mr. Parodi of France had in mind when, referring to the Special Committee on Palestine, on May 13, 1947, he said,

> The position of the members of that committee would lie
> between the two extremes . . . . They would have to act
> according to their conscience, and impartially. I do not
> think they should receive instructions from their govern-
> ments. They should not, however, be described as ex-
> perts so that their governments should not feel in any
> way bound by whatever attitude they may adopt . . . .[128]

In connection with the question of the impartiality of fact-finding bodies, the political background of the Cold War and the division of members of the United Nations into blocs must not be neglected. The Soviet view is that all of the members of the Security Council should be represented on commissions as the Security Council is, in itself, a reflection of the membership of the United Nations.[129]

The question of impartiality is a subjective one. When the Commis-

---

[126]See discussion supra this Chapter under paragraph 2 of the approach to achieving impartiality used by the Organization of American States.

[127]U. N. Doc. A/1100 (November 9, 1948).

[128]U. N. General Assembly Official Records, First Special Session, Vol. III, Main Committee, p. 335.

[129]L. Goodrich and A. Simons The United Nations and the Maintenance of International Peace & Security, (Wash: Brookings 1955, p. 194).

sion of Investigation concerning Greek Frontier Incidents was established, no objection was made by the Western bloc to the inclusion of Communist bloc states as members. In the Cyprus situation, the Greek Government specifically requested socialist state membership in the expectation that these states would be partial to its case.

The objection of impartiality is also affected by the criteria that the principal organs of the United Nations have, at times, used in setting up commissions such as geographic distribution, membership in the Security Council, appointment by the parties and/or direct interest.[130]

In conclusion, it would appear that the functions of a commission, which is composed of Member States, should have a strong bearing on the approach to be used in constituting the commission so as to achieve the greatest possibility of impartiality. Where the functions lean toward conciliation and mediation, the method of balancing directly interested parties with a neutral or neutrals is appropriate. Where the investigation is designed to put an end to hostilities, then only neutral members should compose the investigating body. If the investigation primarily is a fact-finding effort such as occurred in the Palestine situation, again, objective, as well as neutral, members should compose the investigating body.

Whether a commission composed of individuals selected on the basis of personal qualifications is more likely to be impartial than one composed of states is still open to question. The establishment of a panel for inquiry and conciliation by the United Nations General Assembly would indicate that those Member States voting for resolution 268D (III) providing for the panel were of the opinion that it was. The practice of the League of Nations would also indicate support for the position that commissions of inquiry composed of individuals selected on the basis of personal qualifications are more likely to be impartial.

Yet the experience of the United Nations with most of its commissions of investigation composed of Member States shows a high degree of objectivity in many of the inquiries that were undertaken. Perhaps this was due to greater reliance on small nations considered to be objective and neutral. The problem of finding such objective nations has been eased, somewhat, by the universality of the United Nations.

Perhaps the best guarantee of impartiality is illustrated by the approach taken by the Organization of American States which, incidentally, designates states as members of its commissions of investigations. In the Inter-American System, the guarantee of impartiality is achieved by approaching the task with a common interest in hemispheric peace and a recognition of the limitations imposed by the principle of sovereign equality.

4. Universality and Geographic Distribution

The universality of the United Nations is reflected in its practice of selecting commissions of investigation in contrast to that of the League of Nations, which was, apparently, a predominantly European institution. For example, of nine commissions of investigation of the League of Nations, composed of a total of thirty-four members, twenty-eight were of European origin, three were from the United States of America and three were from other areas. In United Nations' practice, of ten commissions examined, composed of a total of forty-one members, eighteen members were of European origin, three were from the United States of America and twenty were from other areas.

The principle of universality of representation on commissions is related to the criterion of geographic representation used by United Nations in setting up such commissions.

---

[130]U. N. Doc. A/AC. 18/SC. 6/6, p. 11.

Once the principle is accepted that a broad spectrum of states must exist on such commissions, it is only one step further to claim that equitable geographical distribution has to be preserved. The membership of the United Nations Special Committee on Palestine was based on such a criterion.[131] A similar idea was expressed in a Cuban draft resolution in the Mindszenty case, in 1949, to "appoint a Special Committee consisting of the representatives of fifteen nations representing different geographical areas and the main religious beliefs in order to elucidate the acts alleged . . . ."[132]

The matter of great power representation on commissions of investigation is of interest in comparing League of Nations' and United Nations' practice. Out of the above mentioned nine League of Nations commissions, composed of a total of thirty-four members, fourteen were representative nations of major powers (mainly European--of these fourteen, two were from the U.S.A.). Of the ten United Nations commissions, referred to above, consisting of a total of forty-one members, only six were from major powers (of these, the U.S.A. appointed three members and Japan appointed one, leaving France as a member on two other commissions).

The idea of great power representation on fact-finding bodies was considered essential on some of the League of Nations commissions of inquiry when nationalities of its members were being considered. The Lytton Commission was composed exclusively of nationals of big powers. A British Ambassador was appointed by the Council as chairman of the Demir-Kapu incident inquiry, concerning a dispute between Bulgaria and Greece in 1925. The Memel Commission, in 1924, was presided over by an American citizen, Norman H. Davis. An American, Abraham J. Elkus, served on the Aaland Islands Commission. French and British officers served on the Chaco and Spanish Commissions, and an Italian Ambassador served on the Chaco Commission. In all those instances, it was probably felt that the nationality of such members would add to the prestige and authority of their findings and would not impair the impartiality of their work. American nationality was at that time considered a guarantee of neutrality. In the Lytton case, particularly, dealing with an aggressive action by a big power, such prestige was essential, and considerations of exclusively appointing nationals of disinterested countries had to be sacrificed.

On the other hand, while the United Nations is based on the assumption of the primary responsibilities of the permanent members of the Security Council for the maintenance of international peace and security, the United Nations' practice shows that only the Commission of Investigation Concerning Greek Frontier Incidents included representatives of all five permanent members of the Council. China and France, of these powers, were also members of the Spanish Sub-Committee, and the United States served on the Commission for India and Pakistan.

One outstanding aspect of United Nations' practice in the composition of commissions of investigation, then, has been the universality of commission membership as reflected in (1) wider geographical distribution, (2) very little great power participation and (3) greater reliance on smaller neutral nations.

The practice of the Organization of American States, a regional or-

---

[131]U. N. General Assembly Official Records, Fourth Session, Supplement No. 11A, p. 15.

[132]U. N. General Assembly Official Records, Third Session, Ad Hoc Political Committee. (U.N. Doc. A/A6/24/48, Rev. 2, April 20, 1949).

ganization, has been to include the United States on almost all commissions of investigation with only two exceptions, in recent years, in one
of which the United States was a party.[133] This has been an indication of
the prominent position of the United States in the peaceful settlement of
such disputes and is a reflection of its vital interest in the Carribean
and its larger interest as a leader in the Organization of American States
and in peaceful settlement anywhere in the western hemisphere.[134]

[133]The United States has also been included on the sub-committees
of the Inter-American Peace Committee.

[134]Henry Myron Blackmer, The United States Policy and the Inter-
American Peace System 1889-1952, Paris: 1952, p. 193.

# CHAPTER VI

## OPERATION OF FACT-FINDING BODIES

A.  Rules of Procedure[1]

The rules of procedure of a commission of inquiry are of vital importance to the smooth functioning of the commission. The question revolves mainly about what rules are desirable, in light of the experience of the League of Nations and the United Nations. Perhaps this question has been recognized as of more urgency in the United Nations' practice than in the League's practice because of the more formal constitution of United Nations commissions.

In all instances, United Nations commissions of investigation - or commissions to some extent concerned with fact-finding - have been authorized to establish rules of procedure. Not all have adopted written rules, however. In such cases, as far as possible, the commission has tended to follow procedural practices of the principal organ, either of the Security Council or of the General Assembly, as the case might be. Five commissions which adopted formal rules of procedure from the beginning were the United Nations Special Committee on Palestine, the United Nations Palestine Commission, the United Nations Temporary Commission on Korea, the United Nations Special Committee on the Balkans, and the United Nations Commission for India and Pakistan.[2]

Four commissions which did not adopt any written rules of procedure were the Commission of Investigation Concerning Greek Frontier Incidents, its Subsidiary Group, the Security Council Truce Commission for Palestine and the Security Council Consular Commission at Batavia. One commission that began operations without any formal rules of procedure but felt compelled to adopt them later was the Security Council Committee of Good Offices on Indonesia. These, however only applied to meetings of the Committee with the parties. Provisional rules of procedure were used when the Committee sat along.

The problem of whether or not to have a set of formal rules can delay the work of a commission as occurred in the case of the Commission on

---

[1]The material in this section has been taken from the studies made by the United Nations Interim Committee of the organization and procedure of United Nations commissions and from information obtained from members of the United Nations Secretariat who have served on the staff of United Nations commissions.

[2]Rules of procedure were also adopted by the United Nations Commission to Investigate Conditions for Free Elections in Germany, the Special Committee on the policies of apartheid of the Government of the Republic of South Africa, the United Nations Mission to the Republic of South Viet-Nam, the Security Council Sub-Committee on Incidents in the Corfu Channel and the Security Council Sub-Committee on Laos.

Eritrea. The Commission of Investigation Concerning Greek Frontier Incidents, which did not adopt formal rules, encountered problems in its operation which required the time of a special sub-committee and sometimes of the entire commission because it was compelled to operate by decisions on procedure. The Subsidiary Group of the United Nations Commission of Investigation Concerning Greek Frontier Incidents followed the practices and precedents established by the main Commission.

The advantages of a set of formal rules of procedure are (1) the saving in time for the commission at its inception and during its operation and (2) a certain amount of continuity in the event of changes in personnel. The use of model sets of rules, based on the experiences of previous commissions, as a basis for adoption of a set of rules of procedure is both practical and efficient.[3] A small commission can work well, however, without frequent resort to its rules of procedure.

The most important points of procedure which should be clarified at the inception of a commission are: (1) chairmanship, (2) agenda, (3) keeping of records, (4) methods of taking decisions, (5) publicity and press releases, (6) appointment of liaison officers and (7), gathering of documentary and testimonial evidence.

1. Chairmanship

The device of rotation of chairmanship in the alphabetical order of the names of countries represented was followed by the Council of the League of Nations, itself, in its rules of procedure.[4] This was an expression of the political character of the Council and a mechanical application of the principle of equality. However, in the case of commissions of inquiry since they consisted of individuals and not of states, it was only natural for them to elect a chairman for the entire period of their work. The League followed, in practice, as does the Organization of American States, the principle of having a permanent chairman for each commission of inquiry.

Under the United Nations, the device of rotating chairmanship was used by most of the investigating commissions. It was taken over from Security Council practice by the Commission of Investigation Concerning Greek Frontier Incidents, for example, and shortened to a one week rotation.[5]

The practice of rotation of chairmanship weekly was also adopted by the Subsidiary Group of the Greek Frontier Incidents Commission and by the Security Council Committee of Good Offices on Indonesia. The Commission to Investigate Conditions for Free Elections in Germany adopted a rule providing for the rotation of the chairmanship every month and the United Nations Commission for India and Pakistan rotated the chairmanship every three weeks.

The Commission For Eritrea of the General Assembly almost appointed a permanent chairman. It elected its Norwegian member as chairman at its third meeting as permanent chairman but, at its thirty-sixth meeting, switched to weekly rotation. This change created difficulties in one of its sub-commissions. Sub-Commission 1 on economic aspects elected its South African member as chairman. After the rules of procedure of the main Commission had been amended, the Guatemalan delegation re-

---

[3]Interim Committee of the General Assembly Organization and Procedure of United Nations Commissions (XII) Comparative Tabulation of the Rules of Procedure of United Nations Commissions, (1950); also, see Interim Committee of the General Assembly, Sub-Committee 2, Proposal submitted by China & the U. S., Part III Rules of Procedure for Commissions. (U. N. Doc. A/AC. 18/SC. 2/2.) Appendix B. infra.

[4]L. of N. Doc. C93. 1933 V, p. 900.

[5]U. N. Doc. S/360, p. 6 (May 23, 1947).

quested that the rotation of chairmanship rule be applied in Sub-Commission 1. The Chairman refused to apply this rule on the grounds that the rule concerning election of officers of subsidiary bodies had not been amended.[6]  One true exception to the practice of rotating the chairmanship was the Special Committee on Palestine which elected as permanent chairman its Swedish member, Justice Emil Sandstrom. [7]

The rotation rule of chairmanship applied to investigating bodies is of a political nature and may possibly result in reducing their efficiency. In view of the difficulties, it was reported, that were encountered, at times, in the matter of chairmanship, it would be better for the organ constituting the investigating commission to consider the question of chairmanship of the commission or for a permanent chairman to be chosen by the investigating body itself. As one member of the Secretariat with extensive experience with investigating bodies pointed out, the competence of the chairman is an important factor in a commission's activities, particularly, in the matter of close cooperation with the staff, the witnesses and the authorities.

2. Agenda

The rules of procedure of the Palestine Commission, the Temporary Commission on Korea, the Commission for India and Pakistan and the Commission of Investigation Concerning Greek Frontier Incidents provided that the provisional agenda be drawn up by the secretariat in consultation with the Chairman. The Special Committee on the Balkans, in its rules of procedure, provided that the provisional agenda be drawn up by the Principal Secretary and approved by the Chairman.

With regard to notification, the rules of procedure of the Temporary Commission on Korea, the Commission for India and Pakistan and the Palestine Commission required that the provisional agenda be communicated to the representatives of the Commission. As to time of notification, the rule of the Palestine Commission noted "as early as practicable before the opening of the meeting" while the Commission for India and Pakistan rules provided "when practicable in advance of the meeting".[8]

The provisional agenda should include
  (1) Items proposed by the commission at a previous meeting
  (2) Items proposed by a member of the commission
  (3) Items proposed by the principal organ
  (4) Items proposed by a sub-commission of the organ
  (5) All items, communications or reports which the chairman or the secretariat may deem necessary to put before the organ[9]
The first item on the provisional agenda of any meeting of a commission should be the adoption of the agenda.[10]

The need for an agenda is not always present to an equal degree but a proper agenda is important or useful discussion may not be possible. The Security Council Committee of Good Offices on Indonesia realized the need for rules of procedure and of an agenda as it proceeded. Certainly, adoption of a detailed agenda at the initial meetings will serve to focus attention on any points in the terms of reference which need clarification. The use of an initial detailed agenda to underline the task of the commission and as a basis for setting up its schedule of operations is also desirable.

3 Keeping of Records

The rules of procedure of the Special Committee on the Balkans, the

---

[6]U. N. Doc. A/1285 (June 8, 1950), p. 4.

[7]U. N. Doc. A/364 (September 3, 1947).

[8]Organization and Procedure of United Nations Commissions XII.

[9]Idem.

[10]Idem.

Special Committee on Palestine, the Palestine Commission, the Temporary Commission on Korea and the Commission for India and Pakistan provided that only summary records of public and private meetings should be drawn up unless the necessity for verbatim records in respect of a specific meeting or part of a meeting was recognized by the Commission. The Temporary Commission on Korea and the Commission for India and Pakistan added the proviso to this rule: "after consultation with the Secretariat".

As to the availability of the records, the rules of procedure of the Palestine Commission, the Special Committee on the Balkans, the Commission for India and Pakistan and the Temporary Commission on Korea provided that the records shall be made available as soon as possible to the members of the Commission. The rules of the Special Committee on the Balkans provided for summary records of each meeting to be made available, also, to representatives of any States which have participated in the meeting. The Security Council Committee of Good Offices on Indonesia provided with respect to conferences with the parties that copies of summary records should be transmitted to the Committee of Good Offices and to the parties.

In one case, the failure of the Indonesian Committee of Good Offices to inform one party of its meeting with the other party led to serious misunderstandings which were dispelled only by assurance on the part of the Committee that it would automatically transmit to both parties records of future meetings. Usually, the practice has been, in the case of private meetings, to distribute the records only to those who participated in the meetings.[11]

The Commission of Investigation Concerning Greek Frontier Incidents, in its rules of procedure, provided that documents and records pertaining to public meetings should be distributed to liaison representatives but that, unless a decision to the contrary was taken, documents and records pertaining to private meetings should be distributed only to representatives present at the meetings.[12]

Two commissions, the Special Committee on the Balkans and the Special Committee on Palestine, further provided that verbatim records would be taken of evidence or hearings and made available to members of the Commission.

With respect to corrections, the Palestine Commission, the Temporary Commission on Korea and the Commission for India and Pakistan provided that members should inform the secretariat, not later than twenty-four hours after the receipt of the records, of any corrections they wished to be made. The rules of the Commission for India and Pakistan also provided that each representative would have the right to annex verbatim or explanatory statements to the summary records. The Special Committee on the Balkans provided a period of four working days after the records had been made available to them in which members of the Special Committee who had participated in meetings could inform the Principal Secretary of any corrections or additions they wished to have made in the records.

Records in which no corrections have been requested or which have been corrected in accordance with the rules of procedure were considered as the official records of the Commission according to the rules of the Palestine Commission, the Commission on India and Pakistan and the Temporary Commission on Korea. This was also provided for in the rules of the Security Council Committee of Good Offices on Indonesia which applied to conferences with the parties. The rules of procedure of the last

---

[11]U. N. Doc. A/AC. 18/SC.6/6, p. 20.

[12]Organization and Procedure of United Nations Commissions XII.

committee contained the following rule which is a good example of possible treatment of records:

Communications shall be considered as having an official
status when they bear the signature of a representative
of the Committee of Good Offices or the Head of the delegation of either party or their authorized deputies. Working papers shall be clearly marked as such, shall be
classified and marked as confidential, and shall not have
any binding character. Copies of such documents may be
given a symbol number and be distributed to the Committee
of Good Offices and to the parties at the discretion of the
Chairman in consultation with the Secretary. Other papers
shall be considered as oral notes and shall be destroyed
after use, no reference to them being permitted in any
meeting or in any document having an official status.[13]

The keeping of records, and their distribution is the work of the
secretariat of a commission. It is helpful to the work of a commission
to keep summary records of all formal meetings. This practice has
been followed by several commissions. Keeping verbatim records of oral
testimony in the field has been the practice in some cases and is also to
be recommended. The prompt distribution of records to all interested
parties has been found to contribute to the efficiency of operations.

4. Methods of Taking Decisions

A number of resolutions of the United Nations Security Council and
the General Assembly have specified, in establishing commissions, that
the decisions of the commission should be taken by majority vote. Examples are the Special Committee on Palestine, the Special Committee
on the Balkans and the Temporary Commission on Korea.

In practice, many commissions although empowered by their rules of
procedure to reach decisions by a majority vote, elected to employ the
principal of unanimity. These included the Commission on India and Pakistan, the Commission to Investigate Conditions for Free Elections in
Germany, the Fact-Finding Mission to the Republic of South Viet-Nam
and the Committee of Good Offices on Indonesia.

The Commission of Investigation Concerning Greek Frontier Incidents
attempted to reach decisions without a formal vote. Only when it was impossible to reach a decision by general agreement, did the Chairman call
for a simple majority vote.

The inclusion in resolutions establishing commissions of a provision
specifying that decisions may be taken by a majority vote is suggested.
Or if not specified in the enabling resolution, then such a provision specifying majority voting should be incorporated in the Commission's rules
of procedure. In the event that a commission may decide thereafter to
follow a rule requiring unanimity, as in the case of the United Nations
Commission for India and Pakistan, it may still do so. In practice, most
commissions have observed the principal of unanimity voluntarily.

For the purposes of the rules, five commissions regarded the phrase
"members present and voting" as meaning members casting affirmative
or negative vote, with the consideration that members who abstained from
voting were considered as not voting.[14]

With respect to the mechanism of voting, four commissions provided
for a vote by show of hands unless a member requested a roll-call.[15] The

---

[13]Idem.

[14]Palestine Commission, Temporary Commission on Korea, Commission for India and Pakistan, the Special Committee on the Balkans,
Special Committee on Palestine.

[15]Special Committee on the Balkans, Special Committee on Palestine,
Temporary Commission on Korea, Commission for India and Pakistan.

rules of these commissions, in addition, provided that the vote of each member participating in any roll-call should be inserted in the record.

The rules of procedure of several commissions also contained detailed provisions for voting on parts of a proposal, on amendments, on two or more proposals and with respect to where the vote is equally divided.[16] It would appear that the question of voting lends itself to detailed coverage in the rules of procedure of commissions.

5. Publicity and Press Releases

The rules of procedure of four United Nations commissions endorsed the principle that meetings of the commission should be held in public unless the commission decided otherwise.[17] However, the Palestine Commission provided, in its rules of procedure, that the Commission was to decide in each instance which of its meetings were to be open to the public. But the Security Council Committee of Good Offices on the Indonesian Question followed a rule that provided, with respect to conferences with the parties, that unless otherwise decided by the Steering Committee, meetings of the conference were to be held in private.[18]

The usual practice has been to take the testimony of witnesses in closed sessions although all commissions have endorsed the principal of open meetings. It is also customary to discuss procedural matters and to draft reports in closed meetings.

The matter of publicity is related to the efficient functioning of a commission. A certain amount of notification is necessary in order to bring the activities of the commission to the attention of interested parties who may wish to contribute information. This has not presented a problem in practice. The Special Committee on the Situation in Angola, for example, was amazed at the extent to which its activities, purpose and whereabouts had been circulated through private contacts, in an area it was not permitted to visit.

It is more likely that notification of a commission's visit would be channelled through the usual media of information. In the case of the United Nations Malaysia Mission, for example, the widest publicity by means of radio, press and government announcements was given in Sarawak regarding the Mission and its terms of reference.[19]

Rules of procedure do not refer specifically to "notification". The rules with respect to "press releases" cover that aspect of a commission's work requiring that notification of the commission's arrival and task be communicated to interested parties. Such information is usually conveyed through information media by means of press communiques issued with the approval of the chairman of a commission.

The question of approval of press communiques and the manner of their release has been dealt with in various ways by United Nations commissions. The rules of procedure of the Special Committee on the Balkans, the Temporary Commission on Korea and the Commission for India and Pakistan provided that official press releases should be previously approved by the Chairman while unofficial press releases or verbal briefings might be issued by the press officer unless instructions to the contrary were given by the Commission. The Special Committee on the Balkans also provided for official press releases to be approved by the Chairman

---

[16]Organization and Procedure of United Nations Commissions XII.

[17]Temporary Commission on Korea, Commission on India and Pakistan, Special Committee on Palestine, Special Committee on the Balkans. The Commission of Investigation Concerning Greek Frontier Incidents endorsed the same principle by decision.

[18]Organization and Procedure of United Nations Commissions, XII.

[19]U. N. Doc. A/5694 (May 1, 1964), p. 125.

as did the Commission of Investigation concerning Greek Frontier Incidents and the Committee of Good Offices on the Indonesian Question. However, the rules of procedure of the Palestine Commission merely stated that press releases would be issued as a rule following each closed meeting, in such form as circumstances might require. [20]

6. Appointment of Liaison Officers

The problem of liaison is a two-way problem. Its importance, cannot be underestimated. Usually United Nations commissions of investigation have invited the parties to appoint permanent liaison officers or delegations. The rules of procedure of the Special Commitee on Palestine provided that the mandatory Power, the Arab Higher Committee, and the Jewish Agency for Palestine might appoint liaison officers to the Committee who would supply such information or render such other assistance as the Committee might require. It was also provided that the liaison officers might present on their own initiative, at the discretion of the Committee, such information as they might think advisable.

Under its rules of procedure, the Special Committee on the Balkans had similar provisions with regard to the appointment of liaison officers by the Albanian, Bulgarian, Greek and Yugoslav Governments. The Palestine Commission also provided, in similar fashion, for the appointment of liaison officers designated by the mandatory Power, the Arab Higher Commitee and the Jewish Agency for Palestine with the additional provision, that such representatives, on being invited by the Commission to attend a meeting, might speak only when called upon by the Chairman.

A decision on rules of procedure of the Commission of Investigation Concerning Greek Frontier Incidents permitted the liaison representatives of Albania, Bulgaria, Greece and Yugoslavia to participate in the discussions as the representatives of those countries had participated in discussions in the Security Council during consideration of the Greek complaint. Although the Commission determined the selection of witnesses, precedence was given to those presented by the respective liaison representatives.[21]

There have been exceptions to the practice of appointing liaison officers. The Security Council Consular Commission at Batavia dealt directly with representatives of the Governments of the Netherlands and the Republic of Indonesia, resorting to the same channels the individual members used in performing their consular duties. The United Nations Mediator for Palestine sent personal representatives to Tel Aviv and the capitals of the states bordering on Palestine as well as sending a similar representative to Jerusalem to maintain contact with the Truce Commission. The representatives of the Secretary-General in Yeman, Cyprus and Jordan maintained contacts with the governments in the respective capitals.

Where commissions have invited the parties to appoint liaison officers, in some cases one or more of the parties have refused or delayed the appointment. This occurred in the cases of the United Nations Special Committee on Palestine, the United Nations Special Committee on the Balkans, the Palestine Commission, the United Nations Temporary Commission on Korea and the United Nations Commission for India and Pakistan.

Commissions should provide in their rules of procedure for the appointment of liaison officers by the interested parties and the relationship of the liaison officers with the commission covering such topics as attending public meetings, presenting information and participating in discussions.[22]

---

[20]Idem.

[21]Idem.

[22]Organization and Procedure of United Nations Commissions XII.

## 7. Oral and Written Testimony

The rules of procedure are usually general in referring to oral and written testimony. The United Nations Special Committee on Palestine incorporated in its rules of procedure the following general principles concerning oral and written testimony:

> The Committee may, at its discretion, invite representatives of governments or organizations, or private individuals, to submit oral or written testimony on any relevant matter. Requests for oral hearing shall contain an indication of the subject or subjects on which the witness desires to testify. The Committee may refer to a sub-committee for examination and recommendation such requests to present oral testimony as it deems advisable.

> The Committee shall in each case decide the time and place of the hearing of any witness from whom it may decide to receive oral testimony. The Committee may advise any witness to submit his testimony in writing. The Committee, on the basis of the time available to it, may limit either the number of witnesses or the time to be allowed to any witnesses.

> The Committee may refer to a sub-committee for study and report such written testimony as it may deem advisable.

Similar practice was later followed by the United Nations Special Committee on the Balkans, the United Nations Temporary Commission on Korea, and the United Nations Commission for India and Pakistan.[23]

The Commission of Investigation Concerning Greek Frontier Incidents provided by a decision on rules of procedure that all requests for a hearing were to be referred to a Committee of Experts which, without having the power to censure, was to ascertain the standing and purpose of such bodies as were not known beforehand. In addition, the Commission itself, was to advise any individuals or organizations to limit statements to such points as might be of some use to the Commission in the completion of its task.[24]

The valuable portion of a hearing is the oral testimony adduced through interrogation. Where written statements are read by a witness, time that could be used for interrogation is lost. It would be well to incorporate in the rules of procedure a provision prohibiting the reading of written statements at hearings. This would forestall the predicament in which the United Nations Special Committee on Palestine found itself, when a witness reading a long prepared statement over the Committee's objections, insisted on equal treatment.[25]

In general, it can be said that the use of oral and written testimony has been within the discretion of the commission of investigation subject only to such limitations as lack of time or failure of a party to cooperate may have imposed.

With respect to the rules of procedure of commissions of investigation, the following basic conclusions can be drawn:

1. The practice has been, and should be, for each commission to establish its own rules.

2. It would be well to include a provision in the rules of procedure that they are applicable to subsidiary organs of the commission.

3. The studies by the United Nations Interim Committee of rules of

---

[23]U. N. Doc. A/AC. 18/SC. 6/6, pp. 29-30.

[24]Organization and Procedure of United Nations Commissions XII.

[25]U. N. Doc. A/364 (September 3, 1947).

procedure used by previous United Nations commissions can be useful to a commission in the preparation of its rules of procedure.

## B. Cooperation of the Parties

There is no question that cooperation of the parties makes easier the fulfillment of its task by the fact-finding body. In most cases, governments have cooperated with commissions of investigation in supplying them with transportation and other facilities. Sometimes the aid has come from neighboring states as was the case of the Congo Republic (Leopoldville) in furnishing facilities to the Sub-Committee on The Situation in Angola.[26] Similar assistance from a neighboring state was also helpful to the Special Committee on the Problem of Hungary.[27]

Where there has been failure to cooperate, such failure may occur on two levels. Either the party may object to the authority of the fact-finding body as not founded on legality or the party, may without openly protesting the legality of the fact-finding body, nevertheless, place obstacles before it in the performance of its task.

Two instances, examples of the second type of non-cooperation, occurred during the period of the League of Nations. The Lytton inquiry in the Manchurian crisis experienced the frustration of having the Chinese assessors attached to the Commission arrested by the Japanese authorities. The close Japanese surveillance of the Commission was also a cause for complaint by Lord Lytton.[28] Obstacles were also created for the Mosul Commission of Inquiry caused by the British authorities insisting that the Commission submit its itinerary in advance for approval; a procedure to which the Commission objected as destroying the possibility of an impartial inquiry.[29]

The practice has been, where there has been failure to cooperate, to base the refusal to cooperate on legal grounds. Such objections may be based on claims as to limitations created by the subject matter of the inquiry as was the case in the Polish-Lithuania dispute over Vilna, in 1920, in which both parties, it was noted by the League Council, though maintaining their acceptance of the Council's resolution of October 18, 1920, had created obstacles to the carrying out of the resolution.[30] Lithuania objected to establishing a commission of inquiry to set up a line of demarcation in the neutral zone on the grounds that Lithuania had not accepted the principle underlying the Council's proposal.[31]

The United Nations has had more experiences with failure to cooperate based upon legal objections than did the League of Nations. These legal objections have centered about Article 2, paragraph 7, of the Charter which states

> Nothing contained in the present Charter shall authorize the United Nations to intervene in matters which are essentially within the domestic jurisdiction of any state or shall require the Member to submit such matters to settlement under the present Charter; but this principle shall not prejudice the application of enforcement measures under Chapter VII.

Article 2, paragraph 7 has not prevented the General Assembly from initiating investigations into matters which, it has been claimed, fall within the domestic jurisdiction of the State against which the complaint was lodged. The refusal of such States, claiming that an investigation constitutes illegal intervention, to co-operate with a commission of investi-

---

[26]U. N. Doc. A/4978 (November 20, 1961).

[27]U. N. Doc. A/3546 (January 10, 1957).

[28]Alexander Victor Lytton, op. cit., p. 212.

[29]L. of N. Doc. C.400.M.147 (1925) VII, pp. 8-9.

[30]L. of N. Official Journal, (1921) Second Year, No. 2, p. 181.

[31]L. of N. Official Journal, (1922), 6, (P II), p. 551.

gation thus created has hindered the conduct of several investigations.

The situation in Hungary in 1956 provides one example of such refusal. On November 4, 1956, the General Assembly adopted a resolution which, among other clauses, contained a request to the Secretary-General [32]

> to investigate the situation caused by foreign intervention in Hungary, to observe the situation directly through representatives named by him, and to report to the General Assembly at the earliest moment . . . .

and called

> upon the Governments of Hungary and the U.S.S.R. to permit observers designated by the Secretary-General to enter the territory of Hungary, to travel freely therein and report their findings to the Secretary-General.

The U. S. S. R. and seven other states with communist governments voted against the resolution.[33] Hungary did not take part in the vote.[34] In subsequent developments, the Hungarian Government rejected the Secretary-General's request that permission be granted for the entry and free travel within Hungary of the observers to be designated by him as asked by the General Assembly.[35] A similar aide-memoire, directed, on November 10, to the Government of the U. S. S. R. asking for its assistance in the fulfillment of his mandate was likewise rebuffed.[36] Both the Hungarian Government and the Soviet Government regarded the situation in Hungary as exclusively within the "internal competence of the Hungarian State."[37] Any resolution of the General Assembly concerning the country's internal political situation was, therefore, according to the Soviet Union's position, an interference in Hungary's internal affairs, and a contradiction of the United Nations Charter provision against intervention in essentially domestic affairs.[38]

The Hungarian and Soviet Governments pursued these arguments in their objection to the subsequent General Assembly proceedings which produced the resolution creating the Special Committee on The Problem of Hungary.[39] The question of the legality of the United Nations' intervention in the Hungary crisis is basic to the determination of the legality

---

[32]U. N. General Assembly Official Records, Resolutions 1955-59, Second Emergency Special Session Nov. 4-10, 1956, p. 2. (Resolution 1004 (ES-11).)

[33]U. N. General Assembly Official Records, First-Second Emergency Special Session, 564th P.M., p. 20.

[34]Idem.

[35]U. N. General Assembly Official Records, Twelfth Session, Supplement No. 1, pp. 35 and 37.

[36]Idem.

[37]Idem.

[38]Ibid., p. 40. The extent to which the legal basis for the Hungarian and Soviet objections influenced other members of the United Nations cannot be stated with certainty. Aside from the negative votes of members associated with the Soviet bloc, fifteen members abstained, many of whom expressed some agreement with the legal position of the Soviet bloc with respect to the lack of power of the General Assembly to deal with a purely internal situation. (Ibid., p. 33.)

[39]The Hungarian position was expressed in U. N. Doc. A/3521 (February 5, 1957).

of the establishment of the Special Committee and of its activities.[40]

The position taken by the Special Committee in its report,[41] which was endorsed by the General Assembly, contradicted the Soviet and Hungarian positions. The Special Committee concluded, after a study of the facts, that

In the light of the extent of foreign intervention, consideration of the Hungarian question by the United Nations was legally proper and, moreover, it was requested by a legal Government of Hungary. In the matter of human rights, Hungary has accepted specific international obligations in the Treaty of Peace. Accordingly, the Committee does not regard objections based on paragraph 7 of Article 2 of the Charter as having validity in the present case. A massive armed intervention by one Power in the territory of another, with the avowed intention of interfering with the internal affairs of the country must, by the Soviet's own definition of aggression, be a matter of international concern.[42]

Austria was the only neighboring country that accepted the United Nations Special Committee on The Problem of Hungary. Czechoslovakia, Romania, the Soviet Union, Yugoslavia and Hungary refused admission to the Committee.[43]

Portugal, also, took a negative position with regard to the Sub-Committee on the Situation in Angola. Considering Angola an integral part of its national territory, Portugal invoked Article 2, paragraph 7 of the Charter more than once.[44] The subsequent failure of efforts by the Sub-Committee to obtain the cooperation of the Government of Portugal in permitting an on-the-spot inquiry in Angola was to be expected.[45]

The Republic of South Africa, on the other hand, while objecting to the jurisdiction of the United Nations over South-West Africa, permitted the chairman and the vice-chairman, but not the entire membership, of the Special Committee on South West Africa to conduct an on-the-spot investigation in the territory. The position the Republic of South Africa took was that it could not permit the entire committee to visit the territory without thereby accepting the jurisdiction of the United Nations.[46]

States have indicated in the past, that in the absence of consent by the parties, no useful purpose could be obtained in establishing a commission. In 1946, a proposed United Nations inquiry into the situation in Indonesia was not initiated because of lack of support from either the Netherlands or the United Kingdom. The majority of members of the General Assembly also decided in 1949 against a commission to study the treatment of Indians in South Africa and against a commission to study

---

[40]For a detailed discussion of the legal aspects of the situation, see Joseph Alexander Szikszoy, The Legal Aspects of The Hungarian Question, Ambilly-Annemasse, France: Les Presses de Savoie, 1963.

[41]U. N. General Assembly, Official Records, Eleventh Session, Supplement No. 18 (U. N. Doc. A/3592).

[42]Ibid., para. 785 (XIII).

[43]Ibid.

[44]U. N. Doc. A/4978 (November 20, 1961), p. 6.

[45]Ibid., pp. 8-10.

[46]U. N. Doc. A/5212 (August 31, 1962). The Government of the Republic of South Africa had also based its objections to the U. N. Commission to investigate the apartheid policy in South Africa on Article 2 (7). (U. N. General Assembly Official Records, Seventh Session, Plenary Meetings, pp. 331-332.)

the question of human rights and fundamental freedoms in Bulgaria and Hungary.

On the other hand, commissions of inquiry were set up over the objections of the State in whose territory the investigation would take place, in the question of the racial situation in South Africa in 1952 and 1962 and in 1961 in the question of Angola and in consideration of the situation in South West Africa.

In between these two attitudes, it is worth noting the attitude of the Assembly with regard to the commission to investigate the charges of bacterial warfare and the commission to investigate the conditions for free elections in Germany. In the first case, the creation of the commission was made dependent on "an indication from all the governments and authorities concerned of their acceptance of the investigation"[47] while in the second case, the investigation of the commission, which was established, was subject to the conclusion of satisfactory arrangements with all the governments and authorities concerned.[48]

There have been three instances in the experience of the Organization of American States when states rejected co-operation with commissions of conciliation and investigation. The first such instance occurred in 1960 when the Dominican Republic, exercising its option under Resolution IV, paragraph 2 of the Fifth Meeting of Consultation of the Ministers of Foreign Affairs,[49] rejected the request of the Inter-American Peace Committee for permission to visit the Dominican Republic.

The other two instances concerned the Government of Cuba. In 1961, that Government refused to co-operate with the Inter-American Peace Committee in its investigation of the facts concerning a complaint by the Government of Peru denouncing acts committed by the Government of Cuba which allegedly were detrimental to the peace and security of the western hemisphere.[50] The Cuban Government, in 1964, rejected a request for information from a committee established by the Council of the Organization of American States to investigate the facts regarding the denunciation by the Government of Venezuela of acts of intervention and aggression by the Government of Cuba which affected the territorial sovereignty of Venezuela. The Cuban Government announced, in rejecting the Committee's request, that it did not recognize the jurisdiction of the Organization of American States.[51]

C. Sources of Information

Few restrictions have been placed on commissions of inquiry with respect to their discretion in determining the sources from which they could seek information. Sometimes, the geographical area within which they were to work has been specified in advance and, on some occasions, the commission has been directed to include specific sources in its inquiry.

For the most part, commissions have been enterprising in seeking information actively, rather than merely evaluating information that was voluntarily submitted. The value of on-the-spot investigations has been accepted and the few instances in United Nations' practice that on-the-spot investigations have not taken place have been due to opposition on the part of states to an investigation in their territory.

For example, the Spanish problem was not investigated by the United

[47]U. N. General Assembly Resolution 706 (VII), April 23, 1952.

[48]U. N. General Assembly Resolution 510 (VI), December 20, 1951.

[49]American Journal of International Law (1961) Vol. 56, pp. 539-540.

[50]Pan American Union Inter-American Treaty of Reciprocal Assistance, Applications, Vol. 2, (Washington: 1964), pp. 69-70.

[51]Ibid., pp. 182-183.

Nations on-the-spot because the Franco Government did not permit a United Nations commission to enter Spain.[52] In the Corfu Channel case, no doubt, whatever, existed that the Soviet Union would block any resolution for an on-the-spot investigation using the same argument as it did, in September 1946, that such a decision implies that the accusation is substantiated.[53] On-the-spot investigations were also blocked in the Hungarian uprising of 1956, the question of apartheid in South Africa and the matter of Angola as well as in the matter of free elections in Germany. The League of Nations did not encounter this problem because the consent of the parties in whose territory the investigation was to take place was obtained in advance.

Where the wishes of the population are to be ascertained, especially, as in the Aaland Islands Inquiry, a visit to the locale is imperative. Ascertaining the wishes of the population was also a requirement in the cases of the Albanian Frontiers, of Memel, of Mosul, and, to some extent, of the Mancurian Situation under the League of Nations, as well as of Eritrea and of Palestine under the United Nations.

The usual sources open to commissions are either written or oral and all can be said to have used both oral and written testimony although in varying degrees. In some cases, oral testimony has been minimal. Contrasted to this are the extensive oral hearings undertaken in Europe and the Middle East by the United Nations Special Committee on Palestine. Where the volume of oral testimony becomes too great, some method of selection must be adopted and effective procedures for taking oral testimony instituted. In the case of the accumulation of written material, the Secretariat of the United Nations (and of the League of Nations) has been very helpful. The United Nations Secretariat prepared for the United Nations Special Committee on Palestine five volumes of material as well as preliminary material for the United Nations Temporary Commission on Korea.

Where governments have cooperated, a large amount of information has been made available to the commissions in the form of documents outlining their positions. In the Palestine dispute many such documents were submitted on the part of the Jewish authorities. The liaison officers attached to commissions of inquiry have also been helpful in obtaining information from their governments.

Where hostilities are in progress, information can be obtained from prisoners, custom officials, other officials in the locale of the warfare, hospital cases, civilian residents in, and refugees from, the area. Captured military equipment as well as the sites of battle, including fortification and documents found there, also provide information.

While the sources open to commissions are similar, certain factors may result in more emphasis being placed on the use of some sources in preference to others. Opposition of a party to an inquiry in its territory would be such an influencing factor. Typical of such an inquiry is that which took place as a result of the Hungarian uprising in 1956, when resort was had to refugees, officials and personnel of non-governmental organizations and governmental sources with diplomatic representation in the locale. The Sub-Committee on the Situation in Angola, also, took testimony from refugees from the territory and from missionaries and business men who had just departed from the territory.

Three other possible influential factors would be:

(1) Whether the facts to be gathered are historical or current and to what extent clarification and evaluation of the information is necessary.

(2) The area of operations of the commission.

(3) The time limit on the investigation.

---

[52]The New York Times, April 13, 1946, pp. 1 and 6.

[53]U. N. Security Council Official Records, First Year, Second Series, No. 16, p. 397.

## D. Logistics and Operations [54]

The operational and logistical problems of fact-finding bodies are mainly concerned with the staff, communication and transportation, and immunity of personnel and witnesses.

The staff and arrangements for travel and operation of commissions of investigation are provided for by the Secretariat of the United Nations. [55] The staff of the United Nations Commission for India and Pakistan, appointed by the Secretary-General, consisted of (1) a principal secretary and personal representative of the Secretary-General, (2) a military adviser, (3) a legal adviser and deputy principal secretary, (4) a personal assistant to the principal secretary, (5) a press officer, (6) a precis writer, (7) an administrative and financial officer (8) a finance officer and (9) six secretary stenographers. [56]

The staffs of commissions have varied in size, the largest possibly being that of the United Nations Special Committee on Palestine in which fifty served throughout the period of the committee's work. [57] An investigating commission requires an adequate staff in order to perform its functions efficiently particularly if a time limit is set for its report and/or it must cover a large territory. The secretariat of commissions have ranged from twenty five to forty five personnel. Sometimes local people are recruited as interpreters although this practice can have its disadvantages. [58]

The position of principal secretary as an administrator is important. As the members of the commission represent the Security Council or General Assembly, as the case may be, the principal secretary is the representative of the Secretary-General. The chairman heads policy making and the principal secretary heads the staff. All communications with the staff should be through the principal secretary.

The principal secretary also performs a function with the commission paralleling one performed by the Secretary-General at the Headquarters with respect to the budget. All matters requiring funds should be submitted to the principal secretary for his assurance that funds are or are not available in the budget of the commission.

Transportation, communications, equipment maintenance, in effect, logistics, are now taken care of by personnel supplied by the United Nations Field Service of the Secretariat. Early missions were handicapped in some repects, but these conditions were improved with time. The Truce Organization of the United Nations in Palestine, for example, was initially handicapped by lack of communication and transport facilities. [59]

---

[54] Much of the material in this section was obtained from information received from members of the Secretariat who have served on the staffs of United Nations commissions.

[55] Similarly, the Pan American Union, which is the Secretariat of the Organization of American States, provides the staff and arrangements for travel and operation of commissions of inquiry of that Organization.

[56] U. N. Security Council Official Records, Fourth Year, Special Supplement No. 7, p. 4.

[57] U. N. Organization and Procedures of United Nations Commissions, III, p. 12.

[58] This was done by the United Nations Temporary Commission on Korea (U. N. Organization and Procedure of United Nations Commissions, VIII, p. 9. On the other hand, in the visit of the Chairman and Vice Chairman of the Special Committee on South West Africa, where an interpreter of the Government of South West Africa was used the testimony may have been stilted or distorted.

[59] U. N. Doc. S/1025 (September 16, 1948), p. 10.

In some cases, facilities are supplied by member states. The Chairman and Vice Chairman of the Special Committee on South West Africa were transported in military planes ordinarily used by government officials which had been furnished by the Republic of South Africa. Facilities are often furnished by neighboring states where a fact-finding body is refused permission to conduct an on-the-spot inquiry as in the cases of Angola and of Hungary.

The question of the status of members of United Nations commissions is usually determined by arrangements made by the Secretary-General with the member states in whose territory the commission will operate. The members of United Nations commissions, in general, are protected by Section 22 of the Convention on the Privileges and Immunities of the United Nations which was approved by the General Assembly in 1949.[60]

The matter of confidential information and the secrecy required in preventing it from reaching unauthorized sources raises the question of providing such physical arrangements as safes, the employment of guards and the use of codes and mail pouches.[61]

E. The Report
    1. Structure of the Report
The structure of a report of an investigating commission may vary according to the function of the commission. The practice of the League of Nations and of the United Nations shows consistently thorough and exacting workmanship on the part of investigating bodies in the preparation of their reports.

The Aaland Islands inquiry would be a good example of such a thorough report. The report of the Committee of Rapporteurs, consisting of 53 large printed pages, gave an exhaustive account of the economic, historic and political aspects of the question.[62] It then stated the position of the three parties, the Aaland Islanders, Finland and Sweden. It also dealt with the question of the competence of the Council in support of the Commission of Jurists' decision that the Aaland Islands question was of an international nature. The report then posed and answered basic questions pertinent to the study. A summarization of arguments and considerations followed and, finally, came the Committee's recommendations. Several annexes containing information supplied by the parties were attached to the report.

Most reports of commissions of investigation include a discussion of the terms of reference as well as a summary of the events surrounding the creation of the commission as well as outlining the positions of the parties.

The reports of commissions of inquiry engaged in putting an end to hostilities may include a formal final report such as in the case of the United Nations Commission of Investigation Concerning Greek Frontier Incidents.[63] The final report of that Commission to the Security Council consisted of 460 pages in 3 volumes with four parts and nine annexes. As a rule, the reports submitted by commissions of inquiry established to put an end to hostilities, or commissions whose purpose it is to keep the Security Council informed, are in the form of interim reports. Such interim reports may vary from a short cable to a more detailed document. The resolution authorizing the establishment of a commission or the appointment of a mediator usually specifies the desired frequency of reports.

    2. Submission of the Report
The report of an investigating body, in United Nations' and League of

---

[60]U. N. Doc. A/43 (February 9, 1946), pp. 687-693.
[61]U. N. Doc. A/AC.18/SC.6/6, p. 22.
[62]L. of N. Official Journal, Second Year, No. 7, p. 699.
[63]U. N. Doc. S/360 (May 23, 1947).

Nations' practice, either has been formally presented to the principal organ by having the full commission proceed to the seat of the principal organ or by having the charman or rapporteur present the report. The former procedure was followed, in United Nations' practice, by the Committee of Good Offices on Indonesia, the Commission of Investigation Concerning Greek Frontier Incidents and the United Nations Commission for India and Pakistan. The latter procedure was followed, with the chairman or rapporteur presenting the report, by the United Nations Temporary Commission on Korea, the United Nations Special Committee on Palestine and the United Nations Palestine Commission.[64]

During the existence of the League of Nations, in the case of the Polish-Lithuanian dispute over Vilna, the Committee of Three considered it absolutely necessary that the League Council should hear Col. Chardigny and some of the members of the Committee who would be able to give the Council all the information collected on-the-spot.[65] In the discussions of the Lytton Report, also, the Secretary-General of the League pointed out that as a general rule all commissions of inquiry set up by the League of Nations had been asked to come to Geneva and had held themselves at the disposal of the Council, citing the Greco-Bulgarian dispute in which, after Greek and Bulgarian observations had been made, the commission chairman was invited to say whether he had anything to add.

In the case of the Commission of Investigation Concerning Greek Frontier Incidents before the United Nations, although the Commission proceeded to New York, it was the rapporteur who, on June 27, 1947, presented the Commission's report to the Security Council.[66] With respect to such a presentation, Mr. Johnson, the U. S. Delegate, said "it would retard a decision on the report not to have the Commission, or at least a representative group from the Commission, in New York at that time," referring to the possibility that the Council as a body, or individual members of the Council, might wish to ask questions of the Commission during examination of the report.[67]

The presence of the chairman or rapporteur of a commission is of advantage in presenting reports. He is available for questions from the principal organ, his presence provides personal contact with the commission and he can engage in private conversations.[68] In addition, the League of Nations' practice of having the members of commissions come to the seat of the principal organ to hold themselves at its disposal is also good practice, especially, where various views are present in a commission's report.

3. Effect of the Report

The measure of the effect of the report of a commission of investigation is not equivalent to the measure of effectiveness of the commission's work in toto. It is easier to trace the direct action taken as a result of the report of a commission of inquiry than to find a similar correlation between the presence of the commission and developments in a situation.

The usual practice with respect to the report of a commission of investigation of the General Assembly or Security Council of the United Nations has been for a State which is a member of the commission or of a subsidiary organ considering the commission's report to present in

---

[64]This problem does not exist with the Organization of American States where the individuals who are members of an investigating body also sit on the Council of the Organization.

[65]L. of N. Council Minutes, Twelfth Session, Annex 163, p. 97.

[66]U. N. Security Council Official Records, Second Year, No. 51, p. 116.

[67]Ibid., No. 39, p. 834.

[68]U. N. Doc. A/AC. 18/SC. 6/6, p. 24.

the Assembly or the Council, as the case might be, a draft resolution based upon the report. In the case of a minority report, a second draft resolution incorporating the minority view might also be presented by one of the States supporting such position.

In some instances, the organ initiating the investigation may set as the goal of the investigation, recommendations of a basis for settlement. The Aaland Islands question was in this category. The report of the Commission of Inquiry and the recommendations contained in it formed the basis of the recommendations of the Council of the League of Nations which, in turn, provided the basis for the agreements into which the parties eventually entered.[69] The Mosul dispute was similarly resolved.[70]

In the experience of the United Nations, the question of the future government of Palestine and the matter of the disposal of Eritrea fell into a similar category. In the former case, the recommendation for partition with economic union which was supported by the majority of the membership of the Special Committee on Palestine was approved by a majority of the General Assembly and incorporated in a resolution.[71] The Eritrean Commission with five members produced three different recommendations as well as three different interpretations of the facts. The solution supported by two members proposing federation of Eritrea with Ethiopia was approved by the Assembly.[72]

In a number of instances, the immediate purpose of the international organ was to obtain a cessation of hostilities. Examples from the experience of the League of Nations are the Demir Kapu matter and The Sino-Japanese dispute. In the first case, the parties agreed to a cease-fire and the recommendations in the report of the commission of investigation were incorporated in a resolution adopted by the League Council.[73] In the second case, the report of the commission of investigation was influential in the considerations which led to the adoption of subsequent resolutions by the Council and Assembly of the League with regard to the matter.[74]

The reports of commissions of investigation established by the Provisional Organ of Consultation or Organ of Consultation of the Organization of American States have resulted invariably in the adoption of resolutions by the Council of the Organization of American States calling upon the parties to observe their treaty obligations. The parties have also agreed to take certain actions to restore tranquility and, in some cases, further observation procedures have been set up in accordance with recommendations contained in a commission's report.

In two instances, the Provisional Organ of Consultation has made specific reference to treaty obligations of the parties with a view toward achieving a pacific settlement of the dispute. In the dispute between Honduras and Nicaragua, in 1957, an ad hoc committee of the Provisional Organ of Consultation succeeding in persuading the Governments of Honduras and Nicaragua to place the question before the International Court of Justice in accordance with the Pact of Bogotá.

Reference was also made to the Pact of Bogotá by the Provisional Organ of Consultation in urging the Governments of Costs Rica and Nicaragua, in 1955, to appoint their respective members of the Commission of Investigation and Conciliation provided for under that treaty.

---

[69] L. of N., Official Journal, 1921, No. 7, p. 699.

[70] L. of N., Official Journal, 1926, No. 2, p. 192.

[71] U. N. General Assembly Resolution 181 (II), November 29, 1947.

[72] U. N. General Assembly Resolution 390 (V), December 2, 1950.

[73] L. of N. Official Journal, 1926, No. 2, pp. 197-205.

[74] L. of N. Official Journal, 1933, Special Supplement No. 112, p. 24.

The United Nations has had a varied experience with respect to the effect of its commission's reports where hostilities were in progress. The Security Council was unable to take any action with respect to the report of the Commission of Investigation Concerning Greek Frontier Incidents. However the resolution of the General Assembly on the Balkan question was in many respects similar to the draft resolution which the United States had introduced into the Security Council based largely on the majority recommendations of the Commission of Investigation Concerning Greek Frontier Incidents.[75]

The reports of the Commission for India and Pakistan and the Commission for Indonesia kept the Security Council informed of the developments in each situation. In the former case, the Security Council, basing its action on the recommendation of the Commission, appointed a single representative to continue attempts at mediation.[76] These two commissions were primarily commissions of good offices and mediation.

The United Nations Commission for Korea, the United Nations Special Committee on the Balkans, the Palestine Commission and the United Nations Mediator in Palestine, were also a means of supplying the Security Council and the General Assembly with information on developments in the area in which each operated. A report of the United Nations Commission for Korea was useful in providing the Security Council with a basis for recommending to its members that they furnish armed assistance to the Republic of Korea.[77]

In one instance, no action at all was taken on a report. The Commission to investigate the conditions existing in Germany with respect to the holding of free elections, in its report, indicated that it did not see any possibility for the Assembly to take further action that would produce a change in the situation.[78] The Assembly did not even consider the report of the Commission.

In another instance, although action by the Council was thwarted, the General Assembly, subsequently seized of the question, adopted a resolution. This occurred in the case of the Sub-Committee on Franco Spain. Although a Soviet veto, prevented the Security Council from taking action, the General Assembly, in its resolution on the question, cited the unanimous findings of the Security Council Sub-Committee. The Assembly resolution was milder, however, in its recommendations than those contained in the Sub-Committee's report.[79]

The effect of reports of commissions of investigation upon world opinion as expressed by the delegations of Member States in their votes in the General Assembly can possibly be traced. One example is the Hungarian question in 1956 and 1957.

As a result of reports of an exodus of refugees from Hungary, of mass deportations, of the use of tanks by Soviet troops, the sentiment expressed in the General Assembly reflected the change in public opinion within the various countries which had remained aloof from the Hungarian situation. The representative of Burma spoke in the General Assembly to condemn Hungary. The Indian representative, V. K. Krishna Menon said, that the rebellion in Hungary had India's sympathy.[80] Ceylon and Tunisia,

[75]U. N. General Assembly Resolution 109 (II), October 21, 1947.

[76]U. N. Doc. A/1469 (March 14, 1950).

[77]U. N. Doc. S/1511 (June 27, 1950).

[78]U. N. Doc. A/2122 (August 11, 1952).

[79]U. N. General Assembly Resolution 39 (I), December 12, 1946.

[80]U. N. General Assembly, Official Records, Eleventh Session, Plenary Meetings, (A/PV 608, December 4, 1956) p. 522.

as members of the Special Committee signed the unanimous report of the Committee.[81]

The General Assembly, on September 14, 1957, adopted a resolution endorsing the report of the Special Committee, noting the conclusion of the Committee that the events which took place in October and November 1956 constituted a spontaneous national uprising, and called upon the Union of Soviet Socialist Republics and "the present authorities in Hungary" to "desist from repressive measures against the Hungarian people".[82]

In the Angola situation, similarly, the General Assembly adopted a resolution based upon the report of its Sub-Committee.[83] The report of the Sub-Committee was conciliatory in tone expressing the hope that bloodshed could be ended, that measures to remove legitimate grievances would be initiated and that this could be accomplished by constructive co-operation between the Government of Portugal and the United Nations.[84] The resolution of the General Assembly was expressed in much stronger terms deprecating "the repressive measures and armed action against the people of Angola" and urging Portugal to undertake, immediately, "extensive political, economic and social reforms and measures".[85] The resolution requested the Member States to use their influence to secure the compliance of Portugal with the resolution. In addition, the Member States, of the United Nations and members of the specialized agencies were requested "to deny Portugal any support and assistance which may be used by it for the suppression of the people of Angola".[86]

The Special Committee on South West Africa had been set up by the General Assembly for the purpose of achieving in co-operation with the mandatory Power certain goals preparatory to obtaining for the territory full independence.[87]

The report of the Special Committee noted that the mission of the Committee could not be accomplished without force and that the population desired immediate United Nations administration and eventual independence.[88] The resolution of the General Assembly on the question, noting the report, reaffirmed the right of the people of South West Africa to eventual independence and condemned the continued refusal of the Government of South Africa to co-operate with the United Nations in providing for the independence of South West Africa.[89] The functions of the Special Committee for South West Africa were transferred, by the same resolution, to the Special Committee on the Situation with regard to the

---

[81]U. N. General Assembly, Official Records, Eleventh Session, Supplement No. 18 (A/3592).

[82]U. N. General Assembly Resolution 1133 (XI), September 14, 1957.

[83]U. N. General Assembly Resolution 1742 (XVI), January 30, 1962.

[84]U. N. General Assembly, Official Records, Sixteenth Session, Supplement No. 16 (A/4978) pp. 48-49.

[85]U. N. General Assembly Resolution 1742 (XVI), January 30, 1962.

[86]Idem.

[87]U. N. General Assembly Resolution 1702 (XVI), December 19, 1961. In resolution 1704 (XVI), December 19, 1961, the General Assembly dissolved the Committee on South West Africa which had been set up under resolution 749 A (VIII), November 28, 1953, to investigate the situation in South West Africa. Subsequent resolutions e.g., U. N. General Assembly Resolution 1568 (XV), December 18, 1960 and U. N. General Assembly Resolution 1596 (XV), April 7, 1961, had reaffirmed this goal as well as enlarging theCommittee's function to make proposals for restoring peace for preparing the indigenous inhabitants for self government and complete independence.

[88]U. N. Doc. A/5212 (August 31, 1962).

[89]U. N. General Assembly Resolution 1805 (XVII), December 14, 1962.

Implementation of the Declaration on the Granting of Independence to Colonial Countries and Peoples.[90]

Subsequent efforts by the General Assembly although important to the question of South West Africa will not be discussed as it is felt that such discussion would not fall into the limited purpose of this study which is to confine itself to direct casual relationships.

Another example of activity by the General Assembly in the field of human rights is the resolution adopted by the General Assembly after submission of the second report[91] of the United Nations Commission on the Racial Situation in the Union of South Africa. The Assembly, noting that the policy of apartheid was "contrary to the United Nations Charter and to the Universal Declaration of Human Rights" and constituted "a grave threat to the peaceful relations between ethnic groups in the world", invited "the Government of the Union of South Africa to reconsider its position: and to "take into consideration the suggestions of the Commission for a peaceful settlement of the racial problem".[92]

Upon submission of the third report of the Commission,[93] the General Assembly again adopted a resolution noting that "the Government of the Union of South Africa again refused to co-operate with the Commission" and called upon that Government to observe the obligations contained in Article 56 of the Charter.[94]

The General Assembly, on October 11, 1963, adopting a harsher attitude, adopted a resolution which, taking note "of the reports of the Special Committee on the Policies of apartheid of the Government of the Republic of South Africa", condemned that Government for "its failure to comply with the repeated resolutions of the General Assembly.[95] It also requested "all Member States to make all necessary efforts to induce the Government of South Africa to release all political prisoners and persons interned for having opposed the policy of apartheid.[96]

On August 7, 1963, the Security Council adopted a resolution which noting the reports of the Special Committee, called upon "all States to cease" the sale of arms, ammunition and military vehicles to South Africa.[97] The Security Council, on December 4, 1963, again noting the reports of the Special Committee, enlarged the call for sanctions to include equipment and materials for the manufacture and maintenance of arms and ammunition in South Africa.[98]

The General Assembly, on December 16, 1963 adopted a resolution which noting the reports of the Special Committee, appealed to all States to

> take appropriate measures and intensify their efforts,
> separately and collectively, with a view to dissuading
> the Government of the Republic of South Africa from
> pursuing its policies of apartheid, and requests them,
> in particular, to implement fully the Security Council
> resolution of 4 December 1963;[99]

[90]Idem.

[91]U. N. General Assembly, Official Records, Ninth Session, Supplement No. 16 (A/2719), August 26, 1954.

[92]U. N. General Assembly Resolution 820 (IX), December 14, 1954.

[93]U. N. General Assembly, Official Records, Tenth Session, Supplement No. 14 (A/2953), August 26, 1955.

[94]U. N. General Assembly Resolution 917 (X), December 6, 1955.

[95]U. N. General Assembly Resolution 1881 (XVIII), October 11, 1963.

[96]Idem.

[97]U. N. Doc. S/5386 (August 7, 1963).

[98]U. N. Doc. S/5471.

[99]U. N. General Assembly Resolution 1978 (XVIII), December 16, 1963.

In conclusion, an attempt has been made here to trace the reports of commissions of investigation to resolutions adopted by the Security Council and the General Assembly. Indirect effects upon a situation or dispute which might have resulted from the operation of an investigating body would be impossible to measure. In this category, would fall any temporizing effects which operations of investigating bodies may have had, on a short or a long term basis, in situations such as the Hungarian question, the matter of Angola, the question of South West Africa and the question of racial conflict resulting from the policies of apartheid of the Government of the Union of South Africa. This would apply equally to the results of resolutions adopted by the Security Council and the General Assembly based upon the reports of such investigating bodies. The direct effects and the implementation of such resolutions of the Security Council and of the General Assembly are not pursued, also, primarily because such pursuit would be outside the scope of this study.

# CHAPTER VII

## SUMMARY AND CONCLUSIONS

Fact-finding in the maintenance of international peace has taken two courses of development. One line of development has been as a method or procedure in the pacific settlement of disputes. The second line of development has been in the exercise of collective responsibility for the maintenance of international peace. The separation between the two lines of development has not always been clearcut but for the purposes of analysis it will help to observe the distinction.

The first line of development may be said to have begun with the Hague Convention of 1899. The concept was to use inquiry on a bilateral basis as a means of promoting the pacific settlement of disputes where neither arbitration nor diplomacy were suitable or adequate. The Hague Convention of 1907 further nurtured this concept of inquiry by providing detailed rules of procedure.

The Bryan treaties gave new impetus to the use of inquiry in the pacific settlement of international disputes. They added, however, concepts which were the beginning of attempts to attach a collective nature to the use of inquiry. The first of these was the compulsory submission of disputes to inquiry. In addition, the obligation not to resort to war during the period of investigation and for a limited time thereafter, by implication, was a limited renunciation of war.

Independent inquiry as a method in the pacific settlement of disputes was then absorbed into conciliation procedures. Or to put it another way, inquiry was expanded to include conciliation. Fact-finding was no longer a procedure standing alone but along with the elucidation of the facts it was expected that recommendations of a basis for settlement would be made.

In Europe, the expression of this trend toward conciliation was less pronounced than in the western hemisphere. The elucidation of the facts was still considered basic and preliminary to the conciliation efforts. In the western hemisphere, in the conciliation procedure, the elucidation of the facts was regarded as of less importance and in some instances dispensed with where considered unnecessary.

The League of Nations, promoted the use of procedures of investigation and conciliation, and adopted a resolution, on September 22, 1922, recommending that the Members of the League conclude separate agreements for the establishment of commissions of conciliation. As a result, a large number of bilateral treaties incorporating investigation and conciliation were entered into during the period between the first and second World Wars. Outstanding examples of this effort toward the promotion of the use of conciliation and investigation were the Locarno Treaties of 1926 and the General Act for the Pacific Settlement of International Disputes of 1928.

The imposition of a collective nature to conciliation and investigation procedures was strongest and most explicit in the League Covenant itself. Article 12, provided that the Members of the League were obligated to submit a dispute likely to lead to a rupture to either arbitration or judicial settlement or to inquiry by the Council. Under Article 15, the Members agreed to submit "any dispute likely to lead to a rupture which is not submitted to arbitration or judicial settlement in accordance with Article 13", to the Council. Paragraph 3 of Article 15 stated that the Council was to "endeavor to effect a settlement of the dispute". The Council of the League, under these provisions of the Covenant, became a mediating and conciliating agency and, through its subsidiary organs, a fact-finding body, as well.

A parallel development occurred in the western hemisphere with respect to the promotion of the use of conciliation and investigation procedures in the pacific settlement of disputes. The Central American Treaty of 1923 was intended by the parties to unify and recast in a single convention the treaties that had preceeded it, viz., the Bryan treaties. But it was the "Gondra Treaty" of 1923 which sought to give a truly collective character to the obligation to submit controversies of "whatever nature to the procedure of investigation".

In 1929, with the General Convention of Inter-American Conciliation, the collective character of the "Gondra Treaty" was extended to cover conciliation. The commission created by the "Gondra Treaty" was expanded by adding to its investigatory powers the further power to propose bases for the settlement of controversy. With the Inter-American Anti-War Treaty of Non-Aggression and Conciliation, sometimes referred to as the "Saavedra Lamas Treaty", the emphasis on securing conciliatory settlement of a dispute rather than on elucidating the facts was further strengthened.

The American Treaty on Pacific Settlement (Pact of Bogota), signed April 30, 1948, was to be the final step in consolidating and superseding previous instruments in assigning a collective character to procedures for pacific settlement. Chapter III of the Pact of Bogota is entitled "Procedure of Investigation and Conciliation". Unfortunately, only ten states have ratified the Pact of Bogota.

The United Nations Charter, is also an example of assigning a collective character to the pacific settlement of international disputes. Chapter VI of the Charter expresses the concern of the United Nations with any dispute or situation which is likely to endanger the maintenance of international peace and security. In addition, the responsibility of the parties to such a dispute to seek means for pacific settlement and of the Security Council to either recommend appropriate procedures or methods of adjustment or such terms of settlement as it may consider appropriate is also contained in Chapter VI.

More specifically, Article 33 provides that it is the responsibility of the parties to such a dispute to seek a solution by any peaceful means of their choice, inquiry being specifically listed as one possibility. Under Article 34, the Security Council is given the power to investigate in order to determine its competence.

The authority given the Security Council to recommend terms of settlement, under Article 37, or to recommend appropriate procedures or methods of adjustment, under Article 36, indicates that the powers of the Security Council to investigate under Chapter VI must be more extensive than those specifically contained in Article 34.

The collective nature attached to pacific means of settlement, of which inquiry is one, under the Charter, is most strongly and directly emphasized in treating the use of inquiry, or other measures for peaceful settlement, as a step in a process leading towards the possible application of collective measures. In this respect, the treatment of the powers of investigation and conciliation given to the Security Council under Chapters VI and VII of the Charter are similar to the treatment of the powers of investigation and conciliation assigned to the League Council by the Covenant. Basically, both under the Charter and under the

Covenant, a process is provided for which introduces into the promotion of the use of pacific methods of settlement the possibility of the application of collective measures in the event of failure to achieve a peaceful solution to the dispute. The similarity, of course, ends in the provisions for collective action. These are more detailed and stronger under Chapter VII of the Charter with respect to the powers of the Security Council than those assigned to the League Council by the Covenant.

Articles 15, 16 and 17 of the Covenant of the League of Nations provided for the application of sanctions after certain steps had been taken of which inquiry and attempts at conciliation by the Council were basic and preliminary. The United Nations Charter does not place as much emphasis on inquiry and conciliation but considers any of several methods of pacific settlement as a possible preliminary step.

In addition, a further weakening of this collective approach to pacific settlement appears in the Charter. Apparently, the United Nations Charter does not display a continuity of procedures between Chapters VI and VII to indicate that failure to arrive at peaceful settlement might lead to collective action.

The Dumbarton Oaks proposals were actually more similar in approach to the provisions of the Covenant of the League of Nations which provided for the possible use of inquiry as a step in the application of collective measures. The powers of the Security Council in the Dumbarton Oaks proposals concerning action with respect to threats to the peace were linked with the failure of the parties to settle their dispute by peaceful means.[1]

At San Francisco, Chapter VIII of the Dumbarton Oaks proposals was revised and incorporated into Chapters VI and VII of the United Nations Charter. The failure to comply with recommendations, made under Chapter VI of the Charter, for the pacific settlement of disputes and the powers of the Security Council to take action under Chapter VII of the Charter appeared less closely related than in the Dumbarton Oaks proposals.

The failure to settle a dispute by peaceful means, using inquiry or otherwise, as a basis for further action by the League Council was thus more clearly stated in the Covenant of the League. The failure to show such close relationship in the United Nations Charter, however, does not, vitiate the intention to do so which was contained in the Dumbarton Oaks proposals. The Security Council, under Article 39 of the Charter, can make a determination as to the seriousness of a dispute or situation thereby indicating the failure of attempts at pacific settlement.

The second line of development of fact-finding, that is, in the maintenance of international peace, may be said to have begun with the "cooling off" provisions of the Bryan treaties. The purpose of the "cooling off" provisions of the Bryan treaties was to postpone hostilities for as long a period as possible. The concept was later referred to as "Inquiry and Delay"[2] and as such incorporated in Article 12 of the Covenant of the League.

The need for "Inquiry and Delay" would appear to have disappeared with the United Nations Charter which provides in Article 2, paragraph 4 that

All Members shall refrain in their international relations
from the threat or use of force against the territorial integrity or political integrity of any state, or in any other
manner inconsistent with the Purposes of the United Nations.

---

[1]U. S. Department of State, Dumbarton Oaks Documents on International Organization (1944), p. 16, Chapter VIII, Sec. B (1).

[2]Alfred Zimmern, The League of Nations and The Rule of Law 1918-1935, London: MacMillan, 1936, pp. 129, 243.

While this may be so in theory, in practice, the respite which comes with "Inquiry and Delay" allows tempers to cool and frictions to subside.

Another aspect of fact-finding which is useful in the maintenance of international peace is that which has been referred to as the "hue and cry". It is a principle which has long been regarded as an effective deterrent against crimes of violence.[3] The principle of "hue and cry" was originally applicable to arrest. The application of it by the League of Nations, the Organization of American States and the United Nations to draw attention to the actions of certain Members does not fall into this category. As a form of moral suasion and a possible deterrent, however, it does possess possibilities.

The use of fact-finding as a basis for action on the part of an international organ is a development which began with the League of Nations. In the case of the League, the action was in the form of a process beginning with inquiry and conciliation and leading, possibly, to recommendations for the imposition of sanctions. Inquiry in this context is in the concept of the Hague Convention with a collective nature attached.

The United Nations Charter retains this concept. Under the Charter, investigation has, in addition, become a more specific mode of action. Under Article 39 the Security Council, impliedly, may investigate in order to determine whether there exists "any threat to the peace, breach of the peace, or act of aggression". Article 40 states that, in application of provisional measures, the Security Council "shall duly take account of failure to comply with such provisional measures". Investigations conducted solely in accord with Articles 39 or 40 would fall under the category of "maintenance of international peace" rather than that of pacific settlement". Although the purpose of each of these categories is designed to achieve the other, for the purpose of analyzing the examples of fact-finding in international disputes, it would be well to observe the distinction between the two categories of fact-finding.

The history of fact-finding in the peaceful settlement of international disputes and in the maintenance of international peace does not show such clear cut distinctions as indicated in the foregoing analysis. In the case of inquiry on the style of the Hague Conventions, there are very few examples and these, consisting of seven in all were confined to very narrow areas of investigation.[4] With one exception, the commissions were composed entirely of naval officers and limited to investigating incidents at sea.

By contrast, the large number of experiences in fact-finding of the League of Nations, the United Nations and the Organization of American States is striking. It is in these cases, that the distinction between inquiry as a basis for recommending terms of settlement in the modified[5] style of the Hague Conventions becomes interwoven with inquiry as a basis for collective action in the maintenance of international peace.

The issue between the concept of equal sovereignty of states and the collective responsibility for the maintenance of international peace and security thus becomes relevant to the use of inquiry by international organs in the maintenance of international peace. It should be noted that in the development of inquiry on a bilateral basis, this issue did not arise.

In practice, investigations conducted by the League of Nations were directed toward arriving at a pacific settlement with the League Council acting in its capacity as a conciliatory agency. Commissions of investi-

---

[3]Ibid., p. 176.

[4]Five commissions of conciliation were also created and functioned, but inquiry was minimal in these cases. (See Chapter II supra.)

[5]"Modified" in the sense of imbuing with a collective nature.

gation established by the League Council were created only with the prior consent of the parties in accordance with the concept of the sovereign equality of the Members of the League.

The Council of the Organization of American States, when acting as Provisional Organ of Consultation in accordance with the provisions of the Treaty of Rio, established, in many cases, a commission to "elucidate the facts of the dispute". These commissions, without exception, obtained the consent of a party before proceeding to conduct an on-the-spot investigation within the territory of that party.

Commissions of investigation established by the Security Council or General Assembly of the United Nations have similarly sought the permission of a party to a dispute to conduct an investigation within its territory.[6]

Where the Security Council engages in an investigation under either Article 34, 39 or 40, it would appear, under the Charter, that there is an exception to the application of the principle of national sovereignty. In such cases, the obligation is present to co-operate in providing information to the Security Council and in assisting it to discharge its responsibility for the maintenance of international peace and security.

The existence of the obligation to co-operate in investigations conducted under Article 34 is rendered difficult to determine, however, because of the wide scope of the investigations undertaken by the Security Council. With the exception of the Commission of Investigation Concerning Greek Frontier Incidents which was established under Article 34,[7] investigations conducted by the Security Council have not been confined to the narrow scope expressed in Article 34. Nor was the Greek investigation confined within this narrow scope for long after its inception.

The obligation to co-operate in an ascertainment of certain facts by the Security Council under Article 40 has not been tested. In practice such ascertainment of fact has been entrusted by the Council to certain agencies already in operation within the area such as the Good Offices Committee, or the Consular Commission, in Indonesia, or the Truce Commission in Palestine.

It should be noted that undue stress need not be placed upon the obligation to co-operate in an investigation under Articles 34, 39 or 40. Firstly, the Security Council is not required to conduct an investigation in order to arrive at a determination of its competence under Article 34 nor to arrive at the determinations which it is empowered to make under Articles 39 and 40. Refusal to consent to an on-the-spot investigation or to co-operate in the ascertainment of the facts would probably enter into the deliberations of the Security Council in arriving at its decisions.

The issue of equal sovereignty or collective responsibility for the maintenance of international peace, therefore, has the most direct bearing on the use of inquiry in pursuing a peaceful solution to disputes through the intervention of an international organ. The experiences of the League of Nations, the Organization of American States and the United Nations have shown a desire for flexibility in investigations which is apparently a response to the problems posed by the conflict between the limitations imposed by the concept of equal sovereignty and the requirements of collective responsibility. Resort to investigation has attempted to include all possibilities ranging from the minimal cessation of hostilities to a permanent solution of the dispute.

As this study was found, it is easier to achieve a cessation of hostili-

---

[6]For a discussion of The United Nations and Domestic Jurisdiction, see Leland M. Goodrich, The United Nations, New York: Thomas Y. Crowell Co., 1959, pp. 74-79.

[7]See Ernest J. Kerley, op. cit., for a discussion of the obligation to co-operate in an investigation as related to the narrow scope of Article 34.

ties than a permanent solution to the dispute which had inspired the use of force. Permanent settlements which the Council of the League of Nations was successful in achieving, utilizing inquiry, were confined to the question of sovereignty over the Aaland Islands, the dispute over the Mosul territory and the Demir Kapu incident, if one disregards the territorial arrangements referred to the Council on the basis of World War I treaties or prior arrangements. Of the three instances above, the question of the Mosul territory was also so referred. The United Nations General Assembly employed inquiry in arriving at recommendations for the solution of disputes in the question of Palestine and in the matter of the disposal of Eritrea.

The recommended settlements, in all cases, rested upon the consent of the parties to submission of the dispute for the purpose of a recommended settlement. In each case, the consent was obtained directly or was transferred as a result of treaty obligations. In the Aaland Islands case such consent was given by Finland and Sweden in agreeing to submit the question to the Council. Consent of the parties to the Demir Kapu Incident was obtained after the application of pressure by the major powers, particularly France and the United Kingdom. The Mosul territory dispute was submitted on the basis of the Treaty of Lausanne of 1923 and the matter of the disposal of Eritrea was submitted on the basis of the Peace Treaty with Italy terminating that country's role as a belligerent in World War II.

The reference of the Palestine problem by the United Kingdom, as the mandatory Power, to the General Assembly of the United Nations, on April 2, 1947, was unique. Initial consent of the parties was impliedly obtained by submission of the international problem of the disposition of a mandate by the mandatory Power. Problems in the implementation of the recommendations of the General Assembly developed, however, as a result of the reluctance of the United Kingdom to support, and direct opposition by the Arabs to, a solution with which they were not in accord.

Consent of the parties has also been regarded by the Organization of American States as preliminary to conducting an investigation for the purpose of recommending either methods or terms of settlement. Such consent has been implied from the adherence of the parties to the Pact of Bogotá.

Although investigations have been conducted in almost all cases of complaints addressed to the Council of the Organization of American States in which it constituted itself Provisional Organ of Consultation, in only three such cases has the Provisional Organ of Consultation recommended methods or terms of settlement. These cases concerned Costa Rica and Nicaragua in 1955, Honduras and Nicaragua in 1957 and the Dominican Republic and Haiti in 1963-1965. The practice of the Provisional Organ of Consultation was to remind the parties of their obligations under the Pact of Bogotá to which they had adhered and then to suggest establishing a conciliation committee in accordance with the Pact of Bogotá. The dispute between Honduras and Nicaragua was referred to the International Court of Justice on a point of law.

The importance of attaching a collective character to inquiry in the pacific settlement of international disputes appears to be justified by contrasting the successes of collective efforts at achieving peaceful solutions, however few, to the lack of implementation of the many treaties for the pacific settlement of international disputes which appeared in the period between the two World Wars.

On the other hand, even these few results do not justify undue optimism when it is to be noted that in all instances the consent of the parties, express or implied, to submission of the dispute for recommendation of methods or terms of settlement was obtained. In the case of the Organization of American States, a regional organization, it would appear that such consent is more easily construed. Reference to the Pact of Bogotá, where the parties have ratified that Treaty, has provided the basis for specific recommendations of the Provisional Organ of Consultation with respect to procedures for settlement.

There is apparently a reluctance on the part of members of international organs to support steps to recommend methods or terms of settlement in the absence of consent of the parties to submission of a dispute for that purpose. This reluctance forms the conditions surrounding the establishment of commissions of inquiry and limits the results which can be obtained through investigations of fact.

The experience of international organs in fact-finding, from the functional point of view is more encouraging. In the area of the development of techniques in conducting investigations, the work of commissions of investigation established by the League of Nations, the Organization of American States and the United Nations reveals a dedication and expertise on the part of the members and the staff of such commissions which indicate the possibilities in the investigative procedure.

Conclusions

Experience has shown that there are two aspects to pursuing a procedure directed toward obtaining the pacific settlement of an international dispute. The first aspect is concerned with the elimination of the use of force or the threat of force as an alternative procedure. The second aspect deals with the mechanics of arriving at a permanent solution to the problem which created the frictions giving immediate stimulus to the dispute. Inquiry or investigation of fact has been utilized in either one or in both of these aspects in the history of international relations in the twentieth century.

The use of inquiry, under The Hague Conventions, in the incidents which occurred prior to 1920,[8] was related to arriving at a settlement of a dispute concerning subject matter of a very limited nature. The subsequent experiences of the League of Nations, the United Nations and the Organization of American States in fact-finding indicate that in a great number of instances in which fact-finding commissions have been used by the political organs of these organizations, the immediate objective was the cessation of hostilities. It should not be overlooked, however, that the primary objective in all such instances was finding a permanent solution.

The use of inquiry by the Organization of American States to prevent hostilities or to obtain an end to hostilities is especially outstanding. On the other hand, the use of formal investigation has not been considered by the Security Council of the United Nations as prerequisite to ordering a "cease-fire". Fact-finding used in connection with the imposition of such "cease-fire" and other provisional measures should be considered as part of such provisional measures and should be distinguished from the use of inquiry to bring about a cessation of hostilities. The distinction lies in the limited nature of observation as part of the imposition of provisional measures. Inquiry directed at achieving a halt to hostilities can - and has - incorporated in its terms of reference a search for more permanent solutions.

Where hostilities are in progress between two States, formal inquiry is not considered as a prerequisite to an order by the Security Council demanding an immediate end to hostilities. In those instances in which the hostilities are not so clearly defined as in situations in which guerilla activity is present, then investigation has been used to contribute toward stabilization of the area concerned. Such stabilization while not a peaceful solution in itself, enables the parties concerned to work towards elimination of the conditions out of which the dispute arose.

---

[8]See Chapter II supra.

The use of inquiry by the three international organizations cited earlier as a means of seeking pacific solutions to international disputes has not been confined solely to instances in which a cessation of hostilities was an immediate requirement. There have been examples of immediate and direct concern with achieving permanent solutions. The post World War I border settlements directed by the League Council can be cited as such examples. The solutions recommended by the Council in the Aaland Island question and the Mosul Territory dispute are further examples in League experience. One can point to the disposition of Eritrea and of the Palestine mandate territory as examples of recommended solutions in United Nations experience.

An analysis of the use of inquiry in international relations in the twentieth century indicates that the major limiting factor upon such use is the principle of sovereign independence of states. The expression of that principle with respect to fact-finding manifests itself in three ways: first, it is related to the subject matter of the inquiry; second, it acts as a limitation upon the exercise of collective responsibility; and third, it underlines the necessity of obtaining the consent of the parties concerned in seeking more permanent solutions.

The relationship of the principle of sovereign independence of states to the subject matter of an investigation was shown in the introduction to this study as it manifested itself in various restrictive clauses excluding matters affecting the "vital honor" of the parties. The instances of commissions of inquiry being used under the Hague Conventions to dispose of disputes arising out of naval incidents gave rise to the hope that disputes involving subject matter of a limited nature could be resolved in this fashion. In the opinion of the writer, international machinery such as the International Court of Justice has superceded commissions of inquiry of limited subject matter and is better adapted to render judgment in such cases.

With respect to other types of inquiry, limiting the subject matter of an investigation to very finite incidents would not create greater use of commissions of investigation. On the other hand, extending the range of subject matter of an investigation will tend to limit the possibility of obtaining the consent of the parties concerned to the investigation. It is necessary to determine the range of subject matter which states are disposed to submit to inquiry. This of course depends on many factors but in the ultimate, it rests on the views of each foreign office on the special interests of its government in this area.

With respect to the limitation which the principle of sovereign independence states imposes upon the exercise of collective responsibility for maintaining international peace, the limitation is brought out by the distinction between obtaining a "cease-fire" and achieving a permanent solution to the problem creating the frictions between the parties to the dispute. Attempts to constitute commissions of inquiry with wide scope against the wishes of a state in whose territory an investigation has been proposed have not succeeded in achieving permanent solutions. As was pointed out earlier, cessation of hostilities does not, according to the practice of the Security Council of the United Nations, require preliminary formal investigation as a prerequisite to Security Council action. But achieving a "cease-fire" is not a permanent solution. While insisting upon a halt to hostilities, the League of Nations, the United Nations and the Organization of American States have avoided exercising collective responsibility to impose terms of settlement where consent of the parties was not present.[9]

---

[9]This is not to minimize the importance of obtaining a cease-fire as a pre-requisite to seeking a more permanent solution. The cessation of hostilities in the Indonesian question led to negotiations which resulted in the independence of Indonesia.

And finally, the most direct relationship between the use of inquiry and the expression of the principle of sovereign independence is contained in the requirement that the consent of the parties concerned be secured. Obtaining the consent of the parties in initiating an investigation is essential to conducting the investigation but even more so in securing acceptance of the recommendations based upon such investigation. The examples of investigations conducted by the General Assembly of the United Nations show that where the consent of a party was lacking, the commissions of investigation were unable to function properly and that the recommendations which were subsequently adopted by the General Assembly were subject to the limitation that implementation without the use of force was impossible.

The importance of obtaining the consent of the parties is further illustrated by the attitude of the Organization of American States toward disputes in the western hemisphere. As a unique regional organization, the Organization of American States has a long tradition of co-operation between Latin American countries and their attachment to certain common ideas and policies which are rooted in their history. Yet the activities of the Organization of American States, based as they are on the principle of non-intervention, display an extraordinary respect for the sovereignty of all governments in the area.

The recognition of the importance of the consent of the parties concerned was recognized in the creation of the United Nations Charter. In this connection, the parallelism between waiver of the unanimity rule for voting in international conferences and the absence of any such exception to sovereign independence with respect to the use of inquiry in the pacific settlement of disputes should be noted. In only a limited application, that of an investigation under Article 34, is acceptance of an investigation by the parties concerned deemed obligatory.[10]

Finding permanent solutions to international disputes requires a process of peaceful procedures. The commission of inquiry was originally conceived by Professor de Martens as an important and essential prerequisite in promoting the efficiency of subsequent arbitration. Secretary of State Bryan saw the commission of inquiry as an aid in insuring the successful outcome of later or concurrent negotiations - an idea which developed from his experience in labor negotiations. In both cases, the major proponents of the independent international commission of inquiry regarded finding the facts as a preliminary step in the process of peaceful resolution and not as a means of settlement or a settlement procedure in itself.

The recognition of the limitations imposed upon compulsory forms or methods of pacific settlement by the principle of sovereign equality of independent states provided the background and encouragement for the initiation and preservation of the concept of the independent international commission of inquiry. These limitations, in turn acted as a restraining factor on the use of commissions of inquiry. Strangely enough, the several instances in which commissions of inquiry in the format of the Hague Conventions were created the commissions did not actually conform to the formula of the Hague Conventions. The function of the independent international commissions of inquiry was to submit a report elucidating the facts. In the several instances in which such commissions of inquiry operated, they submitted reports, in some cases, assigning responsibility and, in some cases, assessing liability. Certainly, the Hague Conferences did not intend that the independent international commission of inquiry possess quasi-judicial functions.

Nevertheless, considering all of the incongruities and modifications in the history of the independent international commission of inquiry, the

---

[10]See discussion in Chapter V supra.

preservation of the concept of fact-finding in that form or in other modes is of extreme importance to peaceful settlement and to the process of peaceful change. The question, essentially, is how to encourage the use of fact-finding in international relations.

As has been discussed earlier, the major limitation upon the use of inquiry in the pacific settlement of international disputes is the principle of sovereign independence of states. How can that limitation be lifted? The answer is by obtaining the consent of the parties concerned to the use of pacific means of settlement where inquiry may be an element in such procedure. The question then becomes one of how to obtain the consent of the parties.

Various answers have been discussed earlier herein. One such answer was to limit the subject matter. The individual states must agree upon what limitations are within their interest. Another suggestion is to improve the functioning of commissions of investigation. The experience of the United Nations, particularly, has accumulated excellent information as to practice and a valuable reservoir of trained personnel within the Secretariat.

As to whether there can be an extension of collective responsibility to induce conventional acceptance or individual acceptance of fact-finding in the pacific settlement of international disputes, the experience of the United Nations and of the Organization of American States indicates that there is a general reluctance to restrict the sovereign independence of Member States.

The recent proposal by the Netherlands delegation to the Sixth Committee of the General Assembly of the United Nations providing for the creation of a permanent fact-finding center[11] creates interesting possibilities for further studies. Would the existence of such a permanent fact-finding body which would by its very existence be based upon consent of the Member States increase the possibility of a greater use of inquiry? Would the general consensus thus achieved and the impartiality of such a body induce specific consent in particular disputes to the use of inquiry? Certainly, this path toward obtaining the consent of the parties should be thoroughly explored. Such avenue of consideration of ways of encouraging the use of fact-finding may be termed the "mechanistic" approach.

Not without significance is the use of methods of obtaining information embodying investigative procedures contained in the Statutes creating International Tribunals and International Administrative Agencies and in various treaties dealing with specific subject matter or territory as the Fisheries Conventions and the Antarctica Treaty.[12] The most striking and common aspect of these categories is that fact-finding procedures are accepted as essential elements in areas of agreement dictated by mutual and common interests.

Employment of investigative procedures to ensure compliance with the provisions of a treaty or in the process of an adjudication of a question which States have voluntarily submitted to an international tribunal, is indicative of a second approach to securing greater use of fact-finding procedures - the creation of more international agencies and international regulatory bodies in specific areas. Perhaps this might be designated as the "functional" approach.

The unique aspect of the concept of the international commission of inquiry which originated at the Hague Convention of 1899 was the "political" approach which it initiated towards finding the facts in international disputes. By encouraging a consideration of inquiry in international disputes it set the course for many future studies and deliberations on a political

---

[11]See discussion in Chapter I supra.
[12]Discussed in Chapter IV supra.

and legal basis. The practical value of these studies and deliberations may be minimized with regard to charismatic results or basic developments in international organizations and relations. But the educational impress of this approach upon constructive thought in international relations can only be indicated by the observation that after almost seven decades the subject was of sufficient interest to initiate a new series of studies and deliberations by the United Nations General Assembly in 1963.

To sum up our observations, then, we must conclude that all three avenues to encouraging the use of inquiry in international disputes should be pursued - the mechanistic, the functional and the political. We should keep in mind, however, that common to all of these approaches is the limitation imposed by the principle of sovereign equality of States on the use of inquiry in international relations. It is also clear that as the mutual and common interests of States dictate agreement on common goals, the establishment of impartial fact-finding machinery becomes in the long run inevitable.

# APPENDIX A

## HAGUE CONVENTION OF 1907

### PART III    INTERNATIONAL COMMISSIONS OF INQUIRY

ART. 9.  In disputes of an international nature involving neither honor nor vital interests, and arising from a difference of opinion on points of fact, the contracting Powers deem it expedient and desirable that the parties who have not been able to come to an agreement by means of diplomacy, should, as far as circumstances allow, institute an international commission of inquiry, to facilitate a solution of these disputes by elucidating the facts by means of an impartial and conscientious investigation.

ART. 10.  International commissions of inquiry are constituted by special agreement between the parties in dispute.
The inquiry convention defines the facts to be examined; it determines the mode and time in which the commission is to be formed and the extent of the powers of the commissioners.
It also determines, if there is need, where the commission is to sit, and whether it may remove to another place, the language the commission shall use and the languages the use of which shall be authorized before it, as well as the date on which each party must deposit its statement of facts, and, generally speaking, all the conditions upon which the parties have agreed.
If the parties consider it necessary to appoint assessors, the convention of inquiry shall determine the mode of their selection and the extent of their powers.

ART. 11.  If the inquiry convention has not determined where the commission is to sit, it will sit at The Hague.
The place of meeting, once fixed, can not be altered by the commission except with the assent of the parties.
If the inquiry convention has not determined what languages are to be employed, the question shall be decided by the commission.

ART. 12.  Unless an undertaking is made to the contrary, commissions of inquiry shall be formed in the manner determined by Articles 45 and 57 of the present Convention.

ART. 13.  Should one of the commissioners or one of the assessors, should there be any, either die, or resign, or be unable for any reason whatever to discharge his functions, the same procedure is followed for filling the vacancy as was followed for appointing him.

ART. 14.  The parties are entitled to appoint special agents to attend the commission of inquiry, whose duty it is to represent them and to act as intermediaries between them and the commission.
They are further authorized to engage counsel or advocates, appointed by themselves, to state their case and uphold their interest before the

commission.

ART. 15. The International Bureau of the Permanent Court of Arbitration acts as registry for the commissions which sit at The Hague, and shall place its offices and staff at the disposal of the contraction Powers for the use of the commission of inquiry.

ART. 16. If the commission meets elsewhere than at The Hague, it appoints a secretary general, whose office serves as registry.

It is the function of the registry, under the control of the president, to make the necessary arrangements for the sittings of the commission, the preparation of the minutes, and, while the inquiry lasts, for the charge of the archives, which shall subsequently be transferred to the International Bureau at The Hague.

ART. 17. In order to facilitate the constitution and working of commissions of inquiry, the contracting Powers recommend the following rules, which shall be applicable to the inquiry procedure insofar as the parties do not adopt other rules.

ART. 18. The commission shall settle the details of the procedure not covered by the special inquiry convention or the present Convention, and shall arrange all the formalities required for dealing with the evidence.

ART. 19. On the inquiry both sides must be heard.

At the dates fixed, each party communicates to the commission and to the other party the statements of facts, if any, and, in all cases, the instruments, papers, and documents which it considers useful for ascertaining the truth, as well as the lists of witnesses and experts whose evidence it wishes to be heard.

ART. 20. The commission is entitled, with the assent of the Powers, to move temporarily to any place where it considers it may be useful to have recourse to this means of inquiry or to send one or more of its members. Permission must be obtained from the State on whose territory it is proposed to hold the inquiry.

ART. 21. Every investigation, and every examination of a locality, must be made in the presence of the agents and counsel of the parties or after they have been duly summoned.

ART. 22. The commission is entitled to ask from either party for such explanations and information as it considers necessary.

ART. 23. The parties undertake to supply the commission of inquiry, as fully as they may think possible, with all the means and facilities necessary to enable it to become completely acquainted with, and to accurately understand, the facts in question.

They undertake to make use of the means at their disposal, under their municipal law, to insure the appearance of the witnesses or experts who are in their territory and have been summoned before the commission.

If the witnesses or experts are unable to appear before the commission, the parties will arrange for their evidence to be taken before qualified officials of their own country.

ART. 24. For all notices to be served by the commission in the territory of a third contracting Power, the commission shall apply direct to the Government of the said Power. The same rule applies in the case of steps being taken on the spot to procure evidence.

The requests for this purpose are to be executed so far as the means at the disposal of the Power applied to under its municipal law allow. They can not be rejected unless the Power in question considers they are calculated to impair its sovereign rights or its safety.

The commission will equally be always entitled to act through the Power on whose territory it sits.

ART. 25. The witnesses and experts are summoned on the request of the parties or by the commission of its own motion, and, in every case, through the Government of the State in whose territory they are.

The witnesses are heard in succession and separately, in the presence of the agents and counsel, and in the order fixed by the commission.

ART. 26. The examination of witnesses is conducted by the president. The members of the commission may however put to each witness questions which they consider likely to throw light on and complete his evidence, or get information on any point concerning the witness within the limits of what is necessary in order to get at the truth.

The agents and counsel of the parties may not interrupt the witness when he is making his statement, nor put any direct question to him, but may ask the president to put such additional questions to the witness as they think expedient.

ART. 27. The witness must give his evidence without being allowed to read any written draft. He may, however, be permitted by the president to consult notes or documents if the nature of the facts referred to necessitates their employment.

ART. 28. A minute of the evidence of the witness is drawn up forthwith and read to the witness. The latter may make such alterations and additions as he thinks necessary, which will be recorded at the end of his statement.

When the whole of his statement has been read to the witness, he is asked to sign it.

ART. 29. The agents are authorized, in the course of or at the close of the inquiry, to present in writing to the commission and to the other party such statements, requisitions, or summaries of the facts as they consider useful for ascertaining the truth.

ART. 30. The commission considers its decisions in private and t the proceedings are secret.

All questions are decided by a majority of the members of the commission.

If a member declines to vote, the fact must be recorded in the minutes.

ART. 31. The sittings of the commission are not public, nor the minutes and documents connected with the inquiry published except in virtue of a decision of the commission taken with the consent of the parties.

ART. 32. After the parties have presented all the explanations and evidence, and the witnesses have all been heard, the president declares the inquiry terminated, and the commission adjourns to deliberate and to draw up its report.

ART. 33. The report is signed by all the members of the commission.

If one of the members refuses to sign, the fact is mentioned; but the validity of the report is not affected.

ART. 34. The report of the commission is read at a public sitting, the agents and counsel of the parties being present or duly summoned.

A copy of the report is given to each party.

ART. 35. The report of the commission is limited to a statement of facts, and has in no way the character of an award. It leaves to the parties entire freedom as to the effect to be given to the statement.

ART. 36. Each party pays its own expenses and an equal share of the expenses incurred by the commission.

## APPENDIX B

## INTERIM COMMITTEE OF GENERAL ASSEMBLY SUBCOMMITTEE 2 PROPOSAL SUBMITTED BY CHINA AND THE UNITED STATES A/AC.18/SC.2/2

### PART III RULES OF PROCEDURE FOR COMMISSIONS

(The topics set out below are intended to suggest all types of rules which might be useful for various types of commissions. When a commission of enquiry, for example, is established, appropriate rules would be selected from this part to enable it to function smoothly. These rules could be rearranged to relate them to each type of commission, or provisions could be added indicating in some detail which rules are appropriate to each type of commission.)

1. Meeting place and travel (Article 9, General Act of 1928).

2. Itinerary (Article 7 and 8, Regulations, General Convention of 1931, Article 4; Report of the Commission of Investigation concerning Greek Frontier Incidents.)

3. United Nations Assistance:
   (a) Assignment of staff.
   (b) Expert assistance from specialized agencies.
   (c) Arrangement for travel in Member States.

4. Languages (Article XI, The Hague Convention of 1907 for the Pacific Settlement of Disputes.).

5. Agents and Counsel (Article 11, General Act of 1928).

6. Liaison officers (Article 10, Regulations, General Convention of 1931, Article 4).

7. Privileges and immunities - qualifying members of commissions for benefits thereof (Section 22, General Convention of the United Nations).

8. Press releases (Report of the United Nations Special Committee on Palestine, A/AC.13/7).

9. Commissions in field:
   (a) Transport (Article 11, Regulations, General Convention of 1931, Article 4).
   (b) Communications (Article 11, Regulations, General Convention of 1931, Article 4).
   (c) Protection (Article 12, Regulations, General Convention of 1931, Article 4).
   (d) Accommodation - billeting (Article 13, Regulations, General Convention of 1931, Article 4).
   (e) Report to the Secretary-General of United Nations (Article 14, Regulations, General Convention of 1931, Article 4).

10. Opening of proceedings - application (Article 7, General Act of 1928).

11. Statement of facts and list of witnesses (Article XIX, The Hague Convention of 1907).

12. Exchange of documents (See: Habicht, "Post-War Treaties for the Pacific Settlement of International Disputes," p. 1016).

13. Right to be heard (See: Habicht, "Post-War Treaties for the Pacific Settlement of International Disputes," p. 1018).

14. Private hearings (Article 10, General Act of 1928).

15. Assessors (Article X, The Hague Convention of 1907).

16. Subsidiary organs (Rules of Procedure, Special Committee on Palestine; Report of Commission on Greek Frontier Incidents).

17. Evidence-documentary and testimonial (Articles XXII and XXIII, The Hague Convention of 1907; Article 11, General Act of 1928; see: Carlston, "The Processes of International Arbitration," pp. 26-27).

18. Municipal assistance - steps necessary to obtain benefit of municipal statutes (for United States Municipal Assistance Statute, see: Title 22 under United States Code, Section 270 d-g).

19. Task of commission - report:
    (a) The elucidation of the questions in dispute and collection of information.
    (b) The obligation to endeavour to bring the parties to an agreement.
    (c) Procès-verbal:
        (i) Commission of enquiry - statement of facts.
        (ii) Commission of conciliation - statement of agreement of parties or of impossibility of settlement.
    (d) Time for terminating procedures of commission (Article XXXII, The Hague Convention of 1907).
    (e) Communication of procès-verbal to parties (Article 16, General Act of 1928).

20. Closing statement

21. Voting:
    (a) Votes necessary for a decision.
    (b) Effect of abstention.

22. Commission's rule-making power.

23. Compensation and expenses (Article XXXVI, the Hague Convention of 1907).

# APPENDIX C

## GENERAL ASSEMBLY RESOLUTION 268 (III) D
### AND ANNEX
### "D"

### Creation of a Panel for Inquiry and Conciliation

The General Assembly,

Mindful of its responsibilities, under Articles 13 (1a) and 11 (1) of the Charter to promote international co-operation in the political field and to make recommendations with regard to the general principles of the maintenance of international peace and security,

Deeming it desirable to facilitate in every practicable way the compliance by Member States with the obligation in Article 33 of the Charter first of all to seek a solution of their disputes by peaceful means of their own choice,

Noting the desirability, as shown by the experience of organs of the United Nations, of having qualified persons readily available to assist those organs in the settlement of disputes and situations by serving on commissions of inquiry or of conciliation,

Concluding that to make provision for a panel of persons having the highest qualifications in this field available to any States involved in controversies and to the General Assembly, the Security Council and their subsidiary organs, when exercising their respective functions in relation to disputes and situations, would promote the use and effectiveness of procedures of inquiry and conciliation,

1. Invites each Member State to designate from one to five persons who, by reason of their training, experience, character and standing are deemed to be well fitted to serve as members of commissions of inquiry or of conciliation and who would be disposed to serve in that capacity;

2. Directs the Secretary-General to take charge of the administrative arrangements connected with the composition and use of the panel;

3. Adopts the annexed articles relating to the composition and use of the Panel for Inquiry and Conciliation.

### ANNEX

#### Articles relating to the composition and use
#### of the Panel for Inquiry and Conciliation

### Article 1

The Panel for Inquiry and Conciliation shall consist of persons designated by Member States who, by reason of their training, experience, character and standing, are deemed to be well fitted to serve as members

151

of commissions of inquiry or of conciliation and who would be disposed to serve in that capacity. Each Member State may designate from one to five persons, who may be private persons or government officials. In designating any of its officials, a State shall agree to make every effort to make such person available if his services on a commission are requested. Two or more States may designate the same person. Members of the panel shall be designated for a term of five years and such designations shall be renewable. Members of commissions appointed in these articles shall not in the performance of their duties, seek or receive instructions from any Government. Membership in the panel shall not, however, render a person ineligible for appointment, as representative of his Government or otherwise, on commissions or other bodies not formed under these articles.

## Article 2

The Secretary-General of the United Nations shall have general responsibility for the administrative arrangements connected with the panel. Each Government shall notify him of each designation of a person for inclusion in the panel, including with each notification full pertinent biographical information. Each Government shall inform him when any member of the panel designated by it is no longer available due to death, incapacity or inability to serve.

The Secretary-General shall communicate the panel and any changes which may occur in it from time to time to the Member States, to the Security Council, the General Assembly and the Interim Committee. He shall, where necessary, invite Member States promptly to designate replacements to fill any vacancies on the panel which may occur.

## Article 3

The panel shall be available at all times to the organs of the United Nations in case they wish to select from it members of commissions to perform tasks of inquiry or conciliation in connexion with disputes or situations in respect of which the organs are exercising their function.

## Article 4

The panel shall be available at all times to all States, whether or not Members of the United Nations, which are parties to any controversy, for the purpose of selecting from the panel members of commissions to perform tasks of inquiry or conciliation with a view to settlement of the controversy.

## Article 5

The method of selecting members of a commission of inquiry or of conciliation from the panel shall be determined in each case by the organ appointing the commission or, in the case of commissions appointed by or at the request of States parties to a controversy, by agreement between the parties.

Whenever the parties to a controversy jointly request the Secretary-General, the President of the General Assembly or the Chairman of the Interim Committee to appoint under these articles a member or members of a commission to perform tasks of inquiry or conciliation in respect of the controversy, or whenever such request is otherwise made pursuant to the provisions of a treaty or agreement registered with the Secretary-General of the United Nations, the officer so requested shall appoint from the panel the number of commissioners required.

## Article 6

In connexion with the constitution of any commission under these articles, the Secretary-General shall give the United Nations organ concerned or the parties to the controversy every assistance, by the performance of such tasks as ascertaining the availability of individuals selected from the panel, and making arrangements for the time and place of meeting of the persons so selected.

## Article 7

Members of commissions constituted pursuant to these articles by United Nations organs shall have the privileges and immunities specified in the General Convention on the Privileges and Immunities of the United Nations. Members of commissions constituted by States under these articles should, so far as possible, receive the same privileges and immunities.

## Article 8

Members of commissions constituted under these articles shall receive appropriate compensation for the period of their service. In the case of commissions constituted under article 4, such compensation shall be provided by the parties to the controversy, each party providing an equal share.

## Article 9

Subject to any determinations that may be made by the United Nations organ concerned or by the parties to a controversy in constituting commissions under articles 3 and 4 respectively, commissions constituted under these articles may meet at the seat of the United Nations or at such other places as they may determine to be necessary for the effective performance of their functions.

## Article 10

The Secretary-General shall assign to each commission constituted by a United Nations organ under these articles, staff adequate to enable it to perform its duties and shall, as necessary, seek expert assistance from specialized agencies brought into relationship with the United Nations. He shall enter into suitable arrangements with the proper authorities of states in order to assure the commission, so far as it may find it necessary to exercise its functions within their territories, full freedom of movement and all facilities necessary for the performance of its functions. The Secretary-General shall, at the request of any commission appointed by parties to a controversy pursuant to article 4, render this assistance to the commission to the extent possible.

Upon completion of its proceedings each commission appointed by a United Nations organ shall render such reports as may be determined by the appointing organ. Each commission appointed by or at the request of parties to a controversy pursuant to article 4, shall file a report with the Secretary-General. If a settlement of the controversy is reached, such report will normally merely state the terms of settlement.

SELECTED BIBLIOGRAPHY

Primary Sources

Documents and Compilations

Annals of the Organization of American States, vols. 1-9.

Carnegie Endowment for International Peace, The International Con-
    ferences of American States 1889-1928, 1931, and First Supple-
    ment 1933-1940, 1940. London: Oxford University Press.

Efremov, Ivan N. Les traites internationaux de conciliation. Paris:
    Les Editions internationales, 1932.

Habicht, M. Postwar Treaties for the Pacific Settlement of Inter-
    national Disputes. Cambridge: Harvard University Press, 1931.

Hackworth, Green H. Digest of International Law. Washington: Govern-
    ment Printing Office, 1940-1944, 8 vols.

Hudson, Manley O. World Court Reports. Washington: Carnegie Endow-
    ment for International Peace, 1934-1943, 4 vols.

Inter-American Peace Committee. Report on the Case Presented by the
    Government of Venezuela. Pan American Union Doc. CIP/4
    (June 7, 1960).

_____. Report on the Controversy Between Guatemala, Honduras,
    and Nicaragua. Pan American Union Doc. CIP-131/54 (July 8,
    1954).

International Court of Justice. The Corfu Channel Case. Judgment
    of April 9, 1949. 5 vols.

_____. Reports of Judgments, Advisory Opinions and Orders.
    1948-----.

_____. Yearbook. 1946-----.

Lange, Christian L. The American Peace Treaties. Kristiania:
    Aschehoug, 1915.

League of Nations. Arbitration and Security. 1926. V. Geneva.

_____. Official Journal. Vols. 1-21 (1920-1940).

_____. Powers and Duties Attributed to the League of Nations by
    International Treaties. C.3.M.3.1944.

_____. Records of the Assembly. 1920-1946. Published as
    Special Supplements to the Official Journal.

_____. Arbitration Security and Reduction of Armaments. L. of N. Doc. A135 (I) 1924 IX.

_____. Essential Facts about the League of Nations. tenth ed., 1939.

_____. Systematic Survey of the Arbitration Conventions and Treaties of Mutual Security Deposited with the League of Nations. Geneva, 1927.

_____. Report of the Special Committee to Study the Application of the Principles of the Covenant. A.7.1938. VII. Geneva.

_____. Treaty Series. 1920-1946.

Malloy, William M. (comp.). Treaties, Conventions, International Acts, Protocols and Agreements Between the United States and Other Powers, 1776-1909. 3 vols. Washington, 1910, 1923.

Moore, John Bassett. History and Digest of the International Arbitrations to which the United States Has Been a Party 53rd Cong., 2nd Sess.; HR Misc. Doc. 212. Washington: Government Printing Office, 1898, 6 vols.

Organization of American States. Americas, vol. 12 (1960).

_____. Applications of the Inter-American Treaty of Reciprocal Assistance, 1948-1964. Pan American Union. Washington, 1964.

_____. Annual Report of the Secretary General 1960.

_____. Annual Report of the Secretary General 1956-1957.

_____. Bilateral Treaty Developments in Latin America, 1953-1955. Pan American Union, Treaty Series 2. Washington, 1956.

_____. Bulletin.

_____. Inter-American Treaties and Conventions. Pan American Union, Treaty Series 9. Washington, 1961.

_____. International Conferences of American States, Second Supplement 1942-1954, Pan American Union. Washington, 1958.

_____. Manual of Inter-American Relations. Pan American Union, Conference and Organization Series 25. Washington, 1953.

_____. Manual of Inter-American Relations. Revised Edition. Pan American Union, Conference and Organization Series 42. Washington, 1956.

_____. Report on the Results of the Conference Submitted to the Governing Board of the Pan American Union by the Director-General (Inter-American Conference for the Maintenance of Continental Peace and Security, Rio de Janeiro, Aug. 15-Sept. 2, 1947). Pan American Union Congress and Conference Series 53. Washington, 1947.

_____. Situation Between Honduras and Nicaragua: Report of the
Investigating Committee. Pan American Union Doc. C-I-341.
Washington, 1957.

_____. Council. Decisions Taken at the Meetings of the Council
of the OAS (English trans.) Vol. I (1948)--. In original language:
Acta de la Sesion . . . . Pan American Union. Washington

Permanent Court of International Justice. Series A. Collection of
Judgments.

_____. Series B. Collection of Advisory Opinions.

_____. Series C. Acts and Documents Relating to Judgments
and Advisory Opinions Given by the Court.

_____. Series D. Acts and Documents Concerning the
Organization of the Court.

Proceedings of the Commission of Inquiry and Conciliation, Bolivia
and Paraguay, March 13, 1929-September 13, 1929. Washington,
1929.

Proceedings of the International Conference of American States on
Conciliation and Arbitration, Washington, December 10, 1928 to
January 5, 1929. Washington, 1929.

Scott, James Brown (ed.). The Hague Court Reports. New York:
Oxford University Press for Carnegie Endowment for International
Peace, 1916, 1932, 2 vols.

_____. (ed.). Instructions to the American Delegates to the Hague
Peace Conferences and Their Official Reports. New York:
Oxford University Press, 1916.

_____. (ed.). The Proceedings of the Hague Peace Conferences.
New York: Oxford University Press for Carnegie Endowment for
International Peace, 1920, 1921, 5 vols.

_____. (ed.) The Reports to the Hague Conferences of 1899 and
1907 (The Official Explanation and Interpretation). Oxford:
Clarendon Press for Carnegie Endowment for International Peace,
1917.

_____. Treaties for the Advancement of Peace Between the United
States and Other Powers Negotiated by the Hon. William J. Bryan,
Secretary of State of the United States. New York: Oxford University Press for the Carnegie Endowment for International Peace,
1920.

United Nations. Administrative Tribunal, Judgments, Judgment No. 74.

_____. Administrative Tribunal Verbatim Records 1955-1958,
Case No. 80.

_____. Handbook of the Legal Status, Privileges, and Immunities
of the United Nations. September 1952.

_____. Report of the Special Committee on Principles of Inter-
national Law Concerning Friendly Relations and Co-operation among
States. U.N. Doc. A/5746.

_____. Organization and Procedure of United Nations Commissions. 1949.X 1 to 9 and 1950.X. 1 to 3.

_____. Report of the Secretary General on Methods of Fact Finding. U. N. Docs. A/5694, A/6228.

_____. Recent Inter-American Experience in the Field of Pacific Settlement. Doc. A/AC.18/SC.9/L.6, 1950.

_____. Repertoire of the Practice of the Security Council, 1946-1951 and Supplement, 1952-1955, New York, 1954, 1957.

_____. Repertory of the United Nations Practice. 1955, 5 vols. and Supplement No. 1, vol. I. May 1958.

_____. Status of Multilateral Conventions in Respect of Which the Secretary-General Acts as Depository. 1959. ST/Leg/3, Rev. 1.

_____. Systematic Survey of Treaties for the Pacific Settlement of International Disputes, 1928-1948. 1949.V.3., 1949.

_____. Treaty Series. 1946-----.

_____. Yearbook of the United Nations, 1946-----.

_____. General Assembly. Memorandum on the Question of the Costa Rican Border Incidents Prepared by the Secretariat. Doc. A/AC.18/SC.6/3, 1949.

_____. _____. Official Records.

_____. _____. Report of the Security Council to the General Assembly. Annual.

_____. _____. Statement of Views and Suggestions by the Secretary-General Regarding the Work of the Interim Committee. Doc. A/AC.18/SC.6/1, 1949.

_____. _____. Interim Committee. Analysis of the Main Features of the Inter-American Peace System. Doc. A/AC. 18/46 and Add. 1, 1948.

_____. _____. _____. Analysis of Provisions in Pacific Settlement Treaties. Doc. A/AC.18/57, 1948.

_____. _____. _____. Analysis of Structure and Working of Arrangements of Inquiry and Conciliation under Existing Treaties. Doc. A/AC.18/64, 1948.

_____. _____. _____. History and Analysis of the General Act for the Pacific Settlement of International Disputes, 26 September 1928. Doc. A/AC.18/56, 1948.

_____. _____. _____. History and Analysis of the General Convention for Improving the Means of Preventing War and the Regulations for the Execution of Article 4 of this Convention. Doc. A/AC.18/55, 1948.

157

. . . Report of the Sub-Committee on International Cooperation in the Political Field. Doc. A/AC. 18/114, 1950.

. . . Study of the Organization and Operation of United Nations Commissions. Doc. A/AC. 18/SC. 6/6 1949.

. . . Study on Methods for the Promotion of International Cooperation in the Political Field. Doc. A/AC. 18/73 and Add. 1, 1948.

. . . Use by the Organs of the League of Nations of Measures and Procedures of Pacific Settlement. Doc. A/AC. 18. 68, 1948.

. . . Use by Organs of the United Nations of Measures and Procedures of Pacific Settlement. Doc. A/AC. 18/61, 1948.

. Security Council. Official Records.

United Nations Conference on International Organization, Documents.

United Nations Information Organizations. Documents of the United Nations Conference on International Organization, San Francisco, 1945. London and New York, 1945, 16 vols.

United States. Statutes at Large.

. Treaty Series.

. Congress. Senate. Committee on Foreign Relations. Hearings, The Charter of the United Nations for the Maintenance of International Peace and Security Submitted by the President of the United States on July 2, 1945 (Revised). July 9-13, 1945. 79th Cong. 1st Sess. 1945.

. Congress. Senate. Judiciary Committee. Report to the Subcommittee to Investigate the Administration of the Internal Security Act and Other Internal Security Laws of The Committee on the Judiciary. 87th Congress, First Session, 1961.

Department of State. American Foreign Policy 1950-1955: Basic Documents, 2 vols. Pub. 6446, General Foreign Policy Series 117, 1957.

. . American Foreign Policy Current Documents. 1956, 1957.

. . Bulletin.

. . Charter of the United Nations: Report to the President of the Results of the San Francisco Conference.

. . Documents and State Papers. Vol. 1 (1948)-----.

. . Dumbarton Oaks Documents on International Organization. Pub. 2349. Conference Series 71, 1945.

158

_____. Inter-American Conference for the Maintenance of Continental Peace and Security, 1947: Report of the Delegation of the United States. Pub. 3016, 1948.

_____. International Agencies in Which the United States Participates. Pub. 2699, 1946.

_____. Ninth International Conference of American States, Bogota, 1948: Report of the Delegation of the United States. Pub. 3263, 1948.

_____. Papers Relating to the Foreign Relations of the United States.

_____. Treaties in Force: A List of Treaties and Other International Agreements of the United States in Force on January 1. 1961. Pub. 7132, 1961.

Whiteman, Marjorie M., Digest of International Law. Washington, D.C.: United States Government Printing Office, 1965, Vol. 5, pp. 134-135.

Wolf, F. C. de. General Synopsis of Treaties of Arbitration, Conciliation, Judicial Settlement, Security and Disarmament Actually in Force Between Countries Invited to the Disarmament Conference. Washington, D. C., 1933.

## Secondary Sources

### Books

Bailey, Sydney D. The General Assembly of the United Nations: A Study of Procedure and Practice. New York: Praeger for Carnegie Endowment for International Peace, 1960.

Beaucourt, Albert. Les commissions internationales après la paix. (Thesis, Paris). Arras: Repesse, Cassel, 1909.

Blackmer, Henry Myron. The United States Policy and The Inter-American Peace System 1889-1952. Paris: 1952.

Bokanowski, Maurice. Les commissions internationales d'enquête. (Thesis). Paris: Pedone, 1925.

Brown, Philip Marshall. La conciliation internationale. Paris: Pedone, 1925

Clark, Grenville, and John, Louis B. World Peace Thru World Law. 3rd Edition Revised, Cambridge: Harvard University Press, 1966.

Carlston, Kenneth S. The Process of International Arbitration. New York: Columbia University Press, 1946.

Commission to Study Organization of Peace. Arthur N. Holcombe, chairman. Strengthening the United Nations. New York: Harper, 1957.

Conwell, Evans, T. P. The League Council in Action. London: Oxford University Press, 1929.

Dickinson, E. D. The Equality of States in International Law. Cambridge: Harvard University Press, 1920.

Dulles, John Foster. War, Peace and Change. New York: Harper and Brothers, 1939.

Dunn, Frederick S. Peaceful Change: A Study of International Procedures. New York: Council on Foreign Relations, 1937.

Fenwick, Charles G. The Organization of American States, The Inter-American Regional System. Washington: Kaufman Printing Co., 1963.

Goodrich, Leland M., and Hambro, Edvard. The Charter of the United Nations. 2nd rev. ed. Boston: World Peace Foundation, 1949.

Goodrich, L., and Simons, A. The United Nations and the Maintenance of International Peace and Security. Washington: Brookings Institution, 1955.

Goodrich, Leland M. The United Nations. New York: Thomas Y. Crowell, 1959.

Hambro, E. The Case Law of the International Court. 2 vols. Leyden: Sijthoff's, 1952, 1960.

Haviland, H. Field, Jr. The Political Role of the General Assembly. New York: Carnegie Endowment for International Peace, 1951.

Hill, Martin. Immunities and Privileges of International Officials. Washington: Carnegie Endowment for International Peace, 1947.

Howard-Ellis, C. The Origin, Structure and Working of the League of Nations. London: G. Allen & Unwin, 1928.

Hudson, Manley O. By Pacific Means. New Haven: Yale University Press, 1935.

_____. International Tribunals, Past and Future. Washington: Carnegie Endowment for International Peace and the Brookings Institution, 1944.

_____. The Permanent Court of International Justice. New York: Macmillan, 1943.

Hull, William I. The Two Hague Conferences and Their Contribution to International Law. Boston: International School of Peace by Ginn, 1908.

Hyde, Charles Cheney. International Law Chiefly as Interpreted and Applied by the United States. 2nd Revised Edition, Boston: Little, Brown, 1945.

Jessup, Philip C. International Security. New York: Council on Foreign Relations, 1935.

_____. The Use of International Law. Ann Arbor: University of Michigan Law School, 1959.

Jimenez, E. Voting and the Handling of Disputes in the Security Council, New York: Carnegie Endowment for International Peace, 1950.

Kaplan, Morton A. and Katzenbach, Nicholas de B. The Political Foundations of International Law. New York: John Wiley and Sons, 1961

Koo, Jr. Wellington. Voting Procedure in International Political Organs, New York: Columbia University Press, 1947.

Ladd, William. An Essay on a Congress of Nations (1840). New York: Oxford University Press for Carnegie Endowment for International Peace, 1916.

Lapradelle, Albert G. de, and Politis, Nicolas. Recueil des arbitrages internationaux. 2 vols. Paris: Pedone, 1905.

Lauterpacht, H. The Development of International Law by the International Court of Justice. New York: Longmans, Green and Co., 1958.

LeRay, Andre. Les commissions internationales d'enquête au XXme siècle. Saumur: Godet, 1910.

Lissitzyn, O. J. The International Court of Justice. New York: Carnegie Endowment for International Peace, 1951.

Martens, Frederick de. La Conference de la Paix a la Haye. Paris: Rosseau, 1900.

Morgenthau, Hans. Politics Among Nations. New York: Knopf, 1954.

Oppenheim, L. F. L. International Law. 8th ed. Edited by H. Lauterpacht. 2 vols. London: Longmans, 1955.

Philipse, A. H. Le rôle du Conseil de la Societe des Nations dans le reglement pacifique des differends internationaux. The Hague: Nijhoff, 1929.

Pollock, Frederick. The League of Nations. London: Sevens, 1920.

Potter, Pitman B. Introduction to the Study of International Law. 1st ed. and rev. ed. New York: Century, 1922, 1925.

Ralston, J. H. International Arbitration from Athens to Locarno. Stanford: Stanford University Press, 1929.

_____. The Law and Procedure of International Tribunals. rev. ed. Stanford: Stanford University Press, 1926.

Sandifer, Durward V. Evidence Before International Tribunals. Chicago: Foundation Press, 1939.

Schwarzenberger, Georg. International Law. 3rd ed. Vol. 1. London: Stevens, 1957, pp. 114-115.

Scott, J. B. The Hague Peace Conferences of 1899 and 1907. 2 vols. Baltimore: John Hopkins Press, 1909.

161

_____ (ed.) Resolutions of the Institute of International Law. New York: Oxford University Press for Carnegie Endowment for International Peace, 1916.

Stone, Julius. Legal Controls of International Conflicts. London: Stevens 1954.

Szikszoy, Joseph Alexander. The Legal Aspects of the Hungarian Question. Ambilly-Annemosse, France: Les Presses de Savoie, 1963.

Vayo, Alvarez del. "The Chaco War," in Pacifism Is Not Enough: Problems of Peace. 9th Series. London: Allen and Unwin for Geneva Institute of International Relations, 1935.

Vulcan, Constantin. La conciliation dans le droit international actuel. Paris: Pedone, 1932.

Walters, F. P. History of the League of Nations. 2 vols. London: Oxford University Press, 1952.

Webster, C. K. and Herbert, Sydney. The League of Nations in Theory and Practice. Boston: Mifflin, 1933.

Yoo, Tae Ho. The Korean War and the United Nations: A Legal and Diplomatic Historical Survey. Louvain: Librarie Desbarax, 1956.

Zimmern, Alfred. The League of Nations and the Rule of Law 1918-1935. London: Macmillan, 1936.

Pamphlets and Periodicals

Alfaro, R. J. "El sistema conciliatoria interamericano y su funcionamento según la Convencion de Washington," Revista de derecho internacional (1939), pp. 32-52.

Alford, Neill H. Jr. "Fact-Finding By the World Court," Villanova Law Review, vol. 4 (Fall 1958), pp. 37-91.

Anderson, Chandler P. "Production of Evidence by Subpoena Before International Tribunals," American Journal of International Law, vol. 27 (1933), pp. 498-501.

Anderson, Chandler P., and Scott, J. B. "Advisory Opinions from Commissions of Inquiry," American Journal of International Law, vol. 26 (1932), pp. 565-568.

Efremoff, Jean. "Organisation de la conciliation comme moyen de prévenir les guerres," Recueil des Cours, l'Académie de droit international de la Haye, vol. 59 (1937), pp. 103-221.

_____. "La conciliation internationale," Recueil des Cours, l'Académie de droit international de la Haye, vol. 18 (1927), pp. 5-145.

Fenwick, Charles G. "Application of the Treaty of Rio to the Controversy Between Costa Rica and Nicaragua," American Journal of International Law, vol. 43 (1949), pp. 329-333.

_____. "The Honduras-Nicaragua Boundary Dispute," American Journal of International Law, vol. 51 (1957), pp. 761-765.

_____. "The Inter-American Peace Committee," American Journal of International Law, vol. 43 (1949), pp. 770-772.

Ferrara, O. "The Practical Significance of the Pan-American Treaties," Current History, vol. 29 (February 1929), pp. 822-824.

Finch, George, "The Bryan Peace Treaties," American Journal of International Law, vol. 10 (1916), pp. 882-890.

Galeano, V. B. "The Gondra Treaty," Transactions of the Grotius Society, vol. 15 (1930), pp. 1-15.

Goodrich, Leland M. "Development of the General Assembly", International Conciliation, May 1951, No. 478.

_____. "Pacific Settlement of Disputes," American Political Science Review, vol. 39 (October 1945), pp. 956-970.

Gross, Leo. "The Question of Laos and the Double Veto in the Security Council," American Journal of International Law, vol. 54 (1960), pp. 118-131.

Hill, N. L. "International Commissions of Inqiry and Conciliation," International Conciliation, No. 278 (1932), pp. 85-134.

Hyde, Charles Cheny. "The Place of Commissions of Inquiry and Conciliation Treaties in the Peaceful Settlement of International Disputes," Proceedings of the American Society of International Law, vol. 23 (1929), pp. 144-157 and British Year Book of International Law (1929), pp. 96-110.

Kelson, Hans. "Limitations on The Functions of The United Nations," Yale Law Journal, vol. 55 (1946), pp. 997-1006.

Jessup, P. "The United States and Treaties for the Avoidance of War," International Conciliation, No. 239 (April 1928), pp. 181-245.

Kerley, Ernest L. "The Powers of Investigation of the United Nations Security Council," American Journal of International Law, vol. 55 (1961), pp. 892-918.

Kirkpatrick, Helen Paull. "The Chaco Dispute: the League and Pan Americanism," Geneva Special Studies, vol. 7 (June 1936), pp. 22-43.

Lake Mohonk Confernce on International Arbitration. Report (s). 1895-1916. Published by Lake Mohonk Conference on International Arbitration, Mohonk Lake, New York.

Liang, Yuen-Li. "The Settlement of Disputes in the Security Council: the Yalta Voting Formula," British Yearbook of International Law, vol. 24 (1947), pp. 330-359.

_____. "Some Aspects of the Work of the Interim Committee of the General Assembly: Pacific Settlement of Disputes," American Journal of International Law, vol. 42 (1948), pp. 895-900.

Lytton, Victor Alexander. "Lessons of the League of Nations Commission of Inquiry in Manchuria," The New Commonwealth Quarterly (1937), vol. 3, No. 3.

Mandelstam, Andre N. "La commission internationale d'enquête sur l'incident de la mer du nord," Revue générale de droit international public, vol. 12 (1905), pp. 161-190 and pp. 351-415.

_____. "La conciliation internationale d'après le Pacte de la jurisprudence du Conseil de la Societe des Nations," Recueil des Cours, L'Academie de droit international de la Haye, vol. 14 (1926-IV), pp. 337-643.

McDougal, Myres Smith and Gardner, Richard N. "The Veto and the Charter; An Interpretation for Survival," Yale Law Journal, Volume 60 (February, 1951).

The New York Times.

Oliveira, Pedro M. "De la investigacion y de la conciliacion en los tratados interamericanos," Revista de derecho y ciencias politicas, 3rd year (1939), pp. 247-282.

"Pacific Settlement of Disputes in the Covenant of the League of Nations and the Charter of the United Nations: A Paper Issued by the Reference Division of the United Nations Information Organization, London," International Conciliation, No. 420 (April 1946), pp. 197-211.

Politis, N. "Les commissions internationales d'enquête," Revue général de droit international public, vol. 19 (1912), pp. 149-188.

Possony, S. T. "Peace Endorsement," Yale Law Journal, Vol. 55 (August 1946), pp. 910-949.

Revel, G. "Role et charactere des commissions de conciliation," Revue generale de droit international public, vol. 5, Series (1931), pp. 564-607.

Schurmann, Carl W. A. A Center for International Fact Finding, a Review and a Proposal. School of International Affairs, Columbia University, July 1963.

Scott, J. B. "Mr. Bryan's Proposed Commission of Inquiry," American Journal of International Law, vol. 7 (1913), pp. 556-570.

_____. "The Pan American Conference on Conciliation and Arbitration," American Journal of International Law, vol. 23 (1929), pp. 143-152.

_____. "Secretary Bryan's Peace Plan," American Journal of International Law, vol. 8 (1914), pp. 565-571.

_____. "Secretary Bryan's Peace Plan," American Journal of International Law, vol. 9 (1915), pp. 175-177.

Simsarian, James. "Inspection Experiences Under the Antarctic Treaty and the International Atomic Agency," A.J.I.L., Vol. 60 (1966) pp. 502-510.

Sohn, Louis B. "The Role of International Institutions as Conflict-Adjusting Agencies," The University of Chicago Law Review, vol. 28 (Winter 1961). pp. 205-257.

Williams, Sir John Fischer. "The Pan-American and League of Nations Treaties of Arbitration and Conciliation," British Yearbook of International Law (1929), pp. 14-31.

# SELECTED BIBLIOGRAPHY

## ADDENDA

### Books

Bloomfield, L. M. and Fitzgerald, Gerald F., Boundary Water Problems of Canada and the United States. Toronto: Carswell, 1958.

Chacko, C. J., The International Joint Commission Between the United States of America and the Dominion of Canada, New York: Columbia University Press, 1932.

Landy, E. A., The Effectiveness of International Supervision: Thirty Years of I.L.O. Experience, Dobbs Ferry, New York: Oceana Publications, Inc., 1966.

White, Gillian M., The Use of Experts by International Tribunals, Syracuse: Syracuse University Press, 1965.

SELECTED BIBLIOGRAPHY

ADDENDA

Pamphlets and Periodicals

Bastid, Suzanne, "La Commission de Conciliation Franco-Siamose." La technique et les principes du droit public: etudes en l'honneur de Georges Scelle, Vol. I, 1950.

Francois, J. P. A., "Le Palais de la Paix en 1955", Nordisk Tijdschrift voor international recht, vol. 3, January 1956, p. 72.

Kenworthy, William S., "Joint Development of International Waters", A.J.I.L., vol. 54 (1960), p. 600.

Report of the Commission of Enquiry in the "Red Crusader" Incident, Bureau International de la Cour Permanente d'Arbitrage, The Hague: Van Langenhuysen Brothers, March, 1962.

Rolin, Henri, European Yearbook, vol. 3 (1957).

Rolin, Henri, "Une conciliation belgo-danoise", Revue generale de droit international public, vol. 24, series 3 (1953)

Rousseau, Charles, "Echec de la procedure d'enquete et de conciliation dans l'affaire de reroulement de l'avion transport de Rabat a Tunis les chefs nationalistes algeriens le Octobre 1956", Revue generale de droit international public, vol. 29, series 3 (October - November, 1958), pp. 691-696.

Timsit, Gerard, "Le fonctionnment de la procedure d'enquete dans l'affaire du 'Red Crusader' ", Annuaire Francaise de Droit International, vol. IX (1963), p. 460.

Van Asbeck, F. M. "La tache et l'action d'une commission de conciliation", Nederlands Tijdschrift voor international recht, vol. 3 (January 1956), pp. 1-9.

    "La procedure suivie par la commission permanente de conciliation franco-suisse", Nederlands Tijdschrift voor international recht, vol. 3, (July, 1956), pp. 209-219.

I N D E X

for

FACT-FINDING

IN THE MAINTENANCE OF INTERNATIONAL PEACE

by

William J. Shore

169

171

172

179

United Nations Palestine Commission
(cont'd)
  and rules of procedure, 113, 116,
    119
United Nations Secretary-General,  107,
  108f., 126
  investigations by,
    and authority to initiate, 84, 95-
      98
    in Hungary,  63
  and Greek question,  96
  and Iranian question,  96
  special representatives of,  96, 97-
    98, 106
    to Oman,  68-69
  and United Nations Malyasia Mission,
    69
United Nations Security Council,  6,
  42, 62, 63, 93, 117, 126
  Advisory Commission on the Congo, 65
  armed assistance to Korea by,  60
  cease-fire orders by,  54-55, 56
  Commission for India and Pakistan,
    101
  Commission of Investigation Con-
    cerning Greek Frontier Incidents,
    51-52, 101
    duration of,  91
    Subsidiary Group of,  52
  Committee of Good Offices on the Indo-
    nesian Question,  55, 138
  competence of, determining, 54, 91-93,
    101
  Consular Commission,
    at Batavia,  113, 119
    in Indonesia,  54-55, 138
  Czechslovak case,  87, 89
  Dispute between India and Pakistan
    over Kashmir, 56-57
  investigation(s),  99
    authority to initiate, 83-84, 87-91,
      135-136
    commissions of,  113-114, 138, 141
    of Franco regime,  86
    limitations on, 84-86, 94
    and obligations of UN Members, 98
  reports to, 128, 130, 133
  sanctions, use of, 132
  Sub-Committee(s),  101-102
    on Incidents in the Corfu Channel,
      53-54, 88, 109
    on Laos,  64, 113f.
    on the Spanish question,  50-51
  terms of reference for commissions,
    100-103, 105-106
  Truce Commission for Palestine, 58,
    113, 119, 138

United Nations Security Council (cont'd
  United Nations Commission for
    Indonesia,  55
  voting, arrangements of,  84-86
United Nations Special Commission on
  Palestine,  106, 109, 111, 115
  oral hearing by,  125
  report, presentation of,  128, 129
  rules of procedure, 113, 116, 117,
    119, 120
  scope of reference of,  103-104
  staff for,  126
United Nations Special Commission on
  the Balkans,
  agenda for,  115
  report of,  130
  rules of procedure for, 113, 115-116,
    117, 118, 119, 120
United Nations Temporary Commission on
  Korea,  96, 125
  agenda for,  115
  report, presentation of,  128, 130
  rules of procedure,  113, 116, 117,
    118, 119, 120
  terms of reference for,  105
United States,  4-5, 19, 35, 48, 73,
  88, 89
  and commissions of investigation,
    111-112
  and dispute with Panama (1964), 47
  International Joint Commission, 74-75
  International Waterways Commission,
    74
  and United Nations,  98-99
    interpretation of Charter provi-
      sions,  91
    proposal to establish Interim Com-
      mittee,  93-94
Upper Silesian Question, 1921,  37


Venezuela,  45-46, 48
  complaint against Dominican Republic
    by,  48-49
  and intervention by Cuba, 47-48
Veto,
  "double",  87
  power of, in Security Council,  85,
  use of,  84
Vietnam, Democratic Republic of,  64
Visscher, Charles de,  18, 35
Voluntary settlement, 2


Waithayakon, Prince Wan,  64
War, restrictions on,  19, 20
Wilson, Woodrow,  1, 19